*Praise for* MERCHANTS OF DESPAIR

*Robert Zubrin's masterful study . . . makes for riveting reading. Mer-*
chants of Despair *is a cautionary tale of what happens when powerful,*
*unprincipled elites are not only alienated from the mass of their fellow*
*men, but come to see them as a barrier to imagined social, evolution-*
*ary, or environmental progress.*

STEVEN W. MOSHER
President, Population Research Institute

Merchants of Despair *is an extraordinary and important book. . . .*
*This fascinating volume carefully traces developments of the Malthusian*
*hypothesis right up to the present: through eugenics to population control*
*and genocide; through the Club of Rome's* Limits to Growth *and extreme*
*environmentalism to climate change and the myth of global warming*
*apocalypse. It is a shocking exposé of a movement whose deadly history*
*has remained hidden far too long. Robert Zubrin has my nomination*
*for a Pulitzer Prize.*

S. Fred Singer
Chairman, Science and Environmental Policy Project
Author of *Unstoppable Global Warming: Every 1,500 Years*

*I believe no one to date has so clearly explained the thread of the anti-*
*human movement throughout history. To read this book is to become*
*a warrior in the battle against antihumanism.*

Jay Lehr
Science Director, Heartland Institute

*The most devastating account and refutation of antihuman environ-*
*mentalism ever written.*

Gregory Benford
Professor of Physics, University of California, Irvine
Contributing Editor, *Reason* magazine

D0018285

Robert Zubrin

# MERCHANTS OF DESPAIR

*Radical Environmentalists, Criminal Pseudo-Scientists, and the Fatal Cult of Antihumanism*

*New Atlantis Books*
ENCOUNTER BOOKS · NEW YORK · LONDON

First American edition published in 2012 by Encounter Books, an activity of Encounter for Culture and Education, Inc., a nonprofit, tax exempt corporation.
Encounter Books website address: www.encounterbooks.com

Manufactured in the United States and printed on acid-free paper. The paper used in this publication meets the minimum requirements of ANSI/NISO Z39.48-1992 (R 1997) (Permanence of Paper).

FIRST PAPERBACK EDITION PUBLISHED IN 2013
PAPERBACK EDITION ISBN 978-1-59403-737-5

LIBRARY OF CONGRESS HAS CATALOGUED
THE HARDCOVER EDITION AS FOLLOWS

Zubrin, Robert.
Merchants of despair : radical environmentalists, criminal pseudo-scientists, and the fatal cult of antihumanism / Robert Zubrin.
    p.    cm. — (New Atlantis books)
Includes bibliographical references and index.
ISBN 978-1-59403-476-3 (hardcover : alk. paper) —
ISBN 1-59403-476-1 (hardcover : alk. paper)
1. Political anthropology. 2. Humanism. 3. Civilization, Modern.
4. Social problems. 5. Science—Philosophy. 6. Pseudoscience. I. Title.
GN492.Z84 2011
306.2—dc23
2011038668

10  9  8  7  6  5  4  3  2  1

# CONTENTS

*TO THE INVENTORS AND DISCOVERERS,*

*BE THEY FAMOUS OR NAMELESS;*

*THAT COMPANY OF HEROES*

*WHOSE NOBLE WORK MUST EVER*

*CONFOUND THE ANTIHUMANISTS.*

*Necessity is the plea for every infringement of human freedom.
It is the argument of tyrants; it is the creed of slaves.*
WILLIAM PITT
Speech in the House of Commons
November 18, 1783

# *Preface*

THERE WAS A time when humanity looked in the mirror and saw
something precious, worth protecting and fighting for, indeed, worth
liberating. Starting with the Biblical idea of the human spirit as the
image of God, taken forward by Renaissance humanists defending the
dignity of man, our greatest thinkers developed a concept of civilization
dedicated to human betterment and "unalienable rights" among which
are "Life, Liberty, and the pursuit of Happiness," proudly asserting that
"to secure these rights, Governments are instituted among Men."

But now, we are beset on all sides by propaganda promoting a radically different viewpoint. According to this idea, humans are a cancer
upon the Earth, a horde of vermin whose unconstrained aspirations
and appetites are endangering the natural order. This is the core idea
of *antihumanism*. Its acceptance can only have the most pernicious
consequences.

1

One does not provide liberty to vermin. One does not seek to advance the cause of a cancer.

Antihumanism is not environmentalism, though it sometimes masquerades as such. Environmentalism, properly conceived, is an effort to apply practical solutions to real environmental problems, such as air and water pollution, for the purpose of making the world a better place for all humans to thrive in. Antihumanism, in contrast, rejects the goal of advancing the cause of mankind. Rather, it uses instances of inadvertent human damage to the environment as points of agitation to promote its fundamental thesis that human beings are pathogens whose activities need to be suppressed in order to protect a fixed ecological order with interests that stand above those of humanity.

Antihumanism has recently enormously expanded its influence by raising hysteria about global warming. This phenomenon, by lengthening the growing season and increasing rainfall and the availability of atmospheric carbon dioxide for photosynthesis, has actually significantly enhanced the abundance of nature, to the benefit of both agriculture and the wild biosphere alike. Nevertheless, according to antihumanism, punitive measures, especially harmful to the world's poor, are required to suppress mankind's activity and economic growth in order to deal with this putative threat. That antihumanism should propose such global oppression as a response to an improvement in the Earth's climate should not be surprising, since, as this book will show in horrifying detail, similar vicious antihuman solutions to fictitious problems have been repeatedly advocated and implemented by antihumanism's followers for two centuries—that is, since long before global warming was an issue at all.

Indeed, while its use of "climate defense" as an agitational issue in support of an antihuman program is novel, antihumanism itself is not. Over the years, it has found other causes to ally with, ranging in diversity from militarism, imperialism, racism, and xenophobia to environmentalism, aesthetic nature appreciation, and even feminism. It has opportunistically sought and found support from political and economic philosophies ranging from *laissez-faire* capitalism to monarchism, socialism, Nazism, and totalitarian communism; worldviews ranging from Darwinian atheism to religious zealotry; and vested interests ranging from colonial expansion to rentier-motivated economic restriction. In some cases it has worked its will through groups that can fairly be described as actual conspiracies, while in other instances it has exerted its effect through its influence on social networks, broadly based parties, or the general shaping of society's ideas. But regardless of its ally of the moment, wherever antihumanism has established a liaison, it has served, like a demonic spirit, to transform its partner for the worse, turning well-meaning causes into pernicious ones and bad movements into catastrophes.

In this book, the ideology of antihumanism will be critically reviewed, and its brutal history thoroughly exposed. Many readers may find this account to be very disturbing, since in the course of its examination, it will become quite clear that some of today's most fashionable political and social ideas are essentially replays of earlier ideological fads that have been continually used over the last two centuries to motivate and justify oppression, tyranny, and genocide. Nevertheless, as those who do not know history are condemned to repeat it, this history must be made known.

Furthermore, while the central lie underpinning all of antihumanism's campaigns has always been the same, its ability to morph into apparently novel guises has allowed it to revive itself to cause new evil, even after a previous form has been defeated at great cost.

The time is long past due to put a stake in the heart of this monster. For that to occur, it needs to be dissected, so that it can be detected, debunked, and destroyed wherever, whenever, and in whatever form it reappears. For this reason, alongside this book's historical account, I shall devote some space to examining the primary pseudoscientific arguments that the antihumanists have voiced over the past two centuries—many of which are still widely accepted—and to refuting them thoroughly. While disputes about overpopulation, racial equality, pesticides, resource limits, nuclear power, biotechnology, and

## CHAPTER ONE

# Thomas Malthus,
# the Most Dismal Scientist

*When a population of organisms grows in a finite environment, sooner or later it will encounter a resource limit. This phenomenon, described by ecologists as reaching the "carrying capacity" of the environment, applies to bacteria on a culture dish, to fruit flies in a jar of agar, and to buffalo on a prairie. It must also apply to man on this finite planet.*

JOHN P. HOLDREN and PAUL R. EHRLICH
*Global Ecology* (1971)[1]

*Here is the difference between the animal and the man. Both the jay-hawk and the man eat chickens, but the more jay-hawks the fewer chickens, while the more men the more chickens.*

HENRY GEORGE
*Progress and Poverty* (1879)[2]

THE FOUNDING PROPHET of modern antihumanism was Thomas Malthus (1766–1834). For three decades a professor at the British East India Company's East India College, Malthus was a political economist who famously argued that human reproduction always outruns available resources. This doctrine served to rationalize the starvation of millions caused by his employer's policy of brutal oppression of the peasants of the Indian subcontinent. The British Empire's colonial helots, however, were not Malthus's only targets.

Rather, his *Essay on the Principle of Population* (first published in 1798 and later expanded in numerous further editions) was initially penned as a direct attack on such Enlightenment revolutionaries as William Godwin and the Marquis de Condorcet, who advanced the notion that human liberty, expanding knowledge, and technological progress could ultimately make possible a decent life for all mankind.

Malthus prescribed specific policies to keep population down by raising the death rate:

> We are bound in justice and honour to disclaim the right of the poor to support. . . . [W]e should facilitate, instead of foolishly and vainly endeavouring to impede, the operations of nature in producing this mortality; and if we dread the too frequent visitation of the horrid form of famine, we should sedulously encourage the other forms of destruction, which we compel nature to use. Instead of recommending cleanliness to the poor, we should encourage contrary habits. In our towns we should make the streets narrower, crowd more people into the houses, and court the return of the plague. In the country, we should build our villages near stagnant pools, and particularly encourage settlements in all marshy and unwholesome situations. But above all, we should reprobate specific remedies for ravaging diseases; and those benevolent, but much mistaken men, who have thought they were doing a service to mankind by projecting schemes for the total extirpation of particular disorders.[3]

In short, Malthus argued that we should do whatever we can to encourage disease, and we should condemn doctors who try to find cures. In addition, everything should be done to keep the wages of working people as low as possible.[4]

It is ironic that today's left, which represents itself as the advocate of the plebeian interest, has embraced Malthus. In the nineteenth century, however, virtually everyone who took a stand as a defender of the poor, social justice, or human equality—from Friedrich Engels

to Charles Dickens to Florence Nightingale—clearly recognized Mal -
thusian doctrine as obviously representing the voice of their enemy.[5]
In his 1879 book *Progress and Poverty*, the American reformer
Henry George explained that Malthus's theory was gaining adherents
because it justified "the greed of the rich and the selfishness of the
powerful," and so was "eminently soothing and reassuring to the
classes who, wielding the power of wealth, largely dominate thought."
"The Malthusian doctrine," George wrote, "parries the demand for
reform, and shelters selfishness from question and from conscience
by the interposition of an inevitable necessity. . . . For poverty, want,
and starvation are by this theory not chargeable either to individual
greed or to social maladjustments; they are the inevitable results of
universal laws, with which, if it were not impious, it were as hopeless
to quarrel with as with the law of gravitation."[6]

George also pointed out a key fallacy underlying the Malthusian
ideology. Human beings are not simply the *consumers* of a pre-existing
gift of nature; they are also the *cultivators* of the bounty on which they
live:

> If bears instead of men had been shipped from Europe to the
> North American continent, there would now be no more bears
> than in the time of Columbus. . . . But within the limits of the
> United States alone, there are now forty-five millions of men
> where then there were only a few hundred thousand; and yet
> there is now within that territory much more food per capita
> for the forty-five millions than there was then for the few hun-
> dred thousand. It is not the increase of food that has caused
> this increase of men, but the increase of men that has brought
> about the increase of food. There is more food, simply because
> there are more men.[7]

An even more masterful refutation of Malthus came from none other
than the young Friedrich Engels, subsequently famous as the coauthor
of *The Communist Manifesto*. In an 1844 work, Engels mocked

Malthus's "vile and infamous doctrine" before zeroing in on the fundamental deceit at its core: its disregard of human creativity.

Malthus ... asserts that population constantly exerts pressure on the means of subsistence; that as production is increased, population increases in the same proportion; and that the inherent tendency of population to multiply beyond the available means of subsistence is the cause of all poverty and all vice. ... Now the consequence of this theory is that since it is precisely the poor who constitute this surplus population, nothing ought to be done for them, except to make it as easy as possible for them to starve to death; to convince them that this state of affairs cannot be altered and that there is no salvation for their entire class other than that they should propagate as little as possible; or that if this is not practicable, it is at any rate better that a state institution for the painless killing of the children should be set up—as suggested by "Marcus"[8]—each working-class family being allowed two-and-a-half children, and the excess being painlessly destroyed. ...

Malthus puts forward a calculation upon which his whole system is based. Population increases in geometric progression—$1 + 2 + 4 + 8 + 16 + 32$, etc. The productive power of the land increases in arithmetical progression—$1 + 2 + 3 + 4 + 5 + 6$. The difference is obvious and horrifying—but is it correct? Where has it been proved that the productivity of the land increases in arithmetic progression? The area of the land is limited—that is perfectly true. But the labor power to be employed on this area increases together with the population; and even if we assume that the increase in output associated with this increase in labor is not always proportionate to the latter, there still remains a third element—which the economists, however, never consider as important—namely, science, the progress of which is just as limitless and at least as rapid as that of population.[9]

Engels hit the nail right on the head, as can be even more clearly seen today than in his time. All predictions based on Malthusian theory have proven false, because, again, human beings are not mere consumers of resources, or even producers from resources—but rather, *we create resources* by developing new technologies that find use for them. The more people there are, the greater the potential for innovation. Every human mouth comes not just with a pair of hands, but with a brain. That is why as the world's population has increased, the standard of living has also increased, and at an accelerating rate.

The human race is not, as later Malthus admirers John Holdren (currently President Obama's science advisor) and Paul Ehrlich sneered in 1971, so many bacteria in a culture dish, doomed to quick extinction unless our appetites can be controlled by wise overlords wielding sterilants to curb our excessive multiplication.[10] Nor are we a swarm of fruit flies in an agar jar, or members of a buffalo herd in need of culling. No: we are creative inventors, and the more of us there are, the better off we are. And the freer we are, the faster we can make the inventions that can advance our condition still further.

## JUSTIFYING OPPRESSION

While history has proven Malthusianism empirically false, however, it provides the ideal foundation for justifying human oppression and tyranny. The theory holds that there isn't enough to go around, and can never be. Therefore human aspirations and liberties must be constrained, and authorities must be empowered to enforce the constraining.

During Malthus's own time, his theory was used to justify regressive legislation directed against England's lower classes, most notably the Poor Law Act of 1834, which forced hundreds of thousands of poor Britons into virtual slavery.[11] However, a far more horrifying example of the impact of Malthusianism was to occur a few years later, when the doctrine motivated the British government's refusal to provide relief during the great Irish famine of 1846.

In a letter to economist David Ricardo, Malthus laid out the basis for this policy: "The land in Ireland is infinitely more peopled than in England; and to give full effect to the natural resources of the country, a great part of the population should be swept from the soil."[12]

For the last century and a half, the Irish famine has been cited by Malthusians as proof of their theory of overpopulation, so a few words are in order here to set the record straight.[13] Ireland was certainly not overpopulated in 1846. In fact, based on census data from 1841 and 1851, the Emerald Isle boasted a mere 7.5 million people in 1846, less than half of England's 15.8 million, living on a land mass about two-thirds that of England and of similar quality. So compared to England, Ireland before the famine was if anything somewhat *underpopulated*.[14] Nor, as is sometimes said, was the famine caused by a foolish decision of the Irish to confine their diet to potatoes, thereby exposing themselves to starvation when a blight destroyed their only crop. In fact, in 1846 alone, at the height of the famine, Ireland exported over 730,000 cattle and other livestock, and over 3 million quarts of corn and grain flour to Great Britain.[15] The Irish diet was confined to potatoes because—having had their land expropriated, having been forced to endure merciless rack-rents and taxes, and having been denied any opportunity to acquire income through manufactures or other means—tubers were the only food the Irish could afford. So when the potato crop failed, there was nothing for the Irish themselves to eat, despite the fact that throughout the famine, their homeland continued to export massive amounts of grain, butter, cheese, and meat for foreign consumption. As English reformer William Cobbett noted in his *Political Register*:

> Hundreds of thousands of living hogs, thousands upon thousands of sheep and oxen alive; thousands upon thousands of barrels of beef, pork, and butter; thousands upon thousands of sides of bacon; and thousands and thousands of hams; shiploads and boats coming daily and hourly from Ireland to feed the west of Scotland; to feed a million and a half people in the

West Riding of Yorkshire, and in Lancashire; to feed London and its vicinity; and to fill the country shops in the southern counties of England; we beheld all this, while famine raged in Ireland amongst the raisers of this very food.[16]

*"The population should be swept from the soil."*
*Evicted from their homes, millions of Irish men, women,*
*and children starved to death or died of exposure.*
(*Contemporary drawings from* Illustrated London News.)

In the face of the catastrophe, the British government headed by Lord John Russell refused to provide any effective aid. According to one biographer, Russell was motivated by "a Malthusian fear about the long-term effect of relief," while the government's representative in Ireland, Lord Clarendon, argued that "doling out food merely to keep people alive would do nobody any permanent good."[17]

Accordingly, Russell gave authority for managing the famine to Charles Trevelyan, who had been indoctrinated by Malthus personally while he received his education at the East India College.[18] Trevelyan elevated his Malthusianism to cult status, explaining that the famine was a "direct stroke of an all-wise and all-merciful Providence."[19]

According to Trevelyan, the famine was simply God's way of redressing an imbalance between population and resources. "Posterity will trace up to that Famine the commencement of a salutary revolution in the habits of a nation long singularly unfortunate, and will acknowledge that on this, as on many other occasions, Supreme Wisdom has educed permanent good out of transient evil."[20]

Trevelyan's claim of divine sanction for his policy of starving a nation shocked the Catholic church. Archbishop John Hughes of New York declaimed:

> They call it God's famine! No! No! God's famine is known by the general scarcity of food, of which it is the consequence; there is no general scarcity, there has been no general scarcity of food in Ireland, either the present, or the past year, except in one species of vegetable. The soil has produced its usual tribute for the support of those by whom it has been cultivated; but political economy found the Irish people too poor to pay for the harvest of their own labor, and has exported it to a better market, leaving them to die of famine, or to live on alms; and this same political economy authorizes the provision merchant, even amidst the desolation, to keep his doors locked, and his sacks of corn tied up within, waiting for a better price.[21]

But it did no good. In the face of massive international criticism, the Malthusian ideologues ruling the British cabinet stuck resolutely to their merciless course. In the course of three years, in scenes of incredible horror the like of which would not be matched in Europe for another century, over one million Irish were starved to death or, weakened by malnutrition, died of rampant disease.[22]

## EXPORTING STARVATION TO INDIA

Three decades later, the death count inflicted on the British Empire's subjects by Malthusian ideology soared into the many millions during another famine, this time on the other side of the globe. From 1876 to 1879, a terrible drought reduced the crop yields in many parts of India, but as in Ireland in the 1840s, there ought to have been plenty left to feed the Indians themselves.[23] Indian grain exports in 1876 were more than double those of the pre-famine year of 1875, and in 1877 they doubled again—hardly a shortage of food. But uncontrolled grain speculation and exports by the colonial pooh-bahs, in addition to rising taxation and a depreciation of the rupee against the new gold standard, combined with natural causes to make it impossible for Indian peasants to obtain food for subsistence.[24]

Having helped precipitate this catastrophe, the British government refused to provide any form of effective succor. Rather, as in Ireland, the imperial government used Malthusian reasoning to help justify its oppressive policy. In 1877, British Viceroy Robert Bulwer-Lytton told the Legislative Council that "the Indian population has a tendency to increase more rapidly than the food it raises from the soil." This line was backed up by Sir Evelyn Baring, the future Lord Cromer, who told Parliament that "every benevolent attempt made to mitigate the effects of famine and defective sanitation serves but to enhance the evils resulting from overpopulation."[25]

As Indian peasants, driven from their land by taxation, a collapsing currency, and crop failure, began to roam the country searching for food, Lytton's government rounded them up and placed them in "relief camps" where they were subjected to hard labor and limited to rations of one pound of rice per day, with no meat, fish, fruit, or vegetables. This daily dole of 1,630 calories was actually less than the 1,750 calories per day provided by the Nazis to the inmates of the Buchenwald concentration camp in 1944–45, and it produced similar results.[26] According to the medical commissioner for the city of Madras (now known as Chennai), monthly mortality in the camps was equivalent to an annual death rate of 94 percent, with postmortem examination showing the chief cause of death to be "extreme wasting of the tissue and destruction of the lining membrane of the lower bowel"—that is to say, starvation—with full-grown men reduced to less than sixty

*Indian Famine Victims, 1876–1879.*

pounds in weight prior to expiration.[27] Indeed, in looking today at photographs of the living, dying, and dead human skeletons taken by British and American missionaries visiting the "relief camps" in 1877, the modern viewer can only be struck by their similarity to the images taken by the liberators of the Nazi death camps in 1945.

As one junior government official later described the scene:

The dead and dying were lying about on all sides . . . for shelter some had crawled to the graves of an adjoining cemetery and had lain themselves down between two graves as supports for their wearied limbs; the crows were hovering over bodies that still had a spark of life in them. . . . The place seemed tenanted by none but the dead and the dying. In a few minutes I picked up five bodies; one being that of an infant which its dying mother had firmly clasped, ignorant of the child being no more; the cholera patients were lying about unheeded by those around; some poor children were crying piteously for water within the hearing of the cooks, who never stirred to wet the lips of the poor things that were in extremis.[28]

As the above testimony suggests, Viceroy Lytton's Malthusian policies were by no means in accord with the traditional sensibilities of Englishmen. There were many who actively rejected the policies born of overpopulation dogma, but their efforts were in vain. For example, outraged by the death-camp horrors, the British community in Madras, under the leadership of the philanthropic Duke of Buckingham, attempted to raise private funds to save the Indians from starvation—but Lytton stopped the plan dead in its tracks.[29] In a series of searing articles denouncing the viceroy for creating "a hideous record of human suffering and destruction" such as "the world has never seen before," Red Cross founder Florence Nightingale called on her nation's government to suspend its merciless taxation policy.[30] She was likewise rebuffed by Lytton. As British officer B. H. Baden-Powell put it, reducing the taxes on the Indian peasantry would only encourage further overpopulation.[31]

Within three years, between 6 and 10 million people died. In 1896–1902, the experience was repeated, this time with as many as 19 million victims in the subcontinent.[32] Similar events would transpire elsewhere in the empire, a truly grim legacy for the ideas of Malthus. But even worse ideas were yet to come.

* * *

*FOCUS SECTION: THE DATA THAT PROVES MALTHUS WRONG*

The theory of Thomas Malthus has provided the scientific pretext for brutal antihuman policies from his own time down to the present. But is it true? On the surface, the idea that the more people there are, the less there will be to go around appears to make sense. It therefore follows that if we get rid of some—especially those we don't like anyway—we'll all be better off. Thus, those interested in eliminating Indians, Irish, Jews, Slavs, Africans, or any other race have argued that their policies, while harsh, are simply necessary to "make the world a better place."[33]

In this section, we will examine this claim critically by looking at historic data that allows us to analyze directly the real relationships between population growth and living standards. It will be shown that the theory of Malthus is completely at variance with the facts.

We begin with Figure 1.1, which shows data for world population, global gross domestic product (GDP), and GDP per capita from the year A.D. 1 down to the year 2000.[34]

In looking at this graph, we can see that while human population has certainly increased over time, GDP has increased even more, and the key metric of average human well-being, GDP per capita, has gone *up* as population has increased, rather than down as Malthusian theory would predict.

In Figure 1.2, we take a closer look at the period starting in the year 1500.

The actual per capita GDP in Figure 1.2 is shown by the thick line marked with squares. The thin line on the bottom marked with triangles represents what Malthus's theory would have predicted at the time of his writing around the year 1800. According to Malthus, the sixfold increase in population after his lifetime should have resulted in a disastrous drop in human living standards. Instead, global per capita GDP actually increased almost fortyfold, from $179 (in 1990 dollars) annually in 1800 to $6,756 by the year 2000.

## World Living Standard and Population Growth

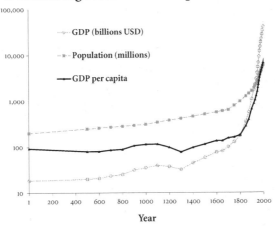

FIGURE 1.1: *Growth of world population, global GDP, and GDP per capita, from A.D. 1 to 2000. Note the logarithmic scale. GDP measured in 1990 dollars.*

## Living Standard vs. Population
### 1500-2000

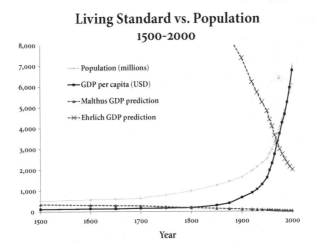

FIGURE 1.2: *Comparison of Malthusian predictions with reality, 1500 to present.*

Well, everyone has the right to be wrong about predicting the future. But the reader will note that I have taken the liberty of extending Malthus's prediction into his past. The world population in 1500 comprised 500 million people, just half of what it was in Malthus's day. If living standards go down with increased population, they should go up with decreased population. Thus, according to Malthusian theory, the world should have been much richer in 1500 than it was in 1800, with per capita GDP in the range of $360, instead of the $114 that historians estimate it actually was. *Malthus was not just wrong about predicting the future, he was wrong about predicting the past*, and not by a small variance, but by a factor of three.

Even more absurd were the predictions based on Malthusian theory that were widely published between 1968 and 1972 by Paul Ehrlich and his protégé John Holdren as well as the Club of Rome.[35] This cohort predicted that the "population explosion" would cause a catastrophic collapse of human well-being by the turn of the century, exactly the opposite of what actually happened.[36] If Ehrlich and company had been right, world GDP per capita would have fallen from $3,200 in 1970 to less than $2,000 today. Instead it rose to over $8,000 by 2010.

This fourfold error in predicting the future was really inexcusable, because these prophets had the advantage of hindsight in knowing about the wild inaccuracy of Malthus's original prediction, which by 1970 had already been shown to be off by a factor of fifty. But even worse, it is evident that Ehrlich, Holdren, and the Club of Rome studiously ignored data readily available to them about the economic history of the recent past. That is, if one takes the trouble of extending their predictive theory backwards in time (as shown by the thin line marked with X marks in Figure 1.2), we see that it indicates an average global GDP per capita of over $7,300 for the year 1900 instead of the $670 that it was in reality. Ehrlich was born in the year 1932. If the world were wealthier in the less-populated 1930s than in the 1960s and 70s, then he would have witnessed it himself. Instead, within his own lifetime, he had seen the world population double and the global standard of living more than triple at the same time. He didn't even have to open an almanac to know he was wrong—he just had to open his eyes.

The first task of any scientist is to compare the predictions of his theory to known data. The fact that Ehrlich, Holdren, and the Club of Rome refused to do this shows that their publications were not science at all. (Ehrlich, Holdren, and the Club of Rome will all be discussed in more detail in Chapter Nine.)

So, having refuted these charlatans, let us examine the data further, to see where it can lead us in developing a true theory that actually predicts the relationship between human well-being and population size.

A standard technique in trying to determine how one variable within a system changes with respect to another is to graph the first variable against the second and see if a clear relationship emerges. With this method, let us graph world population and per capita GDP against one another, using the data of the past five centuries. The results are shown in Figure 1.3.

There obviously seems to be a pattern here, which is *not* the Malthusian claim that living standards decrease as population grows. Rather, what we see is GDP per capita *increasing* with population, with a nearly straight-line direct proportionality holding for the past century. (If instead of talking about GDP per capita we discussed the *total* GDP, as shown in Figure 1.1, we would see that it rises not merely in proportion to population size, but in proportion to the size of the population *squared*.)

Why should this be? How can we explain the fact that as the number of human beings on the planet has grown, we've nearly all become much better off? Why should there be more of everything to go around, when there are more of us to feed, clothe, and house?

Though the trend might at first seem counterintuitive, there are a number of very good reasons why this is what the data show. As economist Julian Simon has noted in his indispensable book, *The Ultimate Resource*, a larger population can support a larger division of labor, and so it is more economically efficient.[37] Ten people with ten skills,

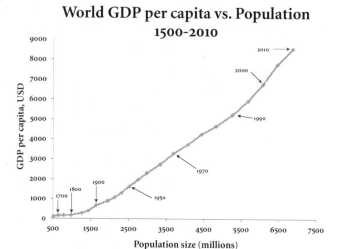

FIGURE 1.3: *How per capita GDP has changed as population has grown, 1500 to 2010.*

working or trading together, can produce far more than ten times as much as one person with one skill. A larger population also provides a larger market, which makes possible mass production and economies of scale. And because they represent a larger market, larger populations drive investment in new plant and equipment much more forcefully than smaller populations. If the market for an item is small, no one is going to build a new factory to produce it or spend much money on research to find ways to improve it. But if the sales opportunity is big, the necessary investment will quickly be made as a matter of course.

And there are other benefits to larger population as well. A larger population can better justify and afford transportation infrastructure projects, such as roads, bridges, canals, railroads, seaports, and airports, all of which serve to make the economy far more efficient and productive. Bigger populations have an easier time affording other kinds of infrastructure, too, like electrification and irrigation systems. And they can better afford the infrastructure of public health, including hospitals, clean water, and sanitation systems, and can act far more effectively in suppressing disease-spreading pests. It takes a large-scale effort to drain a malarial swamp, a reality that puts such projects beyond the capability of small, highly dispersed populations such as still persist in many parts of Africa. Furthermore, "boots on the ground" are necessary to patrol the regions in which we live to prevent ponds and puddles from becoming breeding grounds for mosquitoes and other disease carriers. A thin population will thus in many cases tend to be a much sicker population than a dense population that can marshal its resources against humanity's deadly natural enemies. And of course, a healthy population will be more productive than a sick population, and will reap a much better return on the investment it chooses to make in education (and thus be able to afford more education), since more of its young people will live to employ their education, and be able do so for longer life spans.[38]

That said, it is clear that the primary cause of higher living standards is not population size itself, but rather the overall technological development that it allows. The average living standard can be represented by per capita GDP, which is equal to the production per capita, which relies on technological prowess. So, although it isn't an exact indicator, we can use GDP per capita as a stand-in for technological development.

So then what causes the advance of technology? Clearly, technology does not come from the land; it comes from *people*. It is the product of *human work*. The most general way to measure human work is in terms of person-years. So let us now graph the growth of technology (as represented by GDP per capita) against human person-years expended, from the year A.D. 1 to the present. The results are shown in the next two figures. (Two graphs are used to show this to avoid the necessity of using logarithmic scales, which are harder to read.) Figure 1.4 shows the growth of human technology worldwide from the time of the Roman and Han empires to the late nineteenth century. There is a lot of very interesting history to be seen here, but basically it breaks down into three periods: that before 1500, that from 1500 to 1800, and that after 1800.

From A.D. 1 to 1500, technology does grow, but only at a very slow rate of 17.5 percent over 460 billion person-years, or an average of 0.035 percent per billion person-years. Between 1500 and 1800, the pace picks up substantially, with GDP per capita increasing by 58 percent in 200 billion person-years, or 0.23 percent per billion person-years, a more than sixfold increase over the preceding period. Then, around 1800, technology truly takes off, with GDP per capita growing 116 percent over the next 90 billion person-years.

This story continues in Figure 1.5. We can see a 4,700 percent increase over the entire 500 billion person-year span from 1800 to 2010, for an average growth rate of 0.8 percent per billion person-years.

These results make perfect sense. Before 1500 there really wasn't a world economy in any substantial sense because long-distance trade and communication was so limited. Rather than a world economy, what existed was a number of disparate civilizations including European Christendom, the Islamic world, India, China, Mexico, and Peru, each with its own economy. Important innovations made in one civilization could take centuries or even millennia to reach and be adopted by the others. Thus, for example, it took hundreds of years for such important Chinese inventions as paper, printing, and gunpowder to reach Europe, and thousands of years for European domesticated horses, wheeled vehicles, and numerous other technologies to reach the Americas. Thus, the relevant inventive population size driving the advance of each civilization was not the whole world population, as small as it was, but the much smaller population of the civilization itself.

But around 1500, following the voyages of Columbus, Vasco da Gama, and Magellan, European long-distance sailing ships began to knit together the world economy, creating vastly expanded markets for commerce and making it possible for inventions made anywhere to be rapidly adopted everywhere. Thus the effective inventive population for each civilization was radically expanded virtually overnight to encompass that of the entire world, creating a sixfold increase in the rate of progress per person-year compared to that of prior history. With more inventive people engaged and able to influence one another,

### Growth of Technology vs. Global Person-Years
### A.D. 1 - 1875

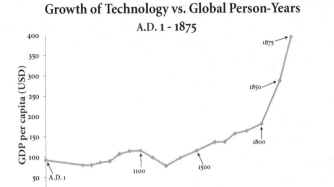

FIGURE 1.4: *Growth of Technology with respect to person-years, A.D. 1 to 1875.*

### Growth of Technology vs. Global Person-Years
### 1400-2010

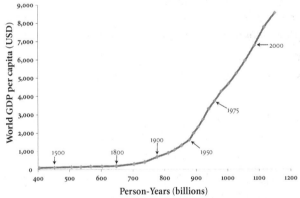

FIGURE 1.5: *Growth of Technology with respect to person-years, 1400 to 2010.*

the world advanced faster. Furthermore, it was precisely those countries with the greatest degree of contact with the largest number of people worldwide, the European seafaring nations, that advanced the fastest.

Then around 1800 the Industrial Revolution began, and the average rate of progress per person-year of human effort quadrupled yet again. This occurred not only because the steam engine allowed human beings to wield vastly greater mechanical power than had ever been possible before, but because particular technologies—most notably steamships, railroads, and telegraphs—radically increased the speed and thus the effective range of transportation, commerce, and communication. By the mid–1800s, innovations made by anyone, anywhere, could spread around the world extremely rapidly, defining a new global reality of accelerated progress that continues to the present day. The fact that any technological advance can now have immediate global impact makes human creativity today far more powerful and valuable than ever before.

The critical thing to understand here is that *technological advances are cumulative.* We are immeasurably better off today not only because of all the other people who are alive now, but because of all of those who lived and contributed in the past. Just consider what the world today would be like if the global population had been half as great in the nineteenth century. Here is a thought experiment: Thomas Edison and Louis Pasteur were approximate contemporaries. Edison invented the electric light, central power generation, recorded sound, and motion pictures. Pasteur pioneered the germ theory of disease that stands at the core of modern medicine. Which of these two would you prefer not to have existed? Go ahead, choose.

Human beings, on balance, are creators, not destroyers. Each human life, on average, contributes to improving the conditions of human life overall. We live as well as we do today because so many people lived in the past and made innumerable contributions, great and small, toward building the global civilization we now enjoy. If there had been fewer of them, we today would be poorer. If we accept

Malthusian dictates and act to reduce the world's population, we will not only commit a crime against the present, but impoverish the future by denying it the contributions the missing people could have made.

The world needs more children.

## CHAPTER TWO

# Darwinism's Moral Inversion

*At some future period, not very distant as measured by centuries, the civilized races of man will almost certainly exterminate, and replace, the savage races throughout the world. At the same time the anthropomorphous apes . . . will no doubt be exterminated. The break between man and his nearest allies will then be wider, for it will intervene between man in a more civilized state, as we may hope, even than the Caucasian, and some ape as low as a baboon, instead of as now between the negro or Australian and the gorilla.*

CHARLES DARWIN
*The Descent of Man*, Chapter VI[1]

BECAUSE THEY ARE so portentous, the ideas of Charles Darwin have been the subject of fierce controversy ever since they were first published. Unfortunately, however, most of those alarmed by the implications of Darwinism have chosen to attack his theories by disputing the fossil record. Such arguments are absurd. Evolution is a fact. To deny the fossil record documenting evolution is simply to deny reality. Furthermore, by defining the argument against Darwinism as a polemic against *evolution*, today's critics of Darwin give him credit for an enormous discovery—the history of life on Earth—that he would never have considered claiming for himself; and, more importantly, they place the defenders of his theory on utterly impregnable ground. Thus fortified, the Darwinists have been able to look down from their high perch as the appointed representatives of the

26

scientific worldview, and dismiss all those who would oppose their ideas and initiatives as irrational religious obscurantists. This misrepresentation of the issues needs to be addressed, for it has been of most pernicious consequence.

Darwin did not discover evolution. Rather, the fact that the complex organisms we see all around us have evolved over long periods of time from simpler forms was known well before Darwin was born, and even posited by some ancient Greek philosophers. Indeed, not only was the concept prominently published by leading Enlightenment biologists such as Georges-Louis Buffon and Jean-Baptiste Lamarck, but it was understood in pre-Darwin popular culture as well. For example, Washington Irving's humorous *Knickerbocker's History of New York: From the Beginning of the World to the Fall of the Dutch Dynasty*, published in 1809 (the year of Darwin's birth), recounts an extended history of the development of the Earth and all its life, starting from a pre-solar system nebula.[2]

Darwin's novel contribution was not the discovery of evolution but the presentation of a plausible explanation for it in the form of his theory of natural selection. Basing his ideas on Malthus's theory of limited resources in combination with Victorian philosopher Herbert Spencer's concept of the "survival of the fittest,"[3] Darwin proposed that all progress, both in nature and among mankind, occurs by superior strains out-competing inferior varieties as part of the "struggle for existence"[4] in the face of limited resources.

While for the Malthusians, the cruel effects of imperial rule could be explained as unfortunate but unavoidable consequences of the constraints of the Earth's bounty, for Darwinians, such horrors were actually seen as a blessing, since they hastened the advance of humanity through the weeding out of "unfit" individuals and races.

To be clear, Darwin was a superb naturalist, and his theory of natural selection represents a significant contribution to biology. With allowance given for a number of errors endemic to the science of his time, his theory does explain some of the phenomena observable in evolution. It does not explain all, however, and subsequent biologists have invoked additional processes, including symbiogenesis, punctuated equilibrium, and ecological succession, to account for the development of the natural world. What is more important for our present discussion, however, is that this purported universal law of nature *when applied to human affairs* leads to wildly incorrect conclusions (some by Darwin himself) and catastrophically unethical policies (by his followers).[5]

In his key work on human social development, *The Descent of Man* (1871), Darwin claims that the advances of various nations and races, and thus the triumphs of one over the other, are due to the inherited traits of their individual members:

> Of the high importance of the intellectual faculties there can be no doubt, for man mainly owes to them his predominant position in the world. We can see, that in the rudest state of society, the individuals who were the most sagacious, who invented and used the best weapons or traps, and who were best able to defend themselves, would rear the greatest number of offspring. The tribes, which included the largest number of men thus endowed, would increase in number and supplant other tribes. . . . At the present day civilized nations are everywhere supplanting barbarous nations, excepting where the climate opposes a deadly barrier; and they succeed mainly, though not exclusively, through their arts, which are the products of the intellect. It is, therefore, highly probable that with mankind the intellectual faculties have been mainly and gradually perfected through natural selection.[6]

As a theory explaining human history, this is sheer nonsense. Nations do not rise in triumph over others due to the genetic superiority of their members. If such were the case, one would be hard put to explain how the Mongols, having lived for thousands of years in degraded obscurity (a fact that the Darwinian theory, as applied to man, would deem a demonstration of genetic inferiority) should suddenly rise in

*"Civilized nations are everywhere supplanting barbarous nations . . . and they succeed mainly . . . through their arts, which are the products of the intellect." Having demonstrated the evolutionary superiority of the Anglo- Saxon race through the liberal use of machine guns, Governor William Maxwell humiliates the Ashanti King and Queen at the end of the Ashanti Campaign in Ghana, 1896 . Acting to advance evolutionary progress still further, the British then stole the Ashanti gold.*

the late twelfth century to conquer most of the civilized world (thereby demonstrating great genetic superiority) only to return to their previous weakness a few centuries later. In their day, the Syrians, Macedonians, Romans, Hungarians, Arabs, Danes, Turks, Castilians, French, and Germans were all awesome conquerors. Yet few fear their military prowess now. In the struggles of nations, genetic endowment matters far less than political organization and leadership, diplomacy, available alliances, economic development, culture, religion, ideology, defense technology, military tactics and generalship, geography, weather, and sheer luck.

The scientific error in ascribing human progress to natural selection of hereditary traits is big enough to drive a train through, for the simple reason that human beings, unlike other organisms, are capable of systematically passing on information through non-hereditary means, such as artifacts and words. While other animals cannot inherit acquired characteristics, let alone obtain beneficial adaptations from those with whom they are unrelated, human beings can. Furthermore, these non-hereditary human means of transferring adaptations operate far faster than adaptations based on biological heredity, and thus completely dominate them in effective control of social development. Finally, because people can use their minds to create novel adaptations varying from technological inventions to better forms of social organization, human progress is chiefly governed by what people accomplish during their *lives*, rather than chiefly through the process of their winnowing out by *death*.

By ignoring the ability of human beings to rapidly transfer information, ideas, and inventions from one nation to another, the Darwinian view denies a fundamental material relationship underlying the brotherhood of man. According to the Darwinian view, since America and China represent competing races, an invention that advances the American economy should harm China. This is false. The Americans and Chinese cooperate in countless ways, transferring many useful inventions (in biological terms, acquired adaptive traits) from one nation or race to another. American advances—from telegraphs, electric lighting, telephones, and airplanes to electronics, nuclear power, satellite communications, personal computers, and agricultural biotechnology—have enormously benefited the entire world, China included. Indeed, America has suffered greatly because most of the rest of the world has not been as inventive, thus depriving us of a huge number of comparable inventions that we might have received in return. The best thing that could possibly happen to the United States would be for China, India, Africa, and the rest of the world to become fully developed and well-educated so those peoples can contribute a greater share to global human progress. But according to the Darwinian view, we should not want the sons and daughters of Chinese or African peasants to become scientists or engineers, intellectually equipped to make new inventions or launch new industries. Rather, we should do everything possible to keep them down or wipe them out.

Where a *true* understanding of the human condition would lead to love, Darwinism prescribes hate. In place of international friendship between diverse nations sharing the benefits of the talents of all, it calls for genocide, falsely warranted by putative scientific law.

## THE DESCENT OF MAN

However, while counterfactual, Darwin's theory of victory through racial superiority—and of human progress being based on such triumphs of "higher races" over "lower races"—did a perfect job of justifying brutal European imperial looting of the less developed world. It should be no surprise, then, that virtually instantly after the publication of his *On the Origin of Species by Means of Natural Selection, or the Preservation of Favoured Races in the Struggle for Life* in 1859, Darwin became an international scientific superstar.

Many on the political left today hold Darwin to be a hero because of the blow his theory inflicted on those holding to Biblical creationism. In his 2007 bestseller, *God Is Not Great*, Christopher Hitchens goes so far as to say: "Charles Darwin was born in 1809, on the very same day as Abraham Lincoln, and there is no doubt as to which of them has proved to be the greater 'emancipator.'"[7] But more astute leftists among Darwin's own contemporaries had much greater insight into what the excitement over natural selection was really all about. As Karl Marx shrewdly observed to Friedrich Engels in 1862: "It is remarkable how Darwin rediscovers, among beasts and plants, the society of England with its division of labour, competition, opening of new markets, 'inventions,' and the Malthusian 'struggle for existence.'"[8] In an 1875 letter to another leftist intellectual, Engels put the matter even more bluntly:

The whole Darwinist teaching of the struggle for existence is simply a transference from society to living nature of [philosopher Thomas] Hobbes's doctrine of *bellum omnium contra omnes* [the war of all against all] and of the bourgeois-economic doctrine of competition together with Malthus's theory of population. When this conjurer's trick has been performed . . . the same theories are transferred back again from organic nature into history and it is now claimed that their validity as eternal laws of human society has been proved. The puerility of this procedure is so obvious that not a word need be said about it.[9]

Darwin's supporters were, if anything, even clearer as to the basis for their enthusiasm. As Darwin's first translator, Clémence Royer, spells out in her preface to the French edition of *The Origin of Species*:

The findings of the theory of natural selection cannot leave us in any doubt but that higher races are progressively produced; and that, by consequence, according to the law of progress, they are destined to supplant the lower races by progressing further, and not to mix and combine with them in a way that would lower the average level of the species. In a word, human races are not distinct species, but they are very well-defined and highly unequal varieties; and we should think twice before proclaiming political and civic equality among a people composed of an Indo-European minority and a majority of Mongols or Negroes.[10]

Like Malthus before him, but going further, Darwin did more than provide a scientific justification for extreme exploitation, racism, imperialism, and genocide. In *The Descent of Man*, he also produced a forceful argument for those wishing to be free of the constraints of Christian or Enlightenment humanist ethics in dealing with their fellow man at home:

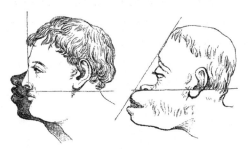

[*Profile of Negro, European, and Oran Outan.*]

IRISH IBERIAN  ANGLO-TEUTONIC  NEGRO

*Darwinian popularizations purporting to show the*
*similarity of Negroes to orangutans (top),*
*and Irish to Negroes.*

With savages, the weak in body or mind are soon eliminated; and those that survive commonly exhibit a vigorous state of health. We civilized men, on the other hand, do our utmost to check the process of elimination; we build asylums for the imbecile, the maimed, and the sick; we institute poor-laws; and our medical men exert their utmost skill to save the life of every one to the last moment. There is reason to believe that vaccination has preserved thousands, who from a weak constitution would formerly have succumbed to small-pox. Thus the weak members of civilized societies propagate their kind. No one who has attended to the breeding of domestic animals will doubt that this must be highly injurious to the race of man. It is surprising how soon a want of care, or care wrongly directed, leads to the degeneration of a domestic race; but excepting in the case of man himself, hardly any one is so ignorant as to allow his worst animals to breed.[11]

Thus for Darwinism, human compassion toward the unfortunate was not merely useless (as per Malthus) but actually morally *wrong*. This is exemplary of a broader inversion of ethics inherent in Darwinism. As Darwin put it in the penultimate sentence of *Origin of Species*: "Thus, from the war of nature, from famine and death, the most exalted object which we are capable of conceiving, namely, the production of the higher animals, directly follows."[12]

For thousands of years, the Judeo-Christian civilization had held life to be good, and death to be evil. Based on this ethic, Europeans had always viewed death as an enemy to be overcome, not a beneficial force. By rejecting the truth that the advance of humanity is achieved through what people accomplish during life, in favor of evolution by elimination, Darwinism reversed this.

Instead of being evils, war, disease, and famine were now good and necessary. Without famine and disease, the unfit could not be culled. Without war, the superior could not rid the world of the inferior. Peace, plenty, care, and compassion were interferences in the course of nature. All progress was based on death.

The twentieth century would see plenty of it.

## CHAPTER THREE

# The Birth of Eugenics

*It might not be unreasonable, perhaps, to intimate that his white blood may have had something to do with the remarkable energy he displayed and the superior intelligence he manifested. Indeed, it might not be altogether unreasonable to ask whether, with more white blood, he would not have been an even better and greater man than he was, and whether the fact that he had any black blood at all may not have cost the world a genius, and be, in consequence, a cause for lamentation instead of a source of lyrical enthusiasm over African possibilities. It is always more or less foolish to credit or discredit a race with the doings, good or bad, of a particular member of that race, but if it must be done, plain justice should see to it that the right race gets the glory or the humiliation.*

Editorial on the death of Frederick Douglass,
*New York Times*, February 27, 1895[1]

DARWIN WAS A reclusive country gentleman scholar of moderate disposition, content to let nature take its course in the inevitable elimination of the inferior—not a political utopian, militarist, robber baron, reactionary, race-baiter, xenophobe, or frenzied fanatic pursuing a political agenda. Nevertheless, such people readily understood that Darwinism gave them precisely the scientific and ethical justification they desired, and they lost no time in putting it to work. Growing lushly in such fertile ground, these ideas then took on a life of their own, evolving further according to their implicit internal logic into ever more ruthless forms, which in turn attracted ever more radical advocates.

One of the first out of the gate was Darwin's cousin, Sir Francis Galton. A well-to-do dilettante who dropped out of medical school upon receiving his ample inheritance, Galton used his book *Hereditary Genius* (1869) to establish the pseudoscience, or, as he hoped, "new religion," that he subsequently named "eugenics."[2] According to Galton, all the human qualities causative of either individual, national, or racial success are inherited, and the same can be said for those traits leading to failure. Furthermore, all successes or failures seen in life are substantially due to the presence or absence of such inbred qualities. Galton marshaled extensive statistical data in support of this proposition, demonstrating beyond question that the offspring of judges, cabinet ministers, and admirals are far more likely to achieve eminence than the children of chimney sweeps, day laborers, and rag pickers.[3] If evolution was to be advanced, it was essential that superior people be encouraged to have more children, and inferior types be constrained to have fewer.

To further the implementation of such a program, Galton provided a grading system to precisely measure the eugenic value of each person. Superior people were graded with capital letters $A$ (just above average) through $X$ (super genius), while inferiors were assigned lowercase letters $a$ (just a bit subnormal) through $g$ (imbecile).[4] To account for the superiority of some races over others, a suitable metric was needed to establish the equivalent merit of various grades across racial lines. The magnitude of such adjustment factors could then be used to assess the value of the races themselves. As Galton explains in his chapter on "The Comparative Worth of Different Races":

Classes E and F of the negro may roughly be considered the equivalent of our C and D—a result which again points to the conclusion, that the average intellectual standard of the negro is two grades below our own . . . the number among the negroes of those whom we should call half-witted men, is very large.

Every book alluding to negro servants in America is full of instances. I was myself much impressed by this fact during my travels in Africa. The mistakes the negroes made in their own matters, were so childish, stupid, and simpleton-like, as frequently to make me ashamed of my own species. I do not think it any exaggeration to say, that their c is as low as our e, which would be a difference of two grades, as before.[5]

To remedy such shortcomings in the native population of Britain's African colonies, Galton recommended their replacement by a more suitable subject race. As he advised in an 1 8 7 3 letter to the *Times* of London:

[In Africa,] as elsewhere, one population continually drives out another.... I wish to see a new competitor introduced— namely the Chinaman. The gain would be immense to the whole civilized world if he were to outbreed and finally displace the negro.... The magnitude of the gain may be partly estimated by making the converse supposition—namely, the loss that would ensue if China were somehow to be depopulated and restocked by negroes.[6]

Even so, native Africans were not the worst of the human lot, according to Galton: "The Australian type is at least one grade below the African negro."[7] Indeed, since, as he explained, "class F of dogs ... is nearly commensurate with the f of the human race, in respect to memory and powers of reason," and "class G of such animals is far superior to the g of humankind," many among the Australian aborigines would have to be considered lower on the evolutionary scale than the better breeds of domestic dogs.[8]

Other inferior races in Galton's view included Orientals, Jews, and, of course, the Irish: "Visitors to Ireland after the potato famine generally remarked that the Irish type of face seemed to have become more prognathous, that is, more like the negro in the protrusion of the

PUCK'S GALLERY OF CELEBRITIES.

THE KING OF A-SHANTEE

*Irish prognathism, as depicted in the American magazine*
Puck *in 1882. The cartoon was entitled "The King of*
*A-Shantee." The pun playing on "Ashanti" served to*
*further link the Irish to black Africans, while the simian*
*features drawn linked both to subhuman primates.*

lower jaw; the interpretation of which was, that the men who survived the starvation and other deadly accidents of that horrible time, were more generally of a low and coarse organization."[9]

Americans of Anglo-Saxon stock were also deemed to be inferior. "England has certainly got rid of a great deal of refuse, through means of emigration,"[10] Galton said, adding that he didn't like American ideals either: "it is in the most unqualified manner that I object to pretensions of natural equality."[11]

Galton went well beyond disparaging the equality of man. According to him, adherents of eugenics must discard any notion of natural human rights as well. On the contrary, as he stated in chillingly prophetic terms, in the face of the state's duty to advance the race, the inferior had no rights, and "if these continued to procreate children, inferior in moral, intellectual and physical qualities, it is easy to believe the time may come when such persons would be considered as enemies to the State, and to have forfeited all claims to kindness."[12]

*Eugenics was put forward as a new universal philosophy.*

While strongly endorsed by Charles Darwin in *The Descent of Man*, Galton's utopian views were initially too much for British morality, practicality, and common sense, and met a cool reception in the press. Reviewing *Hereditary Genius*, the London *Daily News* said "Unfortunately, young men will fall in love, and girls will marry them without considering the effect of the union upon the race."[13] To Galton's answer that, regardless, the proper breeding of humans to meet eugenic purposes could be effected by government oversight and enforcement, the *Times* of London pointedly replied: "The universal knowledge of reading, writing, and ciphering and the absence of pauperism would raise the national grade of ability far quicker and higher than any system of selected marriage."[14]

Nevertheless, Galton kept at it, writing article after article warning of the threat of racial degeneration and arguing for a new eugenic religion to save and elevate mankind. Over time, his persistence paid off, and with the help of his devoted and very able acolyte Karl Pearson, Galton was able to create a substantial following for eugenics among the educated classes in England, Germany, and the United States. Initially, like Darwinism and Malthusianism before it, eugenics found its warmest reception among Britain's *laissez-faire* liberals. Karl Pearson, however, was a man of the left, whose social circle included playwright George Bernard Shaw, Fabian Society leaders Sidney and Beatrice Webb, sexual-liberation radical Havelock Ellis, socialist futurist H. G. Wells, and Karl Marx's daughter Eleanor. As a result of Pearson's successful conversion of this crowd to the creed, English eugenics took on the aspect of a fashionable *avant-garde* radical left-wing movement (to the considerable annoyance of the arch social conservative Galton).[15] There was some logic to this, since, following Sidney Webb's argument that eugenicists could not be *laissez-faire* individualists, many proponents of eugenics believed that their program could only be accomplished under socialism.[16] In other countries, however, it was to assume other guises.

*Francis Galton (right) with his disciple,*
*Fabian Society scientific guru Karl Pearson.*

## CHAPTER FOUR

# Deutschland über Alles

*The support which I receive from Germany is my chief ground for hoping that our views will ultimately prevail.*

CHARLES DARWIN
letter to Wilhelm Preyer, 1868[1]

*Now it seems to me that, among the very numerous philosophical theories current in Germany, and which exert such a real and deep influence on German behavior, one of the most important is the idea of a brutal and ineluctable necessity, inherent in the nature of things, before which all the protestations of human conscience are no more than the vain grizzling of an ill-behaved child. And among these iron laws, one of those that the Germans are most eager to invoke is the "struggle for existence" so powerfully highlighted by Darwin. In the name of Darwinism, they believe they can maintain that science itself, the most modern and solid science, condemns all the nations on earth to be either assimilated or destroyed by the German nation, as the species best equipped for the struggle for existence.*

EMILE BOUTROUX
preface to P. Chalmers-Mitchell,
*Le Darwinisme et la Guerre*, 1916[2]

IT WAS THE good fortune of Darwinism and eugenics, and a catastrophe for the human race, that the new theories recruited as their enthusiastic champion in Germany no less a talent than Ernst Haeckel.

41

A professor of comparative anatomy at the University of Jena, Haeckel was one of the giants of nineteenth-century biology. Among his many other contributions, Haeckel coined the word "ecology" as well as the saying (once recited by high school students everywhere) that "ontogeny recapitulates phylogeny"—meaning that the embryonic development of every organism repeats in truncated form its evolutionary history.[3] Possessing all the power and prestige that went with his stature as the leader of the German scientific establishment, Haeckel was also a brilliant writer, authoring numerous books on science for the general public which sold out in unprecedented runs of hundreds of thousands of copies.[4] To get a sense of the role and influence of Haeckel in Wilhelmine Germany by a more contemporary comparison, take the popularization skills of a Carl Sagan, multiply by ten, and combine them with the authority of an Albert Einstein. For educated and semi-educated Germans interested in the latest ideas that science had to offer, if Haeckel said it, it was so.

Unfortunately, Haeckel was also an extreme racist, virulent anti-Catholic bigot, anti-Semite, anti-Pole, pro-imperialist, Pan-German fanatic.[5] He was also a militant atheist who advocated replacing the worship of God with the worship of Nature. In addition to denying the existence of the human soul, Haeckel's naturalistic atheism also required a denial of any fundamental distinction between human beings and animals, and thus any foundation for the support of human rights, or even the existence of human free will. Instead, human behavior, like that of animals, was governed by heredity, and thus predetermined, with racial identity playing the dominant role.[6]

While Darwin reluctantly conceded that all human beings were ultimately members of the same species, Haeckel denied this. Instead, according to Haeckel, there were no less than twelve different human species, comprising thirty-six different races. These were topped by the white species, which itself included four different white races, among whom the "Indo Germanians" were the best, with the High Germans representing the evolutionary pinnacle of the lot.[7]

These racial differences were by no means immaterial. As Haeckel explained in his 1904 book *Wonders of Life*: "Since the lower races (such as the Veddahs or Australian Negroes) are psychologically nearer to the mammals (apes and dogs) than to civilized Europeans, we must, therefore, assign a totally different value to their lives."[8]

Haeckel argued that Darwinism provided a basis for a new all-encompassing scientific worldview that could replace conventional Christian ethics. Calling this new faith "Monism," for unity, he used his ability as a popularizer to build it into an influential intellectual movement among Germany's elites during the period before World War I.[9] In addition to seeking the furtherance of human evolution through German global conquest, Monists were notable for advocating infanticide of abnormal children and mass murder of invalids for the purposes of racial improvement.[10]

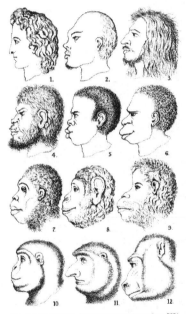

Die Familiengruppe der Katarrhinen (siehe Seite 555).

*"The Family Group of the Apes," showing Germans (top row, left) as the most human and Africans (second row center and left) as closely related to the ape.*

(*Illustrations from Haeckel's* Natürliche Schöpfungsgeschichte, *1868.*)

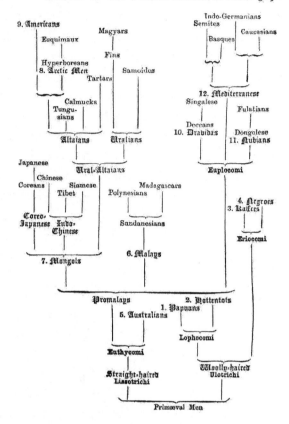

PEDIGREE OF THE TWELVE SPECIES OF MEN. 309

*The human evolutionary tree, as drawn by Ernst Haeckel, 1876. "Indo-Germanians" are the highest branch in the upper right. Africans and aboriginals appear to be much less evolved. The numbers identify twelve different human species.*

As historian Daniel Gasman reported in his landmark 1971 book *The Scientific Origins of National Socialism*:

For most of the Monists the main task of the state was to insure the survival and reproduction of only the biologically fittest individuals.... Successful politics, according to Haeckel, was in reality nothing more than applied biology, and he liked to evoke the memory of the ancient Spartans, who, he maintained, were strong solely because they practiced biological selection. The most "remarkable" aspect of Spartan history, Haeckel wrote [in the 1876 translation of his book, *The History of Creation*], was their "obedience to a special law" whereby "all newly-born children were subject to careful examination or selection." Then, those children [who] were "weak, sickly, or affected with any bodily infirmity were killed." It was only the "perfectly healthy and strong children who were allowed to live, and they alone afterwards propagated the race." In this way the Spartans were "not only continually in excellent strength and vigor," but they also perfected their bodies and increased their strength with every generation. Haeckel concluded, therefore, that the "destruction of abnormal new-born infants" could not be "rationally" classified as "murder" as is "done in modern legal works." One should regard it rather, he wrote, as a "practice of advantage both to the infants destroyed and to the community."[11]

The practice of medicine, according to Haeckel, furthered the spread of disease: "Now, the longer the diseased parents, with medical assistance, can drag on their sickly existence, the more numerous are the descendants who will inherit incurable evils, and the greater will be the number of individuals again, in the succeeding generations ... who will be infected by their parents with lingering, hereditary disease." Haeckel complained that "hundreds of thousands of incurables—lunatics, lepers, people with cancer, etc.—are artificially kept alive ... without the slightest profit to themselves or the general body." Gasman continues:

> He suggested that the number of insane and incurably ill was steadily on the increase and therefore not only was eugenic action necessary for the protection of future generations but the present population of the diseased had to be eliminated. He thus

advocated the setting up of a commission which would decide on matters of life and death for the ill and the deformed. Upon a decision of the commission the "'redemption from evil' should be accomplished by a dose of some painless and rapid poison."[12]

The full meaning of Monism was summed up well by Haeckel's French champion, the Aryan racist ideologue Georges Vacher de Lapouge. In the preface to his 1897 translation of Haeckel's *Monism as Connecting Religion and Science*, Vacher de Lapouge wrote: "We are marching through monism towards the complete elimination of the idea of religion. We are marching, by way of new formulas based on social hygiene, towards the elimination of the idea of morality.... To the celebrated formula that sums up the secular Christianity of the Revolution: liberty, equality, fraternity—we reply: determinism, inequality, selection!"[13]

## WAR OF THE RACES

Haeckel's numerous other protégés and disciples included race scientists Friedrich Hellwald, Wilhelm Schallmayer, Heinrich Ziegler, Ludwig Woltmann, Otto Ammon, Alexander Tille, Ludwig Plate, Max von Gruber, Alfred Ploetz, Eugen Fischer, Ernst Rüdin, and Fritz Lenz.[14] In 1905, Ploetz, Fischer, Rüdin, and Lenz founded the German Society for Racial Hygiene, whose members, notably future *Reichskommissar* Rüdin, were largely responsible for the racist eugenics and anti-Semitic laws of the Third Reich.[15]

Among this vile pantheon, Hellwald is particularly notable as a leading Darwinian apostle of German militarism and anti-morality. In his 1875 bestseller, *The History of Culture in Its Natural Evolution* (dedicated to Haeckel), Hellwald wrote:

Science knows no "natural right." In nature only one right reigns, which is no right, the right of the stronger, violence. But violence is the highest source of law ... properly speaking the right of the stronger has also been valid at all times in human history... [science has proven] that just as in nature the struggle for existence is the moving principle of evolution and perfection, in that the weak are worn away and must make room for the strong, so also in world history the destruction of weaker nations through the stronger is a postulate of progress.[16]

These pro-war ideas were strongly backed by the chorus of Monist leaders that followed, such as prominent biologist Ziegler and anthropologist Ammon. In an 1893 book refuting socioeconomic equality and pacifism, Ziegler says: "according to Darwin's theory wars have always been of the greatest importance for the general progress of the human species, in that the physically weaker, the less intelligent, the morally lower or morally degenerate peoples must give place to the stronger and the better developed."[17] In a book of his own published in 1900, Ammon concurs: "In its complete effect war is *a good deed* for humanity, since it offers the only means to measure the power of nations and to grant the victory to the fittest. War is the highest and *most majestic* form of the struggle for existence and cannot be dispensed with, and thus also cannot be abolished."[18]

Haeckel's followers spanned the political spectrum. Woltmann, for example, was a theoretician of the Social Democratic Party who proposed a grand unification of Marxism and race science. Ploetz defined himself as a man of the left as well.[19] Helene Stöcker, one of Germany's leading pacifists, also followed Monism in her own way, arguing that "war of the white races among themselves immensely threatens the domination of the white race in relation to the yellow and black races."[20] As for Haeckel, though he favored Germany's involvement in World War I, opposed the German peace resolution, and called the war a "violent episode in the universal human struggle for existence," for most of his career he considered himself a pacifist. The reason is not that he believed in peace, but rather that he believed the wrong people die in war: the strong and fit go off to fight and die, while the inferior classes stay home and multiply.[21]

It was, however, among the Prussian militarist establishment that Haeckel's ideas had their most immediate fatal impact. The consequences of this were first made apparent for all to see when the German General Staff ordered a war of extermination against the Herero population of German Southwest Africa (today's Namibia). Targeting every man, woman, and child for butchery, the 1904–1906 German crushing of the Hereros was the first genocide of the twentieth century, and was so brutal as to shock the rather hard sensibilities of imperialist Europe. Even German chancellor Bernhard von Bülow condemned it as "contradictory to all Christian and humane principles." General Lothar von Trotha, in charge of the extermination campaign, dismissed the chancellor's moral indignation: "The philanthropic disposition will not rid the world of the above-mentioned law of Darwin's, the 'struggle of the fittest.'" To this, General Alfred von Schlieffen, the head of the General Staff, added, "Racial war, once it has broken out, can only be ended by the destruction of one of the parties."[22]

Germany's distinguished Darwinian scientific establishment had given its military leaders a global racial mission. As Kaiser Wilhelm II wrote to President Theodore Roosevelt in 1905, "I foresee in the future a fight for life and death between the 'White' and the 'Yellow' for their sheer existence. The sooner therefore the Nations belonging to the 'White Race' understand this and join in common defense against the coming danger, the better."[23]

But it was not just "blacks" and "yellows" who were the militarists' targets. Europe required racial improvement as well. General Friedrich von Bernhardi wrote in his 1912 international bestseller *Germany and the Next War* (also published in an even more popular abridgement *Our Future*), encouraging the German military conquest of Europe, that war was a "biological necessity." Darwinism proves, Bernhardi said, that "everywhere the right of the stronger reigns," and that war was necessary because it "eliminates the weak."[24]

In 1870, as a young officer, Bernhardi had personally led the march through the Arc de Triomphe when the Germans took Paris. Now he was the General Staff's chief intellectual. The chapter titles alone of his book make his chilling thesis clear: "The Right to Make War." "The Duty to Make War." "Germany's Historical Mission." "World Power or Downfall." Germany, Bernhardi said, "is in social-political respects at the head of all progress in culture. . . . Conquest thus becomes a law of necessity."[25]

*"Racial war, once it has broken out, can only be ended by the destruction of one of the parties." Teutonic Austrians exterminate slavic Serbs, 1917.*

Bernhardi's book set off alarm bells in foreign capitals. It seemed insane, but the leaders of the Kaiser's Germany—an empire mighty, prosperous, unthreatened, and nearly unchallengeable on the European continent—appeared to be seeking war almost for the sake of war itself. They were. Soon millions would pay the price.

As horrific as the destruction wrought by the Prussian generals would be, it could not match that set in motion by Haeckel and his legions of Darwinian professorial acolytes. For it was their ideas that were taught in every university in Germany and German-speaking Austria during the Wilhelmine period and the subsequent Weimar years; the graduates of those institutions went on to drum the lessons into schoolchildren across the land. The universities and the German back-to-nature youth movement would thus both become hotbeds of

Darwinian antihumanism. When the schoolchildren grew up, they would take their lessons forward in a way that would make anything that the Kaiser or von Schlieffen had in mind seem very tame indeed.

But perhaps a hint of the insanity that had already been instilled in them could be seen on the fateful evening of August 4, 1914, when it became clear that England would stand by its treaty to defend Belgium from German invasion. A mob of Berliners, enraged by the news, stoned the British embassy, knocking out all the windows. "*Rassenverrat!*" they screamed, venting their hate of the Anglo-Saxons. "Race treason!"[26]

## CHAPTER FIVE

# Eugenics Comes to America

*Our ancestors drove Baptists from Massachusetts Bay in to
Rhode Island, but we have no place to drive the Jews to. Also
they burned the witches but it seems against the mores to burn
any considerable part of our population. Meanwhile, we have
somewhat diminished the immigration of these people.*

CHARLES DAVENPORT
director of the Eugenics Records Office,
letter to Madison Grant, April 7, 1925[1]

AS HAPPENED IN England, Darwin's theory of human progress
through natural selection of superior individuals and races rapidly
became popular among the elite in America. Starting in 1861, a
group drawn from the nation's leading patrician families and finan-
ciers—including J. P. Morgan, Hugh Auchincloss, Theodore Roosevelt, Sr., James Brown and Howard Potter of Brown Brothers (later
Brown Brothers Harriman), Levi Morton and George Bliss of Morton
Bliss, members of the Phelps family, and members of the Dodge family—were induced to generously contribute to the project of establishing the American Museum of Natural History in New York City.
At the founding ceremony, in 1877, Harvard President Charles W.
Eliot explained the purpose of the new institution:

In whose honor are the chief personages of the nation, state,
and city here assembled? Whose palace is this? What divinity is
worshipped in this place? . . . Nothing else than the stupendous

doctrine of hereditary transmission [which will] ... enhance the natural interest in vigorous family stocks ... give a rational basis for penal legislation, and promote both the occasional production of illustrious men and the gradual improvement of the masses of mankind.[2]

Although it would shock the millions of people who now visit it every year, the American Museum of Natural History was for six decades, especially under its long-term president Henry Fairfield Osborn (the nephew of J. P. Morgan), a major center for promoting Darwinism and eugenics in the United States.

The Darwinist ideology gained broader popular traction after 1890, when the U.S. Census announced the closing of the frontier, thereby making the Malthusian view of a world of limited resources seem more generally credible. Soon thereafter, the Immigration Restriction League (IRL) was founded to lobby for legislation that would preserve America's limited natural resources for her existing population, while also preserving that population itself from degradation through intermixing with allegedly inferior immigrant stock. The initial leaders of the IRL came from the elite of New England, but subsequently the group expanded to encompass similar circles across the country.[3]

While anti-immigrant xenophobia had often had some presence in American political life, in the past it could largely be found among laborers fearing job competition, or in the gutter. By contrast, America's business leaders had previously welcomed immigrants, who benefited them greatly by providing both skilled and cheap workers for their industries and settlers to increase the value of their lands. While these material interests still spoke for a pro-immigrant policy, the increasingly prevalent Darwinian antihuman ideology now argued otherwise. As General Francis Amasa Walker, the president of M.I.T., put it in a landmark 1896 *Atlantic Monthly* article that helped launch the new anti-immigration movement:

The problems which so sternly confront us to-day are serious enough without being complicated and aggravated by the addition of some millions of Hungarians, Bohemians, Poles, south Italians, and Russian Jews. . . . These people have no history behind them which is of a nature to give encouragement. They have none of the *inherited instincts* and tendencies which made it comparatively easy to deal with the immigration of the olden time. *They are beaten men from beaten races; representing the worst failures in the struggle for existence.* . . . They have none of the ideas and aptitudes which fit men to take up readily and easily the problem of self-care and self-government, *such as belong to those who are descended from the tribes that met under the oak-trees of old Germany to make laws and choose chieftains.*[4]

The propaganda of the IRL was strongly supported by (supposedly) scientific studies produced by the growing eugenics movement, led most notably by Charles Benedict Davenport. A Connecticut-born biologist who traced his ancestry back to the original Puritan settlers, Davenport traveled to England in 1897 where he met with Galton and was converted to eugenics by the master himself. On his subsequent return to the United States, in 1905 Davenport led in the creation of the human eugenics section of the American Breeders Association, an organization which previously had been devoted to the study of animal stocks.[5] Then, in 1910, Davenport established a very productive social relationship with Mary Harriman (later Mary Harriman Rumsey).[6] Upon her conversion to eugenics, young Mary introduced Davenport to her mother, also named Mary, the spectacularly wealthy widow of railroad magnate E. H. Harriman. Exerting his charm, Davenport not only converted Mrs. Harriman as well, but convinced her to fund the establishment of the Eugenics Record Office (ERO)—an effort to which, over the next eight years, Mrs. Harriman would contribute eighty acres of land near Cold Spring Harbor, Long Island, and over half a million dollars (about $9 million today). With a well-funded staff led by Davenport and superintendent Harry Hamilton Laughlin, and a huge database relating to human heredity, the ERO was to serve as an authoritative voice of the American eugenics movement for the next thirty years.[7]

## ELIMINATING THE HUDDLED MASSES

Among the first projects of the ERO was a campaign to institute laws for the forced sterilization of various categories of allegedly "inadequate" people. These included, according to a Model Eugenical Sterilization Law drafted by Laughlin:

(1) Feeble-minded; (2) Insane (including the psychopathic); (3) Criminalistic (including the delinquent and wayward); (4) Epileptic; (5) Inebriate (including drug-habitués); (6) Diseased (including the tuberculous, the syphilitic, the leprous, and others with chronic, infectious, and legally segregable diseases); (7) Blind (including those with seriously impaired vision); (8) Deaf (including those with seriously impaired hearing); (9) Deformed (including the crippled); and (10) Dependent (including orphans, ne'er-do-wells, the homeless, tramps, and paupers).[8]

As a result of ERO lobbying, variants of Laughlin's model law were passed in thirty states, with over 63,000 institutionalized Americans forcibly sterilized accordingly over the next six decades. Furthermore, hundreds of thousands (possibly millions) of additional poor people were coerced into accepting irreversible sterilization in the face of threatened removal of welfare benefits, until the practice was ruled unlawful by federal judge Gerhard Gesell in 1974.[9]

The ERO also contributed to the cause of American racial purity by acting to suppress knowledge of the cure for pellagra, a vitamin-deficiency disease. During the early part of the twentieth century, approximately 5,000 Americans died every year of pellagra, with an additional estimated 300,000 per year perishing from infectious diseases as a result of being weakened by pellagra. Almost all of these deaths occurred among the poor population of the deep south, with nearly half drawn from the 10 percent of the U.S. population that was black.[10] In a series of experiments in 1914–1915, Dr. Joseph Goldberger of the U.S. Public Health Service discovered that pellagra is caused by a shortage of niacin and can be cured by feeding victims a balanced diet including meat and vegetables. Conversely, limiting a diet to corn, a staple among poor southerners at that time, would invariably produce severe cases of the disease.[11]

Goldberger's findings aroused the ire of the ERO, whose party line was that pellagra and many other diseases result from inferior heredity. ERO Director Davenport, who in 1911 had written that the Irish genetically lack resistance to tuberculosis, and that legislation to improve sanitary and living conditions among Irish communities was therefore misguided, took charge of a campaign to discredit Goldberger's findings.[12] He began with a series of articles in medical journals and the ERO's *Eugenical News* casting doubt on Goldberger's work. Davenport followed this up by commandeering the national Pellagra Commission, and then issuing a report in which he and his ERO staff documented in mountainous detail that in 90 percent of pellagra cases, the stricken individual had at least one parent or grandparent who had been a victim of the disease as well.[13]

This massive statistical fraud carried the day, and it was not until the mid–1930s that Goldberger's findings were accepted into American medical practice. During these two decades of delay, approximately 100,000 Americans died from pellagra, not to mention the millions of deaths attributed to other causes in which pellagra was a contributing factor.[14]

But it was through its role in the immigration debate that the ERO was to have its greatest impact on America and the world. During World War I, the U.S. Army had subjected all of its recruits to Stanford-Binet IQ testing. These tests, designed and promoted by eugenicists, were administered only in English, and contained numerous questions relating to baseball teams and similar Americana. The ERO's Harry Laughlin conducted an extensive statistical analysis of the results of these tests, and lo and behold, discovered that they proved beyond question that native-born Americans were far more intelligent than immigrants. The tests also showed, he said, that the northern and western European ethnic groups which had come to America earlier were more intelligent than the later waves from southern and eastern Europe. Finally, since individual immigrants who had been in the United States for some time scored significantly better than those of the same nation arriving more recently, the tests showed, said Laughlin, that the mental quality of immigrants was getting worse and worse every year. If the Italians, Poles, and eastern European Jews of 1890 were stupid, Laughlin said, those coming now were virtual morons. Unless something could be done quickly to stem the tide, the United States would have its racial stock polluted to the level of imbecility.[15]

Museum of Natural History president Henry Fairfield Osborn hailed Laughlin's results for their profound significance, saying:

> *I believe those tests were worth what the war cost, even in human life*, if they served to show clearly to our people the lack of intelligence in our country, and the degrees of intelligence in different races who are coming to us, in a way which no one can say is the result of prejudice. . . . We have learned once and for all that the negro is not like us. So in regard to many races and subraces in Europe we learned that some which we had believed possessed of an order of intelligence perhaps superior to ours [i.e., Jews] were far inferior.[16] [Italics added.]

The Laughlin IQ study provided weighty scientific support to the Nordic supremacist anti-immigrant campaign spearheaded by Madison Grant, the vice president of the Immigration Restriction League and a trustee of the Museum of Natural History. In his 1916 international bestseller *The Passing of the Great Race*,[17] Grant—a close friend of both Osborn (who wrote the preface) and former president Theodore Roosevelt (who penned a glowing review)—wrote:

> In the Europe of to-day the amount of Nordic blood in each nation is a very fair measure of its strength in war and standing in civilization. . . . In the City of New York and elsewhere in the United States there is a native American aristocracy resting upon layer after layer of immigrants of lower races. . . . It has taken us fifty years to learn that speaking English, wearing good clothes and going to school and to church does not transform a Negro into a white man. . . . Americans will have a similar experience with the Polish Jew, whose dwarf stature, peculiar mentality and ruthless concentration on self-interest are being engrafted upon the stock of the nation. . . . Indiscriminate efforts to preserve babies among the lower classes often result in serious injury to the race. . . . The laws of nature require the obliteration of the unfit and human life is valuable only when it is of use to the community or race. . . . We Americans must realize that the altruistic ideals . . . and the maudlin sentimentalism that has made America "an asylum for the oppressed" are sweeping the nation toward a racial abyss.[18]

Madison Grant was no relation to former President Ulysses S. Grant, but rather was the son of another Civil War hero, Dr. Gabriel Grant. The health commissioner of the city of Newark, Gabriel Grant raised a regiment of New Jersey volunteers to fight for the Union and won the Congressional Medal of Honor by acting with great courage under fire to save the life of abolitionist General Oliver O. Howard (who would later found Howard University, the first college for black Americans) at the battle of Fair Oaks.[19] That the son of such a man should grow up to become one of the leading racist ideologues in America—indeed, in the world; his book was enthusiastically received in Germany, recommended as essential reading by the Nazis, and referred to by Hitler as his "Bible"[20]—spoke volumes for the inversion of morals accomplished through the acceptance of Darwinian ideas by the generation following the publication of *The Descent of Man*.

Beyond raising the alarm over racial purity and declining levels of intelligence, Grant and Osborn brought another argument to the anti-immigrant campaign: environmental concern. According to these gentlemen, non-Nordic immigrants did not share the resident Anglo-Saxon/Teutonic race's deep feeling for Nature (a thesis earlier advanced by Haeckel) and thus represented an unendurable threat to America's remaining pristine wilderness areas. Together with their circle of museum trustees and fellow members of New York gentlemen hunters' Boone and Crockett Club, the two took the lead in launching such early environmentalist groups as the Sierra Club and the Save the Redwoods League (its plaque dedicated to Osborn and Grant still stands in the forest).[21] The most noteworthy supporter of this effort to preserve nature for those who could truly appreciate the aesthetic value of a fine kill was Theodore Roosevelt. In his 1911 review of Houston Stewart Chamberlain's racist masterpiece *Foundations of the Nineteenth Century* (later to serve as another sacred text for the Nazi Party), Roosevelt made crystal clear his own abandonment of the American Founders' ideals in favor of race science:

> Much that [Chamberlain] says regarding the prevalent loose and sloppy talk about the general progress of humanity, the equality and identity of races, and the like, is not only perfectly true, but is emphatically worth considering by a generation accustomed, as its forefathers for the preceding generations were accustomed, to accept as true and useful thoroughly pernicious doctrines taught by well-meaning and feeble-minded sentimentalists.[22]

No indeed, Chamberlain was not the sort of sentimentalist who believed in the equality of the races. In his sixties he befriended the young Adolf Hitler, sending the future Führer fawning letters calling him an "awakener of souls," a "cosmos-creating" force, and "heaven-sent."[23] The admiration was mutual; Hitler "regarded Chamberlain as a prophet."[24]

The combined agitation of the IRL, the museum set, the ERO, and the environmental societies, supported as well by xenophobic elements of the American Federation of Labor and traditional racist groups such as the Ku Klux Klan, was answered in 1 9 2 1 with the passage of the first "scientific" racist immigration law, the Emergency Quota Act, which set standards for admittance into the country based upon the percentage of Americans of a given national origin already present in the U.S. population as measured by the census of 1 9 1 0. This was not exclusionary enough for the eugenicists, so they launched a campaign for an even stricter bill, engineered by Madison Grant, Harry Laughlin, and museum trustee John Trevor, with smaller quotas that moreover would be based on the census of 1 8 9 0 — that is, before substantial immigration had begun from southern or eastern Europe.[25]

*Eugenics Records Office IQ chart alleging inferior intelligence of immigrants from southern and eastern Europe, and Africa.*

To further the lobbying for this more stringent proposal, Grant, Osborn, and Davenport joined forces to organize the Second International Congress of Eugenics at the Museum of Natural History in 1921. (The first congress had been held in London in 1912.) Funding for the conference was provided by the Harriman family, with future high-level diplomat and Democratic Party kingmaker W. Averell Harriman (the son of E. H. Harriman) donating $1,000 out of pocket (about $12,000 in today's money) to cover expenses, and serving on the conference executive committee as well. Other notables in attendance included Osborn's uncle J. P. Morgan, several members of the United States Congress, and future president Herbert Hoover. Mrs. E. H. Harriman co-hosted the Ladies' Committee of the conference with Mrs. Henry Fairfield Osborn, and the two together organized the transportation to New York of the entire immigration committee of the U.S. Congress to view the exhibits and hear scientifically authoritative anti-immigrant tirades from Grant, Osborn, Laughlin, Davenport, Major Leonard Darwin (son of Charles Darwin and one of the most prominent British eugenicists), and a galaxy of lesser eugenics stars. The younger Mary Harriman (Mrs. Charles Cary Rumsey) did her bit by dining and entertaining all the conference attendees and the visiting congressmen together at her own expense at the Piping Rock Club in Glen Cove, Long Island.[26]

After the conference, its exhibits were removed to Washington, D.C. to stand for three years in the Capitol to help educate those members of Congress who had been unable to attend the meeting in New York.[27] Further hard lobbying by Grant and Trevor and repeated expert testimony from Laughlin followed, ultimately reaching success in 1924 with the passage into law of the new, stricter immigration bill. Justifying its racially biased provisions, the ERO's *Eugenical News* opined in February 1924:

Since there were fewer southeastern Europeans here in 1890 than in 1910, a percentage provision based on the former census would decidedly cut down the number of such immigrants.

This provision would change the character of immigration, and hence our future population, by bringing about a preponderance of immigration of the stock which originally settled this country. On the whole, immigrants from northwestern Europe furnish us the best material for American citizenship and for the further upbuilding of the American race.[28]

The deed was done. Ellis Island was effectually shut down, closing the golden door to millions from Europe—including those who would soon have pressing need to escape from the American eugenicists' German counterparts.

Then, with the convening of the Third International Congress of Eugenics at the museum in August 1 9 3 2, organizing openly in support of the coming genocide began.

## EUGENICS SPREADS AMONG THE ELITE

In light of what was to follow, the proceedings of the Third International Congress make fascinating reading today. In addition to assorted Harrimans, Roosevelts, Osborns, Dodges, and other representatives of the social register, the conference was graced by the top intellectual leadership of the eugenics movement from every corner of the globe. These included the American eugenicists Grant, Davenport, Laughlin, Trevor, Henry Fairfield Osborn and his nephew Frederick Osborn, as well as Major Leonard Darwin, British Eugenics Society leader Sir Bernard Mallet, and American Birth Control League founder Margaret Sanger.[29] While hailed as a heroine by liberal feminists today, Sanger's support for legal abortion was strongly based on her argument that it could be used as a means for eliminating undesirable racial stock.[30] In the late 1 9 3 0s, the Nazis would embrace this viewpoint and legalize abortion for Jews.[31]

Also present was Yale professor Irving Fisher, a top economic advisor to President Herbert Hoover, whose post–1 9 2 9 announcements of imminent prosperity would soon prove tragically ludicrous. On the left fringe of the Third Congress's membership were anthropologist Franz Boas, the founder of cultural-relativist anthropology and mentor of Margaret Mead, and geneticist Hermann J. Muller. Muller was an outlier at the conference both because he was actually a real scientist and because he was a hard-core communist with connections at the very highest levels of the Soviet leadership. (In 1936, the American-born Muller, then conducting research in Moscow, would manage to shock the rather tough sensibilities of former seminarian Joseph Stalin by presenting him with a plan for spreading the seed of selected superior fathers to accomplish the eugenic mass breeding of the Soviet Union's human stock. Stalin ordered him killed, but forewarned, Muller fled the country and joined the International Brigades in Spain. Muller went on to win the Nobel Prize for his work in genetics in 1946, help found the Pugwash movement attempting to arrange for collaboration between Anglo-American and Soviet elites, be the university mentor of astronomer Carl Sagan in the 1950s, and help start the institution that would be informally known as the "Nobel Prize sperm bank."[32])

Other members of the Third International Congress who would later prove important in carrying the eugenics movement forward into the postwar era included Population Reference Bureau director Guy Irving Burch, eugenics experts Irene Taeuber and Frank Lorimer, and Colonel Wycliffe P. Draper, the founder of the Pioneer Fund, which would campaign against desegregation laws in the 1960s and which continues to finance race science to the present day.

But the real thrill of the Congress was brought by its German delegation, Professors Eugen Fischer and Ernst Rüdin of the German Society for Racial Hygiene. The Germans' prominence at the conference was only to be expected, for just a few weeks prior to the conference opening, the Nazi Party had won 18 million votes (37 percent of the electorate), catapulting it to leading status in the Weimar Reichstag. Without a doubt, the star of eugenics was on the rise in Germany.

The conference was opened by some introductory remarks by Davenport, whose ERO, by this time, was substantially funded by the Carnegie Institute. Davenport began by giving a progress report on sterilization techniques, and pronounced hopefully that immigration had finally been brought under eugenic control. "Human race crossing" is the cause of "biological disharmony" and "turbulent people," he asserted.[33]

On the other hand, said Davenport,

> the mixture of north Europeans in the United States seems to have produced many especially virile persons of which the Theodore Roosevelt family is a brilliant example.... Meanwhile any people is justified in going slow in bringing together into its land very diverse races of mankind.... Finally, we may inquire: Can we by eugenical studies point the way to produce the superman and the superstate? Progress will come slowly.... But I think we are justified in having faith that the future will bring precise knowledge in human biology, and education will establish the desired mores.[34]

Davenport then turned the podium over to museum president and Eugenics Congress vice president Henry Fairfield Osborn for the keynote address. His speech is still worth reading at length today, as it links together in a single unified theme the Malthusian foundation underlying both Nazism and environmentalism. Osborn said:

> The outstanding generalizations of my world tour are what may be summed up as the "six overs" ...:
>
> Over-destruction of natural resources, now actually worldwide;
>
> Over-mechanization, in the substitution of the machine for animal and human labor, rapidly becoming world-wide;
>
> Over-construction of warehouses, ships, railroads, wharves and other means of transport, replacing primitive transportation;
>
> Over-production both of the food and of the mechanical wants of mankind, chiefly during the post-war speculative period;

Over-confidence in future demand and supply, resulting in the too rapid extension of natural resources both in food and in mechanical equipment;

Over-population beyond the land areas, or the capacity of the natural and scientific resources of the world, with consequent permanent unemployment of the least-fitted. . . .

I have reached the opinion that over-population and under-employment may be regarded as twin sisters. From this point of view I even find that the United States [with 125 million people] is over-populated at the present time. . . . I think the present unemployment figures represent a condition likely to be in part permanent. . . .

While some highly competent people are unemployed, the mass of unemployment is among the less competent, because in every activity it is the less competent who are first selected for suspension while the few highly competent people are retained because they are still indispensable. In nature these less-fitted individuals would gradually disappear, but in civilization we are keeping them in the community in the hopes that in brighter days they may all find employment. This is only another instance of humane civilization going directly against the order of nature and encouraging the survival of the unfittest. . . .

The slogan "not more but better Americans" should have its counterpart in every country in the world . . . accompanied by the consciousness that quality rather than quantity is the essential element of progress in every country and in every race.[35]

Following Osborn's speech, the conference proceeded to elect Rüdin president of the International Federation of Eugenics Organizations.[36] For decades one of Germany's most esteemed scholars of eugenics, Rüdin was a dedicated Nazi. For a clear sense of Rüdin's political outlook, consider the obituary he would pen in 1940 for his former brother-in-law Alfred Ploetz, cofounder of the German Society for

Racial Hygiene: "It is tragic that Ploetz did not live to see the solution of the problem of understanding and cooperation amongst the Nordic races, when he believed so ardently in the purposeful leadership of Adolf Hitler, and in his holy national and international racial hygienic mission. But let it be a consolation to us that until his last breath he maintained the unshakeable hope of a victory of conquest of the German race and that in the then ensuing peace there would follow a victory in racial hygiene."[37]

Adolf Hitler took power in Germany just five months after the New York conference, and Rüdin was soon thereafter appointed *Reichskommissar* for eugenics. Together with Ploetz, Eugen Fischer, and the rest of the gang from the German Society for Racial Hygiene, he would soon show the world exactly what the new science had to offer humanity.[38]

Indeed, by 1935, the new Nazi regime had already accomplished much for the global eugenics movement to celebrate. So, never the sort to miss a chance to throw a party, the Nazis invited race scientists from around the world to come to Berlin to join in the gala occasion of the first International Congress for Population Science. There were more than five hundred participants, with the U.S. delegation led by Eugenics Research Association president Dr. Clarence Gordon Campbell. ERO director Harry Laughlin, an honorary conference vice president, was unable to attend in person, but sent along a paper and exhibits in his stead.[39] Also present were Warren Thompson and Dorothy Swaine Thomas,[40] both of whom, as we shall see in Chapter Seven, would figure prominently (along with Frederick Osborn, Fairfield Osborn, Hermann Muller, other eugenicists, and John D. Rockefeller III) in the founding of the Population Council—the preeminent postwar "population control" organization in 1952.

The keynote of the Berlin conference was given by Nazi Minister of the Interior Wilhelm Frick. "We have been reproached as following a special racial cult and injuring the commands of Christian love for our neighbors by eugenic measures," Frick told the attendees. "But if it was not part of the plan of the original order of things in this world

**Qualitativer Bevölkerungsabstieg**
bei zu schwacher Fortpflanzung der höherwertigen

So würde es kommen,
wenn Minderwertige 4 Kinder und höherwertige 2 Kinder haben.

*Nazi eugenics poster showing how the unfit threatened to
outbreed the fit. The caption speaks of the decline in the
quality of the population if inferior people have twice as
many children as their racial superiors.*

that long life should be given to many sick people through the
progress of science, which had been denied them under primitive
conditions, then it cannot be wrong to prevent this good deed from
becoming a plague to the healthy."[41] Frick would later be hanged by
the Nuremberg tribunal for crimes against humanity.

Eugen Fischer, the conference president, delivered the conference
invocation:

> We may with thankful hearts think today in the beginning of
> our work that man whose strong hand has the will and strength,
> God willing, to save the German nation from the fate of popu-
> lations which led past cultures and peoples to their death. . . .
> With this wish for all as we gather for work on German soil and
> in the Reich capital, we honor and greet the German people's
> Führer and Reich Chancellor, and I would request you to greet
> him with me: Hail Führer and Reich Chancellor Adolf Hitler![42]

The five hundred conference delegates then stood and hailed Hitler.[43]

The leader of the American delegation, Clarence Campbell, reiterated the salute: "The leader of the German nation, Adolf Hitler, ably supported by Dr. Frick and guided by Germany's anthropologists and social philosophers, has been able to construct a comprehensive racial policy of population development and improvement. This policy promises to be epochal in racial history."[44]

That promise would be kept.

## CHAPTER SIX

# The Nazi Holocaust

*If, however, we look around at the course of nature, one author-itative fact becomes distinctly prominent, let us make of it what we may. It is, that the life of the individual is treated as of absolutely no importance, while the race is treated as every-thing, Nature being wholly careless of the former except as a contributor to the maintenance and evolution of the latter.*

FRANCIS GALTON, 1873[1]

*National Socialism is nothing but applied biology.*

RUDOLPH HESS, 1933[2]

*The law of existence prescribes uninterrupted killing, so that the better may live.*

ADOLF HITLER, 1941[3]

AS WE HAVE SEEN, long before Hitler rose to power, the ideas that would form the program of Nazi Germany had been laid out and made respectable by Haeckel and his acolytes in the German scien-tific community. However, with the ascent of Nazism, the roles changed. Instead of serving as a rationale supporting the program of a militarist state, Darwinism became the controlling principle of the state itself. Where once antihuman ideology had been the servant, it was now the master.

Nazi Germany, it must be emphasized, was not just a tyranny that made use of ideological claptrap for propaganda purposes. Rather, it was a tyranny created to *serve* that ideology, the demands of which repeatedly trumped both the economic and military interests of Germany. The Kaiser and his circle had been as anti-Semitic as any traditional bigot could desire. Yet that had not stopped them from accepting the contribution of Germany's Jews to the war effort. Their rationality on that score had been amply rewarded: During World War I, 100,000 out of Germany's 500,000 Jews had served in uniform, with over 42,000 of them being killed, wounded, or decorated for bravery in combat.[4] While comprising only 1 percent of Germany's population, Jews supplied 16 percent of the nation's medical doctors—a vital capability in war.[5] Even more important was the contribution of Jewish scientists, such as Fritz Haber, whose development of the method of artificially fixing nitrates (essential for production of ammunition) from the atmosphere saved Germany from early defeat when the British blockade cut off the Reich's nitrate imports from Chile, and whose subsequent invention of poison gas gave Germany a novel secret weapon that could have won the war, had not the Kaiser's generals wasted its surprise value so foolishly.[6]

By contrast, Hitler killed or drove away all of that capability—an action whose significance can be appreciated in its starkest terms by surveying the roll call of Axis-nation-born emigrant talent that enabled the subsequent American atomic-bomb effort: Albert Einstein, Rudolf Peierls, Otto Frisch, Hans Bethe, Enrico Fermi, Edward Teller, Eugene Wigner, Leó Szilárd, and more.

When the Nazi armies entered the Ukraine, Byelorussia, and even western Russia, they were initially welcomed as liberators by peoples suffering under the weight of the harsh tyranny of Joseph Stalin. But the Germans' genocidal behavior in the conquered areas rapidly convinced their new Slavic subjects that their only hope of survival rested with Soviet victory. Thus, instead of the armies of allies they could have recruited, the Nazis created great forces of partisans to fight against them. Nazi Germany conscripted millions of people into slavery, but then defied economic rationality in systematically slaughtering or starving to death its enormously valuable enslaved workforce. For Nazi Germany, genocide was a higher priority than victory.

## MAN AGAINST MAN

But Darwinian ideology did not merely control Nazi Germany—it created it and enabled its capacity for evil. Contrary to the writings of some postwar German apologists, the atrocities of Nazism were not accomplished in secret by a few satanic fanatics while the rest of the good citizens proceeded with their decent daily lives in well-meaning ignorance. In point of fact, such blissful ignorance was not possible. At the height of the Third Reich, there were over twenty thousand death camps,[7] and most were discovered by Allied forces within hours of their entering newly liberated territory—as the stench of the camps' crematoria made them readily detectable. Hundreds of thousands of Germans were employed operating these facilities, and several million more were members of armed forces or police units engaged in or supporting genocidal operations.[8] Nearly every German had friends or family members who were eyewitnesses to or direct perpetrators of genocide, who could, and did, inform their acquaintances as to what was happening. Many sent photos home to their parents, wives, or girlfriends, depicting themselves degrading, killing, or posing astride the corpses of their victims.[9] Moreover, the Nazi leadership was in no way secretive about its intent; genocide directed against Jews and Slavs was the openly stated goal of the Party *which 17 million Germans voted for* in 1933.[10]

On March 20, 1933, less than two months after the Nazi assumption of power, SS leader Heinrich Himmler announced the establishment of the first formal concentration camp, Dachau, *at a press conference.*[11] The stated purpose of the camp was for "political opponents," but as the implementation got underway, the German public was witness to systematic degradation, beatings, lynchings, and mass murder of Jews done openly for all to see in the Reich's streets from

1933 onward, with the most extensive killings, such as those of the November 10, 1938 *Kristallnacht* pogrom, celebrated afterwards at enormous public rallies and parties.[12] The contention, then, that the Nazi-organized Holocaust took place behind the backs of an unwilling German population is patently false. Rather, the horrifying fact is, as documented beyond doubt by historian Daniel Goldhagen in his book *Hitler's Willing Executioners*, that the genocidal Nazi program was carried out with the full knowledge and substantial general support of the German public.[13]

*Nazism was very popular.*

The question that has bedeviled the conscience of humanity ever since then is: how could this have happened? How could the majority of citizens of an apparently civilized nation choose to behave in such a way? Goldhagen offers German anti-Semitism as the answer. But this explanation fails in view of the fact that anti-Semitism had existed in Germany—and in many other countries, such as France, Poland, and Russia, sometimes to a much greater extent—for centuries prior to the Holocaust, with no remotely comparable outcome. Furthermore,

*Nazis murdering civilians in Lithuania, 1942.*
*Note the spectators.*

the Nazi genocidal program was not directed just against Jews, but also against several other categories of people despised by Darwinian eugenicists, including invalids, Slavs, and Gypsies. Had the Nazis prevailed, it would unquestionably have been expanded to include other non-Nordic Europeans, Africans, and Asians—that is, the entire target list of the eugenics movement.

In other words, as the Nazi leadership itself repeatedly emphasized, the genocide program was not motivated by mere old-fashioned bigotry. It certainly took advantage of such sentiments among rustics, hoodlums, and others to facilitate its operations. But it required something else to convince a nation largely composed of serious, solid, dutiful, highly literate, and fairly intellectual people to devote themselves to such a cause. It took Darwinian science.

## BY THE LIGHT OF PERVERTED REASON

As historian Richard Weikart concludes in his noteworthy study *From Darwin to Hitler: Evolutionary Ethics, Eugenics, and Racism in Germany*: "Darwinism by itself did not produce the Holocaust, but without

Darwinism, especially in its social Darwinist and eugenics permutations, neither Hitler nor his Nazi followers would have had the necessary scientific underpinnings to convince themselves and their collaborators that one of the world's greatest atrocities was really morally praiseworthy."[14]

Again and again, if one reads the memoirs of Germans in the process of becoming Nazified, such as those presented in such important recent works as Michael Burleigh's *The Third Reich: A New History*,[15] or Richard Evans's *The Third Reich in Power*,[16] one witnesses an internal struggle in which the moral calculus is inverted. Those Germans who felt sympathy for their Jewish friends, neighbors, or schoolmates came to view their own inner voice speaking for such compassion as the voice of sentimental weakness, which had to be overruled by their intellectual convictions, which presented themselves as the voice of duty—or dare one say it, the voice of conscience —requiring them to *do the right thing* and be hard. In the face of this moral inversion, only a few with very firmly held alternative belief structures—most typically devoted Roman Catholics—were able to resist, and as a result were generally viewed by the majority to be irrational retrograde religious fanatics.[17]

The Malthusian theory of limited resources, however, had another child besides Darwinism, which also lent its support to the genocide program. This twin was environmentalism, which in Germany, as in the United States, was closely linked via its common parental philosophy to eugenics. One does not ordinarily think of the Nazis, with their lignite-fired synthetic-fuel industries blackening the air and their crematoria smokestacks spewing human ash across the landscape, as being models of environmental concern. Certainly, from a practical point of view, the Third Reich did very little to improve the European environment. But from the ideological standpoint of advancing the argument that the activities of (especially non-Nordic) human beings needed to be constrained in order to preserve the sacred precincts of Nature, the Nazis were as green as could be.

Going back to Haeckel, these ideas were most cogently formulated for the Nazis by anti-Semitic neo-pagan Nietzschean philosopher Ludwig Klages, who in his 1913 tract *Man and Earth*, written for the conclave of the proto-Nazi German back-to-nature youth movement, laid out in full the conservationist case against humanity, technological progress, industrial development, and advanced agriculture that has played a central role in the environmental movement ever since.[18] (In 1980, *Man and Earth* was reprinted, without comment, as one of the founding documents of the West German Green Party.[19]) These ideas were embraced by many leading Nazis, including Hitler, Himmler, Deputy Führer Rudolf Hess, Agricultural Minister Richard Walther Darré, Industry Minister Fritz Todt, and most importantly for the future, Hitler Youth leader Baldur von Schirach.[20] As a result, by 1939, Nazi Party enrollment among the members of German nature preservation societies was six times as prevalent (six in ten versus one in ten) as their representation among the population at large.[21] Not just for the sake of maintaining German racial purity, but for the clear moral necessity of saving the Earth itself, the inferior races of mankind simply had to be eliminated.

Both the population's general knowledge of the genocide, and the moral inversion that allowed them to support it, are most poignantly documented in the writings of the handful of Germans who, on the basis of their religious convictions, were able to resist the tide. Most eloquent among these are the brave college students of the Munich-based White Rose resistance group who bore witness in their series of leaflets issued during the fall of 1942:

> Nothing is so unworthy of a civilized nation as allowing itself to be "governed" without opposition by an irresponsible clique that has yielded to base instinct. It is certain that today every honest German is ashamed of his government. Who among us has any conception of the dimensions of shame that will befall us and our children when one day the veil has fallen from our eyes and the most horrible of crimes—crimes that infinitely outdistance every human measure—reach the light of day? If

the German people are already so corrupted and spiritually crushed that they do not raise a hand, frivolously trusting in a questionable faith in lawful order in history; if they surrender man's highest principle, that which raises him above all other God's creatures, his free will; if they abandon the will to take decisive action and turn the wheel of history and thus subject it to their own rational decision; if they are so devoid of all individuality, have already gone so far along the road toward turning into a spiritless and cowardly mass—then yes, they deserve their downfall.

–The first leaflet of the White Rose[22]

Since the conquest of Poland, *three hundred thousand Jews* have been murdered in this country in the most bestial way. Here we see the most frightful crime against human dignity, a crime that is unparalleled in the whole of history. For Jews, too, are human beings.... All male offspring of the houses of the [Polish] nobility between the ages of fifteen and twenty were transported to concentration camps in Germany and sentenced to forced labor, and all the girls of this age group were sent to Norway, into the bordellos of the SS! Why tell you these things, since you are fully aware of them?... Why do the German people behave so apathetically in the face of all these abominable crimes, crimes so unworthy of the human race?... Each man wants to be exonerated of a guilt of this kind, each one continues on his way with the most placid, the calmest conscience. But he cannot be exonerated; he is *guilty, guilty, guilty!*

–The second leaflet of the White Rose[23]

Every word that comes from Hitler's mouth is a lie. When he says peace, he means war, and when he blasphemously uses the name of the Almighty, he means the power of evil, the fallen angel, Satan. His mouth is the foul-smelling maw of Hell, and his might is at bottom accursed. True, we must conduct the

struggle against the National Socialist terrorist state with
rational means; but whoever still doubts the reality, the existence of demonic powers, has failed by a wide margin to
understand the metaphysical background of this war.... 
Everywhere and at all times demons have been lurking in the
dark, waiting for the moment when man is weak; when of his
own volition he leaves his place in the order of Creation as
founded for him by God in freedom; when he yields to the
force of evil.... We will not be silent. We are your bad conscience. The White Rose will not leave you in peace!

–The fourth leaflet of the White Rose[24]

In the face of a general societal consensus backed up by all authoritative scientific opinion supporting the necessity for genocide, however, such faith-based appeals to conscience and human decency
could make little impression, and the Holocaust went on.

## THE HOLOCAUST BEGINS

After the mass murder of Hitler's political opponents, the first to be
targeted for elimination based on eugenic and Malthusian consider-
ations were Germany's mental patients and invalids. This program
commenced in 1933 with the passage of the law "For the Prevention
of Hereditary Diseases in Posterity." Crafted by Ernst Rüdin and pub-
lic-health director Dr. Arthur Gütt, and based upon the ERO's Model
Eugenical Sterilization law proposed by Harry Laughlin in 1914, the
Nazi law initially prescribed for forcible sterilization of the feeble-
minded, mental patients, criminals, and those with various other
infirmities.[25] However, under the Nazis' "T4" program—designed by
Rüdin and his Society for Racial Hygiene colleagues in the late 1930s—
the remedy was changed to "euthanasia." Thus was born Nazi Germany's first extermination program, in the course of which hundreds
of thousands of hospital patients, orphans, and the elderly were gassed
in an assortment of castles and other secure locations across the

Reich.[26] This slaughter was publicly justified by the Nazis as a proper effort to eliminate *Lebensunwertes Leben*—"life unworthy of life."[27]

Writing from Berlin in 1940, reporter William Shirer speculated on the purpose of the campaign: "What is still unclear to me is the motive for these murders. Germans themselves advance three: 1. That they are being carried out to save food. 2. That they are done for the purpose of experimenting with new poison gases and death rays. 3. That they are simply the result of the extreme Nazis deciding to carry out their eugenic and sociological ideas." Discounting the first two reasons, Shirer concludes, "The third motive seems most likely to me. For years a group of radical Nazi sociologists who were instrumental in putting through the Reich's sterilization laws have pressed for a national policy of eliminating the mentally unfit. They say they have disciples among many sociologists in other lands, and perhaps they have."[28]

Shirer was basically on the mark in choosing reason number three as primary, but the first two reasons cited played their roles as well. While from the standpoint of reality, as Shirer says, the killing of hundreds of thousands could do very little to improve the food supply of a nation of 80 million, from an ideological point of view, the Nazis had deluged the nation (and themselves) with Malthusian propaganda for years, arguing the need to eliminate the unfit to make more food available for the worthy. (Elementary school math textbooks in Nazi Germany even asked students to calculate how much food could be saved via the elimination of various numbers of "useless eaters."[29]) As for the second reason, it was the mass extermination techniques perfected and the personnel trained in the course of the T4 euthanasia program that would subsequently be redeployed to establish greatly expanded killing centers in places such as Auschwitz and Buchenwald.[30]

This larger genocide, directed primarily against the Jews, began in 1935 with the passage of the racial hygiene law "For the Protection of German Blood and German Honor," which made any sexual intercourse between Jews and Aryans a criminal offense, and a related law that defined Jews as non-citizens. This commenced a campaign of systematic degradation, terror, dispossession, forcible impoverishment,

*Nazi propaganda showing precisely how much the inferior
are costing their fellow citizens. The caption points out
that a "person suffering from hereditary defects costs the
community of Germans during his lifetime" a total of
60,000 Reichsmarks. "Fellow Citizen," the poster adds,
"that is your money, too."*

and murder of Germany's highly assimilated Jews and Jewish-descended
Christian population.[31] With the Nazi conquest of Austria in 1938,
this program was greatly expanded in both scope and intensity.[32]


## THE WORLD TURNS ITS BACK

As the 1930s wore on, and conditions for German and Eastern European Jews became ever more catastrophic, many tried to escape by
emigration. While ostensibly acceptable to the Nazis, this option was
made nearly impossible by the rest of the world's governments,
which, influenced by the global eugenics movement, agreed at a 1938

meeting in Évian, France not to receive substantial numbers of Jewish refugees from Nazi Germany. Acting in concert, the British government of Nazi appeaser Neville Chamberlain cut off Palestine as a potential refuge, while the leadership of the U.S. eugenics movement campaigned to keep the American immigration door firmly shut.[33]

Thus, in February 1939, when New York Senator Robert Wagner introduced a bill to allow twenty thousand German Jewish children to come in above quota, to be adopted by American families who had already agreed to take them, it was ERO Superintendent Harry Laughlin and John Trevor, a trustee of the American Museum of Natural History and a director of the ERO's Eugenics Research Association, who helped lead the successful effort to defeat it.

To do this, they organized a Coalition of Patriotic Societies that brought together an assortment of nativist organizations, both real and fictitious, ranging from the Sons and Daughters of the American Revolution to the likes of the Ku Klux Klan to put pressure on Congress. Nearly all of the testimony delivered by the Coalition against the Wagner bill was presented by Laughlin, Trevor, and Guy Irving Burch, the head of the Population Reference Bureau. Twenty thousand Jewish children might not seem like much, said Burch, but "they will increase to 500,000 in only six generations." The children were not admitted. As a result, most of them were gassed.[34]

Then, in May 1939, some 930 German Jews escaped the Nazis on the *St. Louis*, a German ocean liner, and sailed to America to seek refuge despite their lack of welcome. As the *St. Louis* sailed up and down the coast of Florida waiting for permission to land, Laughlin issued a special report on immigration which demanded that "international sentimentality" not cause America to lower its "eugenical and racial standards." Laughlin demanded that the United States cut its quota by a further 60 percent, and that "loopholes" which allowed Jewish immigration to America by excusing the "moral turpitude" of fleeing Jews who had smuggled (their own) money out of the Nazi Reich be closed.[35]

As a result of such racist agitation, the *St. Louis* was turned around, and the 620 of its passengers who could not receive permission to

*Jewish refugees on board the* St. Louis
*on their way to America, 1939.*

debark in Britain were returned to Europe, where 254 of them were eventually annihilated.[36]

Then in September 1939, war broke out, and escape became impossible. With the conquest of Poland, and then large areas of the Soviet Union, millions of Jews and tens of millions of Slavs fell into Nazi hands. In horror that defies telling, countless numbers of them would soon be sacrificed on the altar of Malthusian eugenics.

## CHAPTER SEVEN

# Eugenics Reborn

*It is obvious that fifty years hence the world cannot support three billion people.... Unless population increases can be stopped, we might as well give up the struggle.*

WILLIAM VOGT
*The Road to Survival,* 1948[1]

*We are not primarily interested in the sociological or humanitarian aspects of birth control. We are interested in the use which Communists make of hungry people in their drive to conquer the earth.*

HUGH MOORE
letter to John D. Rockefeller III, 1954[2]

THE AMERICAN EUGENICISTS' sympathy with Nazism caused little concern among their high-society backers during the 1920s and 1930s. But with Hitler's actions forcing first Britain and then the United States into war against the Reich, the Anglo-American elites realized they had to cut their ties. By 1940, the Carnegie Institute had given Davenport and Laughlin the boot from the Eugenics Record Office, and, by renaming it and reorienting it under new management as the Genetics Records Office, essentially shut down the eugenics movement in the United States. Nordic supremacist race science be - came unacceptable discourse in polite society, and those who refused to get the new message had it delivered to them forcibly—as John Trevor and Guy Irving Burch would discover when their Coalition of

Patriotic Societies was indicted for sedition as a pro-Nazi subversive organization in 1942.[3]

However, the ashes of Auschwitz had hardly cooled when elements of the pre-war eugenics movement re-emerged to revive the cause under a new rubric: "population control." Almost immediately after the Axis surrender, eugenicists started to flood America's periodicals with articles warning of the danger of overpopulation of the world's underdeveloped sector.

The first out of the box in launching the new crusade against brown people was Guy Irving Burch himself, who together with fellow eugenicist Elmer Pendell issued the book *Population Roads to Peace or War*.[4] Endorsing Hitler's *Lebensraum* rationale for his acts of aggression and genocide, Burch and Pendell said "if the birth rate is kept high the total population eventually reaches the 'must expand or explode' stage. . . . The way is now prepared for the despot."[5] Then, according to Burch and Pendell, the despot necessarily leads the overpopulated nation into war. The only way to maintain world peace, they argued, was through organized population reduction.

Lest it be unclear to anyone *which* populations should be targeted for reduction, the cover of some editions of the book included endorsements from some of the world's leading eugenicists, including Henry Pratt Fairchild of New York University, E. A. Ross of the University of Wisconsin, Yale professor and former American Eugenics Society president Ellsworth Huntington, and Nazi apologist Lothrop Stoddard, author of the racist classic *The Rising Tide of Color Against White World Supremacy*.[6] Then, in 1948, Fairfield Osborn, the son of the late Henry Fairfield Osborn, stepped into his father's shoes by publishing *Our Plundered Planet*,[7] a three-million-copy blockbuster (and *that* just for U.S. sales) which became the founding manifesto of the postwar environmentalist movement. (This book enjoyed cover endorsements from Albert Einstein, Eleanor Roosevelt, and the eugenicist novelist Aldous Huxley.) Osborn's work was quickly followed by another 1948 bestseller, *The Road to Survival*, by William Vogt, the head of the conservation section of the Pan American Union.[8]

A few quotes are sufficient to reveal the character of the Malthusian ideology underlying these works. From Osborn: "The problem of the pressure of increasing populations—perhaps the greatest problem facing humanity today—cannot be solved in a way that is consistent with the ideals of humanity. . . . The tide of the earth's population is rising, the reservoir of the earth's living resources is falling. . . . Man must recognize the necessity of cooperating with nature . . . the time for defiance is at an end."[9]

Vogt was more explicit:

> One of the greatest national assets of Chile, perhaps the greatest asset, is its high death rate. . . . China quite literally *cannot feed more people*. . . . The greatest tragedy that China could suffer, at the present time, would be a reduction in her death rate. . . . There can be no way out. These men and women, boys and girls, must starve. . . . [The Food and Agricultural Organization of the U.N.] should not ship food to keep alive ten million Indians and Chinese this year, so that fifty million may die five years hence. . . . Mother India is the victim of her own awful fecundity. In all the world there is probably no region of greater misery, and almost certainly none with less hope. Her very hopelessness may be of good augury for the rest of mankind. . . . A heavily industrialized India, backed up by such population pressure, would be a danger to the entire world.[10]

In the immediate postwar period, at least one country filled with non-white undesirables did not need to be *asked* to reduce its population —it could be *told*. This was Japan, then under U.S. military occupation. Arguing that America should seize this opportunity to end the Yellow Peril forever, Vogt made a stark recommendation:

> By 1950, Japan will have a population of 79,000,000. . . . If we attempt to raise her to a standard of living that makes democracy possible, she will remain a world threat—unless

her population is limited. . . . If Japan is to regain anything comparable to her former status as an industrial world power, she will either have to be subjected to harsh policing to contain her war potential—or her population must be systematically reduced by cutting the birth rate, until her own ability to supply her needs is far nearer to the demand than it has been since 1880. Reduced to a population approximately that of Scandinavia, she might well take an honored place in the world, comparable to that of Scandinavia.[11]

Reducing Japan's population to equal that of Scandinavia would require eliminating 80 percent of the Japanese. This was certainly quite a challenge, and not one that General Douglas MacArthur, the head of the U.S. military occupation authority in Japan, wished to pursue.

## REPACKAGING EUGENICS AND POPULATION CONTROL

However, there was one high-ranking American official who thought Vogt's policy had real merit. This was Secretary of the Army General William H. Draper, Jr.

A ranking investment banker at Dillon Read while it had underwritten Nazi Germany's industrial development bonds during the 1930s, Draper was appointed chief of the economics division of the Allied Council for Germany from 1945 to 1947. Once there, he opposed the denazification process, protecting his former clients on the boards of Thyssen, I. G. Farben, and other Nazi concentration-camp cartels from Allied prosecution. Denounced by his fellow officers as a Nazi sympathizer, Draper was transferred back from Germany to the United States, where he was kicked upstairs to assume the post of Under Secretary of the Army.[12] Now he was in a position to do something himself to protect the world from the most dangerous of the racially undesirable.

While MacArthur dragged his feet, Draper, with the backing of

John D. Rockefeller III, sent to occupied Japan a string of veteran eugenicists, including Warren Thompson, Pascal K. Whelpton, Irene Taeuber, and Frank Notestein, to pressure the puppet Japanese government into accepting a population control law.

Arguably the most important of these experts was Thompson. A U.S. delegate to the 1935 Berlin population conference, Thompson was appointed an official advisor to the occupation. From that position, he coordinated a publicity campaign through the Japanese media to organize support for Japan's Eugenic Protection Law, which legalized birth control and abortion for the stated purpose of preventing "the increase of inferior descendants."[13]

As reported by author Matthew Connelly in his noteworthy 2008 book, *Fatal Misconception: The Struggle to Control World Population*, the Japanese government met with Thompson and shortly thereafter announced that birth control was "a fundamental solution to Japan's population problem." The cabinet then set up a Council on Population Problems; the Health and Welfare Ministry deregulated birth control clinics and approved twenty-seven different contraceptives; and the legislature resolved that "Japan is extremely overpopulated" and called for the public to reduce the birth rate.[14]

The dutiful Japanese people obeyed their leaders. By 1955 it was estimated that there were 30 to 50 percent more abortions than live births in Japan,[15] a wave of destruction of human potential that would stop the Japanese economy dead in its tracks when its inevitable consequences—a shrinking and aging workforce—arrived on schedule forty years later.

Meanwhile, Osborn, with his book *Our Plundered Planet* selling like hotcakes, established the Conservation Foundation, where Vogt would later serve as secretary.[16] Making use of his excellent social connections, Osborn was able to secure virtually unlimited monetary support from the Rockefeller and Old Dominion (later Mellon) Foundations.[17] These groups, along with the Milbank Foundation and Princeton's Office of Population Research, used their resources to sponsor decades of television documentaries propagandizing Malthusian environmentalism, as well as dozens of studies of Third World nations designed to justify World Bank and U.N. population-reduction programs directed against those nations.[18] (These studies were led by such scholarly stars as demographer and American Eugenics Society board member Kingsley Davis, a descendent of Confederate States president Jefferson Davis.) The Conservation Foundation would go on to provide funding to the Sierra Club, the Environmental Defense Fund, and many other environmental groups.[19]

The Conservation Foundation counted among its members British Eugenics Society leader Julian Huxley (the grandson of "Darwin's bulldog" T. H. Huxley), who played a central role in setting up the UNESCO anti-population and anti-growth programs, as well as the International Union for the Conservation of Nature. Joining with leading members of the (in some cases quite recently denazified) European nobility, the Conservation Foundation helped create the very influential World Wildlife Fund as well.

This network of like-minded organizations and projects grew again in 1952, when Fairfield Osborn joined with his cousin, American Eugenics Society president Frederick Osborn (who in 1932 had served as the treasurer of the Third International Congress of Eugenics) and John D. Rockefeller III to form the Population Council.[20] The continuity of this organization with the pre-war eugenics movement is striking. In fact, its founding meeting roster reads like a eugenics movement reunion, with the list of thirty-one participants including Warren Thompson, Dorothy Swaine Thomas, Hermann Muller, and Irene Taeuber—all participants in the big eugenics conferences of the 1930s. Other participants included William Vogt, Kingsley Davis, and Frank Notestein. Notestein's work on behalf of Japan's eugenics law has already been mentioned. A protégé of Frederick Osborn and Irene Taeuber since the 1930s, Notestein had been appointed founding director of the Office of Population Research by Osborn in 1936, became head of the U.N. Population Division in 1946 (a position later held by Kingsley Davis), and took over as head of the Population Council in 1959.[21] He thus became the successor to Frederick Osborn, who had served simultaneously as president of the American Eugenics Society and executive vice president of the Population Council in the 1950s. (Another prominent member of the AES in the 1950s and 60s was Dr. Otmar Frieherr von Verschuer, the professor who had supervised the ongoing science experiments of Dr. Josef Mengele at Auschwitz.[22]) Rockefeller, the Population Council's founding president and leading financial backer, was the eldest son of a father who had bankrolled the eugenics movement—in both the United States and Weimar and Nazi Germany—since the 1920s.[23]

*In 1952 Frederick Osborn (left) joined with John D. Rockefeller III (right) to re-launch the eugenics movement under the banner of "population control." During the 1950s, Osborn served as the president of the American Eugenics Society, president of the racist Pioneer Fund, and vice president of the Population Council.*

The Population Council worked together with Margaret Sanger's Planned Parenthood Federation of America (led in the 1950s by *Road to Survival* author William Vogt) to launch and liberally fund an array of "population control" groups. As already noted, Sanger, too, was a longtime supporter of eugenics. As her magazine put it in a 1919 editorial, "More children from the fit, less from the unfit—that is the chief issue of birth control."[24] In her 1922 book *The Pivot of Civilization*, she called for sterilization of genetically inferior races and the "insane and feeble minded."[25] The board of her American Birth Control League included racist ideologues Lothrop Stoddard and Clarence C. Little.[26] Other noteworthy close Sanger supporters included British eugenicists Havelock Ellis and H. G. Wells, Guy Irving Burch, and leading French Aryan supremacist Georges Vacher de Lapouge.[27] At the 1940 convention of the newly-formed Birth Control Federation of America (created when the American Birth Control League merged with the Birth Control Clinical Research Bureau), former American Eugenics Society president Henry Pratt Fairchild (who along with Sanger had been a member of the Third International Congress of Eugenics in 1932) told the assembled membership: "One of the outstanding features of the present conference is the practically universal acceptance of the fact that these two great movements [eugenics and birth control] have now come to such a thorough understanding and have drawn so close together as to be almost indistinguishable."[28] (In 1942, the BCFA changed its name to the Planned Parenthood Federation of America.[29] Its international spinoff, the International Planned Parenthood Federation, was founded in 1952 and headquartered in the offices of the British Eugenics Society, with its most influential American board member, heiress Dorothy Hamilton Brush, also serving simultaneously as a member of the board of directors of the American Eugenics Society.[30])

## THE ESTABLISHMENT EMBRACES POPULATION CONTROL

Another key convert to the population control cause won by Vogt's book was Hugh Moore, a wealthy businessman who had made a fortune in Dixie Cups before devoting his time to various questionable philanthropies. Embracing his newfound faith with enthusiasm, Moore bankrolled a string of population control and eugenics groups including Guy Irving Burch's Population Reference Bureau (he became chairman of the board), Vogt and Sanger's International Planned Parenthood Federation (he became vice president), and Elmer Pendell's Birthright, Inc. (he became president and renamed it the Association for Voluntary Sterilization).[31] In 1954, Moore commissioned an agitational pamphlet entitled *The Population Bomb*, which his Population Action Committee mailed to over a million politicians, journalists, businessmen, professors, and other people of influence. This booklet, which presaged the Paul Ehrlich tract of the same name fourteen years later, featured on its cover a bomb-like globe crowded with humanity, standing-room only, an alarming mass of teeming black Africans front and center, ready to explode in all directions as soon as the lit fuse sticking out of the North Pole sets off the detonation—unless a pair of scissors labeled "population control" can cut the fuse in time.[32]

In 1958, when President Dwight D. Eisenhower appointed General William Draper to head a commission to assess the effectiveness of U.S. military foreign aid, Moore urged his fellow Malthusian and good personal friend to seize the opportunity to push the population control agenda. Draper was only too willing to oblige. Choosing to interpret his commission's mandate very broadly, he had copies of Moore's *Population Bomb* distributed to all the other commissioners and brought in Moore's Population Reference Bureau experts as well as those from Frederick Osborn's Population Council as consultants.[33]

Accordingly, when the Draper commission report was issued in July 1959, it argued that population control was essential for "decreasing opportunities for communist political and economic domination [in developing nations].... No realistic discussion of economic development can fail to note that development efforts in many areas of the world are being offset by increasingly rapid population growth." Therefore, "the United States should make promotion of birth control techniques an explicit item of the technical assistance program.... [Aid should be given to those] developing countries who establish programs to check population growth."[34]

President Eisenhower categorically rejected the report's call for U.S. funding of population control. Speaking at a White House press conference on December 2, 1959, he said, "I cannot imagine anything more emphatically a subject that is not a proper political or governmental activity or function or responsibility. . . . That's not our business."[35]

Senator John F. Kennedy, then running for president, also opposed the Draper report, a stand that drew down on him denunciations by his Democratic party nomination challengers Senators Adlai Stevenson, Hubert Humphrey, and Stuart Symington, who criticized him for trying to impose his Catholic religious values on a pluralistic society. Planned Parenthood leader Margaret Sanger went further: If Kennedy were elected in 1960, she declared, she would leave the country.[36]

As it happened, Kennedy was elected, but Sanger said she'd stick around a year and "see what happens."[37] In 1961, her Planned Parenthood Federation merged with Moore's World Population Emergency Campaign to form the Planned Parenthood-World Population Society.[38] Moore and Draper assumed leadership roles in the new organization; while Draper continued to network among the Washington elite, Moore directed his efforts at propaganda. Through yet another of his numerous organizations, the Campaign to Check the Population Explosion, Moore bombarded the public with full-page ads in major newspapers signed by impressive assemblages of Nobel Prize recipients, eugenicists, theologians, political figures, and show-business celebrities, warning Americans that population growth was a threat to world peace, the environment, and law and order. "Have you ever been mugged?" asked the headline of one such CCPE ad run in the *New York Times*, continuing, "Well, you may be!" The recommended prevention: population control.[39]

On November 23, 1963, President Kennedy was assassinated. Seizing the opportunity to effect a policy shift, Moore and Draper joined forces with Lammot du Pont Copeland (then the president of the DuPont chemical company) to form the Population Crisis Committee, with its powerful funding wing, the Draper Fund.[40] In addition to Moore, Copeland, and Draper, the leadership of this group would come to include Kennedy-Johnson administration insider (and Second International Eugenics Congress bankroller) Averell Harriman,

General Maxwell Taylor, General William Westmoreland, Secretary of Defense Robert S. McNamara, Ambassador Ellsworth Bunker, Ambassador Marshall Green, and Under Secretary of State George Ball—a congeries of Vietnam War figures whose confluence in a population reduction society raises some interesting questions bearing on the origin of the self-defeating "pacification" and "body count" attrition strategies dictated to U.S. military forces out of Washington (particularly by McNamara) during that conflict.

Be that as it may, what is certain is that the recruitment of the top

*Full-page ads were placed by Hugh Moore's Campaign to Check the Population Explosion in the* New York Times *and other major newspapers. Here, the campaign blames crime on overpopulation.*

echelons of the U.S. government to the overpopulation dogma resulted in a change in American foreign aid policy. This was expressed forcefully by President Lyndon B. Johnson in his speech to the United Nations, on the occasion of its twentieth anniversary in 1965: "Five dollars invested in population control is worth a hundred dollars invested in economic growth."[41] Instead of seeking to rid the world of poverty, the new goal would be to get rid of the poor.

By the mid-1960s, the United States Agency for International Development (USAID) was not only providing population control assistance to Third World nations, it was becoming increasingly coercive in doing so. When India suffered crop failures in 1966, the Johnson administration refused to provide famine relief unless India agreed to impose forced sterilization programs on its rural peasantry.[42] Faced with mass starvation, India capitulated. Having helped effect this atrocity, McNamara subsequently left the administration to take a position as head of the World Bank, whose financial leverage he used to continue to target the gonads of poor people worldwide.

Collectively, these entities—the Population Council, the Draper Fund/Population Crisis Committee, the International Planned Parenthood Federation, USAID, the World Bank, and the U.N. Fund for Population Activities (UNFPA, largely funded by USAID)—together with a host of smaller outfits funded by them (including the Population Reference Bureau, the Association for Voluntary Sterilization, the Pathfinder Fund, and many others), would come to form the imposing and influential population control establishment.[43] Disposing of billions of dollars in funds, and backed by respectable opinion, this movement would eventually grow into a global suppression of life of unprecedented dimensions. We shall return to relate that story in Chapter Eleven.

## CHAPTER EIGHT

# In Defense of Malaria

*We have discovered many preventives against tropical diseases, and often against the onslaught of insects of all kinds, from lice to mosquitoes and back again. The excellent DDT powder which had been fully experimented with and found to yield astonishing results will henceforth be used on a great scale by the British forces in Burma and by the American and Australian forces in the Pacific and India in all theatres.*

WINSTON CHURCHILL
September 24, 1944[1]

*My own doubts came when DDT was introduced for civilian use. In Guyana, within two years it had almost eliminated malaria, but at the same time the birth rate had doubled. So my chief quarrel with DDT in hindsight is that it has greatly added to the population problem.*

ALEXANDER KING,
cofounder of the Club of Rome, 1990[2]

IN THE LAST DAYS of September 1943, as the U.S. Army advanced to the rescue of Italian partisans—some as young as nine—battling the Germans in the streets of Naples, the enraged Nazis, in a criminal act of revenge against their erstwhile allies, deployed sappers to systematically destroy the city's aqueducts, reservoirs, and sewer system. This done, the supermen, pausing only to burn irreplaceable libraries, including hundreds of thousands of volumes and artifacts at the University of Naples—where Thomas Aquinas once taught—showed their youthful Neapolitan opponents their backs, and on October 1, to the delirious cheers of the Naples populace, Allied forces entered the town in triumph.

But a city of over a million people had been left without sanitation, and within weeks, as the Germans had intended, epidemics broke out. By November, thousands of Neapolitans were infected with typhus, with one in four of those contracting it dying of the lice-transmitted disease.[3] The dead were so numerous that, as in the dark time of the Black Death, bodies were put out into the street by the hundreds to be hauled away by carts. Alarmed, General Eisenhower contacted Washington and made a desperate plea for help to contain the disaster.

Fortunately, the brass had a new secret weapon ready just in time to deal with the emergency. It was called DDT,[4] a pesticide of unprecedented effectiveness. First synthesized by a graduate student in 1874, DDT went unnoticed until its potential application as an insecticide was discovered by chemist Paul H. Müller while working for the Swiss company Geigy during the late 1930s. Acquainted with Müller's work, Victor Froelicher, Geigy's New York representative, disclosed it to the American military's Office of Scientific Research and Development (OSRD) in October 1942. Examining Müller's data, the OSRD's experts immediately realized its importance. On Guadalcanal, and elsewhere in the South Pacific, the Marines were losing more men to malaria than they were to the Japanese, with the entire 1st Marine Division rendered unfit for combat by the insect-borne disease. Without delay, first Geigy's Cincinnati factory and then the giant DuPont chemical company were given contracts to produce the new pesticide in quantity.[5]

By January 1, 1944, the first shipments of what would eventually amount to sixty tons of DDT reached Italy. Stations were set up in the palazzos of Naples, and as the people walked by in lines, military police officers with spray guns dusted them with DDT. Other spray teams prowled the town, dusting public buildings and shelters. The effects were little short of miraculous. Within days, the city's vast population of typhus-transmitting lice was virtually exterminated; by month's end, the epidemic was over.[6]

*January 1944. The U.S. Army uses DDT to end the typhus epidemic in Naples.*

The retreating Germans, however, did not give up so easily on the use of insects as vectors of death. As the Allied forces advanced north from Naples toward Rome, they neared the Pontine Marshes, which for thousands of years had been rendered nearly uninhabitable by their enormous infestation of virulently malarial mosquitoes. In his most noteworthy accomplishment before the war, Mussolini had drained these marshes, making them potentially suitable for human settlement. The Germans demolished Mussolini's dikes, quickly transforming the area back into the mosquito-infested malarial hellhole it had been for millennia. This promised to be very effective. In the brief Sicilian campaign of early summer 1943, malaria had struck 22,000 Allied troops—a greater casualty toll than that inflicted by the Axis forces themselves.[7] The malarial losses inflicted by the deadly Pontine Marshes were poised to be far worse.

But the Nazis had not reckoned on DDT. In coordination with their ground forces, the Americans deployed airborne crop dusters, as well as truck dusters and infantry DDT spray teams. Success was total. The Pontine mosquitoes were wiped out. With negligible losses to malaria, the GIs pushed on to Rome, liberating the Eternal City in the early morning of June 5.[8]

From now on, "DDT marches with the troops," declared the Allied high command.[9] The order could not have come at a better time. As British and American forces advanced in Europe, they encountered millions of victims of Nazi oppression—civilians under occupation, slave laborers, prisoners of war, concentration camp inmates—dying in droves from insect-borne diseases. But with the armies of liberation came squads spraying DDT, and with it life for millions otherwise doomed to destruction. The same story was repeated in the Philippines, Burma, China, and elsewhere in the Asia-Pacific theater. Never before in history had a single chemical saved so many lives in such a short amount of time.

In 1948, in recognition for his role in this public health miracle, Paul Müller was given the Nobel Prize for Medicine. Presenting the award, the Nobel Committee said: "DDT has been used in large quantities in the evacuation of concentration camps, of prisoners and deportees. Without any doubt, the material has already preserved the life and health of hundreds of thousands."[10]

With the coming of peace, DDT became available to civilian public health agencies around the world, and they lost no time in putting it to good use. One of the first countries to benefit was the United States. In the years immediately preceding World War II, between one and six million Americans, mostly drawn from the rural South, contracted malaria annually. In 1946, the U.S. Public Health Service initiated a campaign to wipe out malaria through the application of DDT to the interior walls of homes. The results were dramatic. In the first half of 1952, there were only *two* confirmed cases of malaria contracted within the United States.[11]

Other countries were quick to take note of the American success, and those that could afford it swiftly put DDT into action. In Europe, malaria was virtually eradicated by the mid–1950s. South African cases of malaria quickly dropped by 80 percent; Ceylon (now Sri Lanka) reduced its malaria incidence from 2.8 million in 1946 to 17 in 1963; and India cut its malaria death rate almost to zero. In 1955, with financial backing from the United States, the U.N. World Health Organization (WHO) launched a global campaign to use DDT to eradicate malaria. Implemented successfully across large areas of the developing world, this effort soon cut malaria rates in numerous countries in Latin America and Asia by 99 percent or better. Even for darkest Africa, hope that the age-old scourge would be brought to an end appeared to be in sight.[12]

But this enormous victory for humanity did not please everyone. For those concerned about the potential inundation of the world with undesirable (that is, non-white) people, the elimination of malaria from the Earth's tropical regions was anything but a blessing.

Among the first to sound the alarm was pro-eugenics author Aldous Huxley. The brother of British Eugenics Society leader Julian Huxley, Aldous Huxley is most famous for his 1932 novel *Brave New World*, which depicts a future society whose members are totally controlled through eugenic caste stratification. Since few would care to live in such a world, most readers interpret this book simply as an anti-utopian warning, along the lines of George Orwell's *1984*. However, an examination of Huxley's career shows that he was a staunch advocate and vigorous promoter of eugenics.[13] His literary output during the 1930s included both a positive review of racist ideologue Madison Grant's second book *The Conquest of a Continent*[14] and a vitriolic attack on Israel Zangwill's anti-eugenicist and pro-immigration play *The Melting Pot*.[15]

In a radio broadcast delivered the same year *Brave New World* was published, Huxley endorsed the book's social system, saying "in a scientific civilization society must be organized on a caste basis. The rulers and their advisory experts will be a kind of Brahmins controlling, in virtue of a special and mysterious knowledge, vast hordes of the intellectual equivalent of Sudras and Untouchables." Taken in context, then, Huxley's *Brave New World* might better be understood not as a warning but as an ironically-styled blueprint.

In 1958, Huxley updated his masterpiece with a new work entitled *Brave New World Revisited*. True to the new eugenics party line, he chose to center his argument on the danger to civilization posed by Third World overpopulation—which, playing on the anxieties of his Cold War readership, he warned would lead to communist revolution. Having thus made the issue of excessive non-white reproduction suitably relevant, Huxley attacked the chemical that was doing more than any other to keep poor people alive. "We go to a tropical island," he wrote, "and with the aid of DDT we stamp out malaria and, in two or three years, save hundreds of thousands of lives. This is obviously good. But the hundreds of thousands of human beings thus saved, and the millions whom they beget and bring to birth, cannot be adequately clothed, housed, educated or even fed out of the island's available resources. Quick death [*sic!*] by malaria has been abolished; but life made miserable by undernourishment and over-crowding is now the rule, and slow death by outright starvation threatens ever greater numbers."[16]

Huxley's argument was remarkable, not only for its representation of mass death via malaria as being a kind of merciful euthanasia, but also because it clearly based the case against DDT on the putative need to eliminate significant numbers of Africans and Asians.

## MASTERFUL PROPAGANDA

Most Americans, however, were not inclined to accept such open antihumanism. A more attractive argument was necessary to justify the banning of a substance that had saved millions of lives. But one was on the way: In 1958, the same year that Huxley published his book, Rachel Carson was given the contract to write *Silent Spring*.[17]

A former marine biologist and accomplished nature writer, Carson based her passionate argument against pesticides on the desire to protect wildlife, rather than an alleged necessity to spread death via insect-borne epidemics. Using evocative language, Carson told a powerful fable of a town whose people had been poisoned, and whose spring had been silenced of birdsong, because all life had been extinguished by pesticides.[18]

Published in 1962, *Silent Spring* was a phenomenal success. As a literary work, it was a masterpiece, and as such, received rave reviews everywhere. Deeply moved by Carson's poignant depiction of a lifeless future, millions of well-meaning people rallied to her banner. Virtually at a stroke, environmentalism grew from a narrow aristocratic cult into a crusading liberal mass movement.

While excellent literature, however, *Silent Spring* was very poor science. Indeed, considered as a scientific work, Carson's book can only be described as a mendacious fraud. Carson claimed that DDT was threatening many avian species with imminent extinction. Her evidence for this, however, was anecdotal, and unfounded. In fact, during the period of widespread DDT use preceding the publication of *Silent Spring*, bird populations in the United States increased significantly, probably as a result of the pesticide's suppression of their insect disease vectors and parasites.[19] In her chapter "Elixirs of Death," Carson wrote that synthetic insecticides can affect the human body in "sinister and often deadly ways," so that cumulatively, the "threat of chronic poisoning and degenerative changes of the liver and other organs is very real." In terms of DDT specifically, in her chapter on cancer she reported that one expert "now gives DDT the definite rating of a 'chemical carcinogen.'"[20] All of these alarming assertions were false as well.[21]

The panic raised by Carson's book spread far beyond American borders. Responding to its warning, the governments of a number of developing countries called a halt to their DDT-based anti-malaria programs. The results were catastrophic. In Ceylon, for example, where, as noted, DDT use had cut malaria cases from millions per year in the 1940s down to just 17 by 1963, its banning in 1964 led to a resurgence of half a million victims per year by 1969.[22] In many other countries, the effects were even worse.

Attempting to head off a hysteria-induced global health disaster, in 1970 the National Academy of Sciences issued a report praising the beleaguered pesticide:

> To only a few chemicals does man owe as great a debt as to DDT. It has contributed to the great increase in agricultural productivity, while sparing countless humanity from a host of diseases, most notably, perhaps, scrub typhus and malaria. Indeed, it is estimated that, in little more than two decades, DDT has prevented 500 million deaths due to malaria that would otherwise have been inevitable. Abandonment of this valuable insecticide should be undertaken only at such time and in such places as it is evident that the prospective gain to humanity exceeds the consequent losses. At this writing, all available substitutes for DDT are both more expensive per crop-year and decidedly more hazardous.[23]

To the environmentalists, however, five hundred million human lives were irrelevant. Disregarding the NAS findings, they continued to demand that DDT be banned. Responding to their pressure, in 1971 the newly-formed Environmental Protection Agency (EPA) launched an investigation of the pesticide. Lasting seven months, the investigative hearings led by Judge Edmund Sweeney gathered testimony from 125 expert witnesses with 365 exhibits. The conclusion of the inquest, however, was exactly the opposite of what the environmentalists had hoped for. After assessing all the evidence, Judge Sweeney found: "The uses of DDT under the registration involved here do not have a deleterious effect on freshwater fish, estuarine organisms, wild birds, or other wildlife.... DDT is not a carcinogenic hazard to man.... DDT is not a mutagenic or teratogenic hazard to man."[24] Accordingly, Judge Sweeney ruled that DDT should remain available for use.

Unfortunately, however, the administrator of the EPA was William

D. Ruckelshaus, who would later go on to be a founding sponsor of the Draper Fund.[25] Ruckelshaus reportedly did not attend a single hour of the investigative hearings, and according to his chief of staff, did not even read Judge Sweeney's report.[26] Instead, one can only conclude, he chose to ignore the science and act in accord with his political bias: overruling Sweeney, in 1972 Ruckelshaus banned the use of DDT in the United States except under conditions of medical emergencies.[27]

Initially, the ban only affected the United States. But the U.S. Agency for International Development (USAID) soon adopted strict environmental regulations that effectively prohibited it from funding international projects that used DDT.[28] Together with similar decisions by other major donor nations, this step turned the foreign aid programs of the United States and Europe into agents of genocide. Around the globe, Third World governments were told that if they

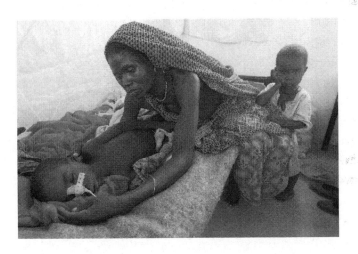

*As a result of the ban on DDT, millions of African children continue to die every year from malaria.*

wanted USAID or other foreign aid money to play with, they needed to stop using the most effective weapon against malaria.[29] Given the corrupt nature of many of the recipient regimes, it is not surprising that many chose lucre over life. And even for those that did not, the halting of American DDT exports (since U.S. producers slowed and then stopped manufacturing it) made DDT much more expensive, and thus effectively unavailable for poor countries in desperate need of the substance.[30] As a result, insect-borne diseases returned to the tropics with a vengeance. By some estimates, the death toll in Africa alone from unnecessary malaria resulting from the restrictions on DDT has exceeded 100 million people.[31]

## FOCUS SECTION: THE TRUTH ABOUT DDT

Over 80 percent of all infectious diseases afflicting humans are carried by insects or other small arthropods.[32] These scourges, which have killed billions of people, include bubonic plague, yellow fever, typhus, dengue, Chagas disease, African sleeping sickness, elephantiasis, trypanosomiasis, viral encephalitis, leishmaniasis, filariasis, and, most deadly of all, malaria. Insects have also caused or contributed to mass death by starvation or malnutrition, by consuming up to 40 percent of the food crop and destroying much of the livestock in many developing countries. Because of its unmatched ability to suppress these horrors, the introduction of DDT in 1943 marked the greatest single advance in public health in human history.

In 1972, following a campaign of wild allegations spearheaded by Rachel Carson through her book *Silent Spring*, DDT was banned by the Environmental Protection Agency in the United States, and international funding for DDT projects abroad was ended, resulting in untold millions of deaths. While critics of *Silent Spring* have tended to focus on the one-sidedness of Carson's case or on those of her claims that have not held up over time, the fraudulence of *Silent Spring* goes beyond mere cherry-picking or discredited data: Carson abused, twisted, and distorted many of the studies that she cited, in a brazen act of scientific dishonesty.[33]

In this section, we shall examine the three central anti-DDT claims made by Carson and her allies. As we shall see, each of their principal accusations is false.

CLAIM #1: DDT CAUSES CANCER IN HUMANS

In the late 1960s and early 1970s, the average American could be expected to ingest DDT in food and drink at levels of around 30 micrograms per day.[34] (Note: 1 gram = 1,000 milligrams = 1,000,000 micrograms.) Numerous studies of workers with intense exposure to DDT in the workplace, sometimes by factors of thousands more than the average dose—either in factories or in the field using DDT to combat malaria—have failed to show any "convincing evidence of patterns of associations between DDT and cancer incidence or mortality," according to the World Health Organization.[35] The thousands of individuals in these studies were regularly exposed to hundreds or perhaps thousands of times the amount of DDT that the average American would have been exposed to, but cancer rates seem not to have been elevated.[36] A great many studies of specific cancers—breast cancer, lung cancer, testicular cancer, liver cancer, prostate cancer, and more—over many decades have failed to show significant evidence of cancer as a result of exposure to DDT.[37]

There is scientific evidence that ingesting DDT or its byproduct DDE can cause mice to develop tumors, but only if they are fed at least ten times the amount per day (by body weight) that a person would normally expect to ingest.[38] Cancer studies of other mammals have been less conclusive.[39] In other studies of the effects of DDT on mammals, rats fed with large doses of the substance were found to have their reproductive lifespans increased by 65 percent (from 8.91 months to 14.55 months).[40] Heavily dosed dogs also experienced no ill effects, and in fact were found to be healthier than the control group, as DDT freed them of infestation by roundworms.[41]

Summarizing all of the relevant research, the U.S. government reported in 2002 that "there is no clear evidence that exposure to DDT/DDE causes cancer in humans."[42] That assessment is a vindication of the legal conclusion of Judge Edmund Sweeney's 1972 report on DDT for the EPA: "DDT is not a carcinogenic hazard to man."[43]

\* \* \*

CLAIM #2: DDT ENDANGERED U.S. BIRDS WITH
EXTINCTION

According to Rachel Carson, DDT was so harmful to birds that someday America's springs would be silent, as all the birds that might enliven
them with song would be dead. Indeed, it was from this poignant image
that she drew the title for her book.[44] As evidence for this claim, Carson
maintained that since the introduction of DDT to the United States
shortly after World War II, the nation's bird populations had fallen
into rapid decline, with even the robin threatened with extinction.[45]

An examination of actual data, however, thoroughly debunks
Carson's claim. This can be seen in Table 8.1, which compares the
Audubon Society's Christmas Bird Count data for 1941 (before
DDT) to that of 1960 (the height of DDT, shortly before the publi-
cation of *Silent Spring*).[46]

It can be seen that far from declining, the number of birds encountered by each observer nearly quadrupled over the period in question.
In the case of the robin, singled out by Carson as "the tragic symbol
of the fate of the birds,"[47] the population count increased twelvefold.

Many other studies show the same pattern of sharp increase of
some bird populations during the DDT years. For example, a bird
sanctuary that has been counting birds over Hawk Mountain, Pennsylvania since the 1930s reported an increase in sightings of ospreys from
less than 200 in 1945 to over 600 by 1970, and an increase in sightings of migrating raptors from 9,291 in 1946 to 29,765 in 1968.[48]
The herring gull population on Tern Island, Massachusetts grew
from 2,000 pairs in 1940 to 35,000 pairs in 1970 (at which point
the Audubon Society displayed its concern for the birds' well-being
by poisoning 30,000 of them, a procedure it said was "kind of like
weeding a garden").[49] And the annual data from the North American
Breeding Bird Survey from 1966 (the year the survey was launched,
in response to the public fear Carson had created about the effects of
DDT on birds) through the end of the 1970s shows no obvious pattern
of overall increasing bird populations as would be expected to follow

TABLE 8.1

*Audubon Society Christmas Bird Count: Counts per Observer*
*1941 (2,331 observers) compared with 1960 (8,928*
*observers)*

COUNTS PER OBSERVER

| SPECIES | 1941 | 1960 | RATIO 1960/1941 |
|---|---|---|---|
| Eagle | 0.08 | 0.10 | 1.25 |
| Gull | 53.40 | 72.00 | 1.33 |
| Raven | 0.29 | 0.30 | 1.03 |
| Crow | 79.59 | 28.04 | 0.35 |
| Pheasant | 0.88 | 1.15 | 1.31 |
| Mourning dove | 2.83 | 2.21 | 0.75 |
| Swatlow | 3.18 | 8.17 | 2.57 |
| Grebe | 6.15 | 27.14 | 4.41 |
| Pelican | 1.07 | 3.12 | 2.92 |
| Cormorant | 1.91 | 1.18 | 0.62 |
| Heron | 0.97 | 1.82 | 1.88 |
| Egret | 0.63 | 1.88 | 2.98 |
| Swan | 7.96 | 3.81 | 0.48 |
| Goose | 78.43 | 78.04 | 0.99 |
| Duck | 916.81 | 306.85 | 0.33 |
| Blackbird | 58.99 | 2,302.01 | 39.02 |
| Grackle | 10.70 | 1,407.98 | 131.59 |
| Cowbird | 17.17 | 368.09 | 21.44 |
| Chickadee | 9.15 | 6.26 | 0.68 |
| Titmouse | 2.16 | 2.05 | 0.95 |
| Nuthatch | 1.81 | 1.50 | 0.83 |
| Robin | 8.41 | 104.01 | 12.37 |
| English sparrow | 22.80 | 40.19 | 1.76 |
| Bluebird | 1.60 | 0.77 | 0.48 |
| Starling | 90.88 | 971.45 | 10.69 |

the 1972 banning of DDT if it were truly harming bird populations.[50]

Although many of Carson's key claims about how DDT affects the health of birds have been disproven in the years since her book was published, there is now evidence, both from field studies and laboratory experiments, that DDT does have an effect on birds that Carson did not know about when she wrote *Silent Spring*: it can cause many bird species to produce eggshells that are thinner and therefore more fragile. This effect has been linked to reduced populations of certain bird species, especially "raptors, waterfowl, passerines, and non-passerine ground birds."[51]

Eggshell thinning is a potential problem, but it should not be overstated. The levels of DDT required for malaria control are much less than those required for crop dusting as practiced in the 1950s. Furthermore, the problem does not affect every bird species—indeed, for some species, there is reason to believe that DDT has an overall beneficial effect, by protecting them from the insect-borne diseases that are a primary cause of bird mortality. For example, some marsh bird populations grew so dramatically during the DDT years that they emerged from their marshes in millions to cause significant damage to crops in the American Midwest.[52] Ultimately, the effects of DDT on bird populations are not nearly as dire as Carson depicted—and offer no justification for the millions of human deaths caused by the unwarranted prohibition of DDT.

### CLAIM #3: DDT THREATENED THE LIFE OF THE OCEANS

The most egregious lie put forth by the anti-DDT crusaders was launched after Carson's death, by Charles Wurster, a cofounder of the Environmental Defense Fund. In a note published in *Science* magazine in 1968, Wurster claimed to have shown that the presence of 500 parts per billion (ppb) of DDT in seawater would stop photosynthesis by phytoplankton.[53] Since phytoplankton are the productive foundation that supports all higher marine organisms, their suppression by DDT seemed to threaten the very existence of all life in the ocean, and possibly on the planet.

This was truly an alarming result. However, the maximum solubility of DDT in seawater is only 1.2 ppb, nowhere near 500 ppb, so the scenario Wurster reported was physically impossible.[54] In fact, in order to get so much DDT to dissolve, Wurster had been forced to use not seawater, but a saltwater/alcohol mixture as the medium for his experiment. It is hardly surprising that marine algae stopped functioning when thrown into such stuff. In contrast, other scientists found no harm or loss of activity of the same species of marine algae that Wurster used when immersed in actual seawater saturated to the limit with DDT.[55]

The Wurster experiment was thus meaningless as science. But as a propaganda tool for those seeking to ban the life-saving chemical, it was quite useful. In 1969, Paul Ehrlich, otherwise famous as the author of the antihumanist bible *The Population Bomb*—about which we shall have much to say in the next chapter—set alarm bells ringing everywhere with a screed entitled "Eco-Catastrophe!" in *Ramparts* magazine.[56] Reporting the history of the world as seen with undisputable authority from the standpoint of the future, Ehrlich wrote:

> The end of the ocean came late in the summer of 1979, and it came even more rapidly than the biologists had expected. There had been signs for more than a decade, commencing with the discovery in 1968 that DDT slows down photosynthesis in marine plant life. It was announced in a short paper in the technical journal, *Science*, but to ecologists it smacked of doomsday. They knew that all life in the sea depends on photosynthesis, the chemical process by which green plants bind the sun's energy and make it available to living things. And they knew that DDT and similar chlorinated hydrocarbons had polluted the entire surface of the earth, including the sea.

For the record, 1979 has come and gone, and life in the world's oceans has continued to flourish gloriously. But, as a result of the mendacity and actions of Carson, Ruckelshaus, Wurster, Ehrlich, and their

## CHAPTER NINE

# Scriptures for the Doom Cult

*We should change the pattern of federal support of biomedical research so that a majority of it goes into the broad areas of population regulation, environmental sciences, behavioral sciences, and related areas, rather than into short-sighted programs on death control. It is absurd to be preoccupied with the medical quality of life until and unless the problem of the quantity of life is solved. . . . India, where population growth is colossal, agriculture hopelessly antiquated, and the government incompetent, will be one of those we must allow to slip down the drain.*

PAUL EHRLICH, 1967[1]

THE ANTI-DDT CAMPAIGN mobilized an unprecedented mass following for American environmental groups. But if the crowds of new supporters were to be consolidated into something more than a transient single-issue movement, they needed to be given a broader systematic catechism that could organize their entire worldview along antihuman lines. Acting on this imperative, in 1967 the Sierra Club commissioned Stanford University insect ecology professor Paul Ehrlich to write a new Malthusian bible for modern times.[2] The result, entitled *The Population Bomb*, was released in May 1968. With the help of extraordinary television, radio, and newspaper publicity organized by the Sierra Club, the tract was turned into a bestseller, unmatched by any other piece of antihuman literature since Adolf Hitler's *Mein Kampf*.

"The battle to feed all of humanity is over. In the 1970s and 1980s hundreds of millions of people will starve to death," Ehrlich began. "At this late date nothing can prevent a substantial increase in the world death rate. . . . Nothing could be more misleading to our children than our present affluent society. They will inherit a totally different world, a world in which the standards, politics, and economics of the past decade are dead." In the face of this reality, freedom is no longer a luxury we can afford. "Our position requires that we take immediate action at home and promote effective action worldwide. *We must have population control at home, hopefully through changes in our value system, but by compulsion if voluntary methods fail.* Americans *must* also change their way of living so as to minimize their impact on the world's resources and environment."[3]

Commenting on the book, many of Ehrlich's admirers noted its unique power, in that it made the reader truly *feel* the threat of overpopulation. Ehrlich's own visceral feelings about Third World people were certainly well conveyed in passages like the following:

> I have understood the population explosion intellectually for a long time. I came to understand it emotionally one stinking hot night in Delhi a few years ago. My wife and daughter and I were returning to our hotel in an ancient taxi. . . . As we crawled through the city, we entered a crowded slum area. The temperature was well over 100, and the air was a haze of dust and smoke. The streets seemed alive with people. People eating, people washing, people sleeping. People visiting, arguing, and screaming. People thrusting their hands through the taxi window, begging. People defecating and urinating. People clinging to buses. People herding animals. People, people, people, people. As we moved slowly through the mob, hand horn squawking, the dust, noise, heat, and cooking fires gave the scene a hellish aspect. Would we ever get to our hotel?[4]

Earlier Nazi biologic propaganda had described non-Nordics as "viruses," "bacteria," or "infections" that endangered the race. Ehrlich demeaned the objects of his revulsion in strikingly similar terms—and recommended a similar surgical solution for dealing with them: "A cancer is an uncontrolled multiplication of cells; the population explosion is an uncontrolled multiplication of people.... We must shift our efforts from the treatment of the symptoms to the cutting out of the cancer. The operation will demand many apparently brutal and heartless decisions. The pain may be intense."[5]

As a specific recommendation, Ehrlich called for the United States to require that the Indian government forcibly sterilize all men with three or more children as a condition for the provision of food aid. "Coercion?" asked Ehrlich, rhetorically. "Perhaps, but coercion in a good cause."[6] In an apparent derisory reference to the public outrage over the decision of the Johnson administration to withhold desperately needed relief from India during the famine of 1966, Ehrlich added: "I am sometimes astounded at the attitudes of Americans who are horrified at the prospect of our government insisting on population control as the price of food aid."[7]

But the Third World was not the only target of *The Population Bomb*. Ehrlich also proposed that a "federal Bureau of Population and Environment should be set up to determine the optimum population

*Antihumanist ideologue Paul Ehrlich (left)*
*and his protégé John Holdren.*

size for the United States, and devise measures to establish it."[8] One way the proposed bureau could enforce its will would be to add "temporary sterilants to water supplies or staple food. Doses of the antidote would be carefully rationed by the government to produce the desired population size."[9] Unfortunately, while "it might be possible to develop such population control tools," political opposition from know-nothing Neanderthals could block implementation of such improvements for some time. "Just consider the fluoridation controversy!" Ehrlich exclaimed.[10]

In the face of such obstacles, therefore, Ehrlich offered a backup plan, which would be for the federal government to revise the tax code. Instead of tax deductions being offered to those with children, rewards would be given to those without. But that would just be the beginning. For Ehrlich, the population control possibilities opened by systems of financial coercion were endless:

> On top of the income tax change, luxury taxes could be placed on layettes, cribs, diapers, diaper services, expensive toys.... There would, of course, have to be considerable experimenting on the level of financial pressure necessary to achieve the population goals. To the penalties could be added some incentives. A governmental "first marriage grant" could be awarded each couple in which the age of both partners was 25 or more. "Responsibility prizes" could be given to each couple for each five years of childless marriage, or to each man who accepted irreversible sterilization (vasectomy) before having more than two children. Or special lotteries might be held—tickets going only to the childless.[11]

While Ehrlich does not make a point of it, it goes without saying that the imposition of financial penalties for having children would represent a much greater deterrent to the poor than to the rich. Thus, under the Ehrlich scheme, the reproduction of low-income racial and ethnic minorities such as blacks and Hispanics would be curtailed more than whites, thereby furthering the long-held goals of the eugenics movement as well.

Finally, however, Ehrlich concludes that the force of governmental coercion alone will not be enough. As in Nazi Germany, the new regime can only truly triumph by the replacement of older values with a radically new worldview that rejects not only Judeo-Christian morality, but all that it implies. "Our entire system of orienting to nature must undergo a revolution," says Ehrlich.

> And that revolution is going to be extremely difficult to pull off, since the attitudes of Western culture toward nature are deeply rooted in Judeo-Christian tradition. Unlike people in many other cultures, we see man's basic role as that of dominating nature, rather than as living in harmony with it. . . . Christianity fostered the wide spread of basic ideas of "progress". . . . Both science and technology can clearly be seen to have their historical roots in natural theology and the Christian dogma of man's rightful mastery over nature. Therefore . . . it is probably in vain that so many look to science and technology to solve our present ecological crisis. Much more basic changes are needed, perhaps of the type exemplified by the much despised "hippie" movement—a movement that adopts most of its religious ideas from the non-Christian East. It is a movement wrapped up in Zen Buddhism, love, and a disdain for material wealth.[12]

By "love," Ehrlich, the advocate of "apparently brutal and heartless decisions," certainly did not mean *caritas*, or loving care for other people. Rather, he meant, as the hippie movement for the most part did, sex. "We need a federal law requiring sex education in schools," he wrote, reserving the design of its curriculum to his federal bureau.

> By "sex education" I do not mean a course focusing on hygiene. . . . The reproductive function of sex must be shown as just one of its functions, and one that must be carefully

regulated in relation to the needs of the individual and society. Much emphasis must be placed on sex as an interpersonal relationship, as an important and extremely pleasurable aspect of being human, as mankind's major and most enduring recreation. . . . If we take the proper steps in education, legislation, and research, we should be able in a generation to have a population thoroughly enjoying its sexual activity.[13]

Thus Ehrlich laid out his brave new world—one whose purported lack of resources requires the abandonment of children, freedom, moral concern, progress, striving, and rational thought, but which, like Huxley's, compensates its inhabitants for these losses with the consolation of unlimited recreational sex. In the context of late 1960s America, such ideas were seen by some as very "hip" and "with it." Ehrlich was made into a star, appearing frequently on *The Tonight Show* with Johnny Carson and similar venues. With Ehrlich as its president, an organization called Zero Population Growth was founded, which soon grew influential enough to inspire such luminaries as Democratic Representative Richard Ottinger and Republican Senator Bob Packwood to introduce population control legislation to both chambers of Congress.[14]

In the place of single-issue campaigns with narrow objectives, the environmental groups now had a broad overarching ideology, which could link all particular points of agitation into a united cause. Instead of "Stop DDT!" the new slogan would be "People Pollute!" The potential for political growth offered by this theme was spectacular. In April 1970, "Earth Day" celebrations were held across the nation, the first demonstrations of a new mass movement dedicated to saving the world from humanity.

Ehrlich's tract did a great job of reaching the masses, but a different approach would be necessary to convince the political class.

In 1968, a group of thirty aristocrats, corporate magnates, and other self-styled elites from around the globe gathered at the Accademia dei Lincei in Rome to discuss "ideas about the global aspects of problems facing mankind and of the necessity of acting at the global level."[15] Following the meeting, Aurelio Peccei, a wealthy former executive at Fiat and Olivetti, reassembled a select few of the participants at his home, a gathering out of which arose the Club of Rome, a prominent propagator of antihumanist dogma.[16] Jointly led by Peccei and Alexander King, the scientific director of the Organization for Economic Cooperation and Development, and armed with generous funding from the Volkswagen Foundation, this cabal initiated a set of studies to raise the alarm about population growth and coming scarcity: that is, to prove scientifically that the era of plentiful resources and thus human freedom was—unfortunately, regrettably, but alas, necessarily—at an end. The most famous of these studies was released in 1972 under the title *The Limits to Growth*.[17]

Making use of its excellent connections throughout the business and media world, the Club succeeded in obtaining unprecedented publicity for *The Limits to Growth*. Indeed, the hype associated with the release of the study was so remarkable that one reviewer was led

*Members of the Club of Rome meeting in 1972. From left,*
*Fiat magnate Aurelio Peccei, OECD Director Alexander*
*King, Swiss Battelle Memorial Institute Director Hugo*
*Thiemann, and Japan Economic Research Center*
*President Saburo Okita.*

to comment, "*The Limits to Growth* is not just a book, it is an event."[18] But then, the Club had a lot to work with. For *The Limits to Growth* presented the results not of a mere human inquiry, but of a study *done by a computer*, which predicted, *with infallible computer accuracy*, that unless global economic growth were quickly brought to a halt, all non-renewable resources would soon be exhausted. Thus, for example, according to the Club's study, in 1972 only 455 billion barrels of oil were left to humanity. Since this was being consumed at a rate of 14.7 billion barrels per year, at then-current rates it would run out within 31 years; and if continued growth were taken into account (this is the part where the computer came in), it would all be gone by 1992. The same was true of every other resource.[19] Only so much of each existed, and if humans were allowed to continue to consume, most would be used up within twenty years, with the inevitable result being the collapse of civilization and the descent of humanity into bottomless impoverishment and misery. Who could fail to see it? The case was open and shut, provable by simple arithmetic verified by the best computer in the world. Neanderthal conservative ideologues and old buzzards from the Chamber of Commerce crowd might try to deny the inconvenient truth, but all enlightened opinion had to concur. Unless humanity repented and accepted severe limits to its aspirations, the end of the world was nigh.

In 1973, the Islamist-led OPEC cartel launched its petroleum embargo, sending the price of oil up fourfold and in the process brutally derailing a global economy that had been growing marvelously for a quarter century. Leaders of the Club of Rome hailed the change as heralding the advent of their age of limits. There was no truth to this—from the publication of *Limits* through to today, humanity has used 600 billion barrels of oil, but total known reserves have *grown* to over a trillion, and all other predictions by the Club of resource exhaustion have proven equally false. Nevertheless, this idea became the underlying theme of the Carter administration. Elected to office in 1976, Jimmy Carter brought into the White House, the Department of Energy, and the Environmental Protection Agency a number of staffers associated with the Club of Rome. Issuing their own version of *Limits* under the title *The Global 2000 Report*, this crowd turned the U.S. government for the first time into a propaganda agency for antihuman ideology.[20]

## FOCUS SECTION: THE FALLACY OF LIMITED RESOURCES

> *In the early 1970s, the leading edge of the age of scarcity arrived. With it came a clearer look at the future, revealing more of the nature of the dark age to come.*
>
> PAUL and ANNE EHRLICH
> *The End of Affluence:*
> *A Blueprint for Your Future, 1974*[21]

In its much-celebrated 1972 *Limits to Growth* manifesto, the Club of Rome predicted the near-term exhaustion of almost every major industrial resource. Among the reserves scheduled to run out were aluminum (by 2003), copper (by 1993), gold (by 1981), lead (by 1993), mercury (by 1985), molybdenum (by 2006), natural gas (by 1994), petroleum (by 1992), silver (by 1985), tin (by 1987), tungsten (by 2000), and zinc (by 1990). Manganese would be the next to go; it was scheduled to run out in the year 2018, followed by the platinum group metals in 2019.[22]

Now, if these predictions had any relationship to reality, the price of all of these supposedly rapidly disappearing commodities would soar to astronomical levels by 1990, if not sooner. Economist Julian Simon found this idea so risible that in 1980 he issued a public challenge, as follows:

> This is a public offer to stake $10,000, in separate transactions of $1,000 or $100 each, on my belief that mineral resources (or food, or other commodities) will not rise in price. If you are prepared to pay me now the current market price for $1,000 or $100 worth of any mineral you name (or other raw material

including grain and fossil fuels) that is not government controlled, I will agree to pay you the market price of the same
amount of that raw material on any future date you now spec-
ify. Will the doomsayers, who now say that minerals and other
raw materials will get more scarce, also put their money where
their mouths are?[23]

Having drunk their own Kool-Aid, Malthusians Paul Ehrlich, John
Holdren, and John Harte quickly announced that they would "accept
Simon's astonishing offer before other greedy people jump in."
Savoring his certain triumph in advance, Ehrlich commented "the
lure of easy money can be irresistible."[24]

As the duelists being challenged, the Ehrlich-Holdren-Harte party
was allowed to choose the items and the date that would settle the
dispute. Accordingly, on September 29, 1980 they selected the key
industrial metals copper, tin, nickel, chromium, and tungsten as the
commodities in question, and September 29, 1990 as the settlement
date.

Ten years came and went, and behold, on the day of settlement,
every single one of the metals Ehrlich, Holdren, and Harte had
selected had fallen in price. Especially noteworthy was tin, whose supply the Club of Rome had predicted would be completely exhausted
by 1987, and which therefore should have skyrocketed to platinum-
like prices by 1990.[25] Instead, its price, which was $8.46 a pound in
1980, was down to $3.86 a decade later.[26]

Utterly befuddled, the three geniuses (Ehrlich and Holdren have
both been recognized with "Genius Awards" by the MacArthur Foundation, and one can only assume that their comrade in the venture,
Harte, must be equally brilliant) paid up $576.07 to settle the wager.
As Ehrlich griped that the result was anomalous, Simon offered to
repeat the bet, this time for $20,000 —but the geniuses demurred.[27]

Commenting on the affair afterwards, Simon said "From my
point of view, the bet was like shooting fish in a barrel."[28] From
geniuses to fish—suckerfish, no doubt—evolution marches on.

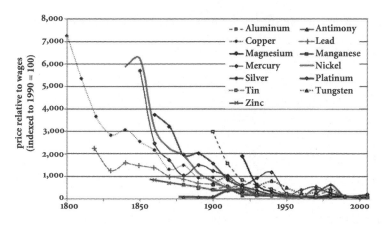

FIGURE 9.1: *Metals prices indexed against U.S. wages,*
*1800–2007.*
(*Courtesy Indur M. Goklany, MasterResource.org.*)

So what did Simon know that the three suckers, assisted as they were by the great all-knowing Club of Rome computer, did not?[29] Did he have secret access to a yet more advanced computer? Nope. He just knew a bit of economic history.

Shown in Figure 9.1 is the history of metals prices for the past two hundred years, indexed against U.S. wage rates.

It can be seen that, despite massive use of these metals over the past two centuries, and a simultaneous sixfold increase in global population, each and every one of the metals considered has become much cheaper—meaning, in real economic terms, more plentiful than in the past. Thus, despite the continued depletion of older mines, the ongoing advance of human technology has made acquisition of the ores for these metals so much easier than before that, regardless of vastly increased demand from an exponentially growing world market, the price of these commodities has simply fallen through the floor.

Furthermore, we are not running out of anything. In his essential book *The Ultimate Resource 2*, Simon provides the following figures for known reserves of the following commodities in 1990, indexed against the size of their known reserves in 1950.

TABLE 9.1

*Known Reserves of Key Industrial Resources*
*(Indexed to 1950 = 100)*[30]

| | |
|---|---|
| Lead | 300 |
| Zinc | 421 |
| Copper | 566 |
| Iron ore | 827 |
| Oil | 1311 |
| Phosphate | 1398 |
| Bauxite | 1657 |

How can this be? According to the Club of Rome's infallible computer analysis, most of this stuff should have been *gone* by 1990. Instead the commodities in question were radically more plentiful than they had been in 1950. In forty years, our copper resources more than quintupled, iron increased eightfold, while the Earth's supply of aluminum-containing bauxite ore multiplied sixteen times over.

Hold on right there, some might say. Aluminum ore multiplied? Now, really. Sure, the Club of Rome's computer may have been mathematically challenged—or misinformed, or whatever—but certainly aluminum ore can't multiply. If we are using it up, the extant amount can only decrease. After all, it is a finite, nonrenewable natural resource, isn't it?

Well, no. In point of fact, our aluminum ore supply is not nonrenewable, not finite, and not a natural resource. In the entire history of humanity, it is doubtful that we have destroyed a single kilogram of aluminum—the only way to do that is nuclear transmutation, a very rare occurrence indeed. All the aluminum we have ever produced is still around, with the large majority in the form of aluminum metal or alloys, making it much more available for future reuse than it ever was in its original form of aluminum oxide. So aluminum is renewable.

Furthermore, there is nothing natural about aluminum's status as a resource. Aluminum comprises 8.3 percent (by weight) of the Earth's crust, yet its existence was not even inferred until 1808 and remained undemonstrated until its isolation by Danish scientist Hans Christian Ørsted in 1825. Until that time, human beings, living on a planet whose third-most-common elemental component is aluminum, had no more knowledge of it or ability to use it than they did of radio signals, coherent laser light, or antimatter. The comparison with coherent laser light is particularly apt, since while both light and aluminum compounds exist in nature, coherent light and metallic aluminum do not. Search where you will; unless you can find the wreckage of a flying saucer, the only aluminum metal you will ever encounter anywhere on this planet will be a human industrial creation.

So aluminum metal is not a natural resource at all; it is an artificial resource, a product of human science and ingenuity. The same is true of "aluminum ore." There was no such thing as aluminum ore until chemists developed techniques for extracting aluminum metal from aluminum oxides. Until that time such materials were not aluminum ore. Instead they were called "rock," or "dirt," or "dust," and had no value beyond what those names connote. Furthermore, even after the first creation of aluminum metal, the question of whether a particular piece of matter was a "rock" or "aluminum ore" was ultimately determined by the level of available industrial technique. Until we developed our first extraction techniques, it was all rock. As techniques advanced, more and more "rock" became aluminum ore. We *created* aluminum ore by advancing our technology.

The same is true of all other metals and materials. During the Bronze Age, what is now iron ore was mere dirt. By developing iron smelting technology, human ingenuity transformed all that worthless rock into iron ore. Until then there was no such thing. People have used silicon compounds for some time to make ceramics and glass, and more recently have expanded the list to include fiberglass structural materials, fiber-optic data transmission lines, and silicon semiconductors. For certain applications, fiberglass can replace steel or

aluminum. For others, fiber-optic cables can replace copper tele-
phone wires—or alternatively, both can be replaced by mobile phones
using tiny amounts of silicon in semiconductors and no transmission
wires at all. Silicon can also be produced as a metal, and undoubtedly
combined with other metals to produce satisfactory structural alloys.
We haven't bothered to do it because we have all the steel and aluminum we want, and they do the job just fine. But if for some reason
we wanted to make silicon metal structural alloys, we could. Then,
very quickly, another 25.7 percent of the Earth's crust would transform from being "dirt" to ore—silicon ore.

## THE AVAILABILITY OF FOOD

So much for metals. But what of food? From the time of Malthus
down to the doomsday prophesies of Ehrlich and the Club of Rome,
antihumanists have insisted that the hungry must die because, if they
don't, there will never be enough to go around.

How would Ehrlich, Holdren, and Harte have fared if, instead of
dwelling on imaginary metal shortages, they had put their money
where their mouths were, and bet on *famine* during the 1980s? The
answer is that their humiliation would have been even worse. This is
shown in Figure 9.2.

In Figure 9.2, we show the affordability of food, defined as the
average per capita income divided by the price of sustenance, in both
the United States and India, from 1900 to 2007. During this period
of time, the population of the world quadrupled, yet despite this (or
rather in part *because* of this), the affordability of food increased eightfold in India and thirteenfold in the United States. Over the wager's
timespan from 1980 to 1990 alone, the affordability of food in India
*tripled*. It then doubled again over the following decade. As a result,
food is fifty percent more affordable in India today than it was in America in 1900. With the advent of biotechnology, there is no reason
why this trend cannot continue, so that in a few more decades, the

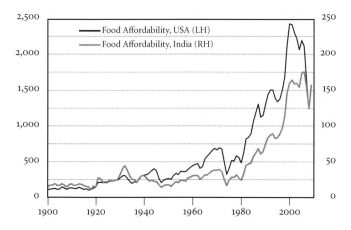

FIGURE 9.2: *Affordability of food in the United States and India, 1900 to 2007. Affordability is per capita income divided by the price of food. United States figures are graphed against the left, India against the right.*
(*Courtesy Indur M. Goklany, MasterResource.org.*)

people of India will be able to eat just as well, with just as little personal sacrifice, as Americans can today.

In 1968, Paul Ehrlich called for letting the people of India die because there would never be enough to feed them. I believe he owes them an apology.

## THE QUESTION OF FINITUDE

Finally we come to "finitude," a quasi-religious concept upon which the Malthusians stake the ultimate truth of their dogma. "Yes," they cry, "you humans may be able to make more food and mine more metal using your clever little tricks that have foiled our predictions so far, but in the end, there is only so much matter in the Earth. It is not infinite! Sooner or later you are going to run out of mass, and when that day comes everyone will see that we were right all along!"

If only the tenacity of those making this argument were devoted to a better cause. In what sense can a resource be regarded as finite if you not only never run out, but never experience any shortage? Our ability to turn the matter composing our planet into useful items is increasing daily. Someday it may all be useful. The Earth has a mass of six trillion trillion ($6 \times 10^{24}$) kilograms. That means that even if the human population expanded a thousandfold, from its current six billion to six trillion, there would still be a trillion kilograms of mass on this planet alone for each and every one of those six trillion citizens. Earth, moreover, is not the only world. We have already taken our first baby steps into space. Long before we have six trillion people, or sixty billion people for that matter, we will have mastered space travel. The mass of the other planets in our own solar system alone exceeds that of the Earth a hundredfold. There are some four hundred billion stars in our home galaxy, most of which have solar systems, and hundreds of billions of other such galaxies in the universe at large. And that is just the part we know about now.

We will never run out of mass, or space, and provided we resist the advice of those who would have us destroy ourselves in order to avoid such imaginary perils, we need never run out of time, either.

## CHAPTER TEN

# The Betrayal of the Left

*I frankly admit that I have extraordinarily little feeling for, or interest in, what is usually termed "the final goal of socialism." This goal, whatever it may be, is nothing to me, the movement is everything.*

EDUARD BERNSTEIN
German Socialist Party leader, 1896[1]

THE TWO MOST essential elements of any modern economy are Labor and Capital. In a democracy, each of these elements needs— and will therefore seek to create and support—political forces to speak for its interests. Thus any healthy democracy will perforce have strong parties representing the left and the right. Sometimes the changes necessary for continued advance will be driven by one, sometimes by the other, but like different sections of an orchestra, each has its role to play.

The American left has a proud history of struggle to advance the human condition. It fought for Independence and the Bill of Rights, against slavery and child labor, for the eight-hour day, the minimum wage, factory and mine safety, public schools, rural electrification, and the right to organize trade unions. It militantly opposed Nazism, some of its members going so far as to volunteer to fight Hitler in Spain long before the rest of the country got involved. During the 1960s, it was in the forefront of the civil rights movement and led the effort to stop the Vietnam War. Many of its efforts are universally acknowledged today as great contributions to America. Others remain controversial.

It certainly was not always in the right. Its economic prescriptions have often been incompetent and its long willful blindness to the evils of Soviet communism was shameful. But taken as a whole, it was a brave and generous movement, devoted, in accord with its own lights, to defending and improving the condition of *people.*

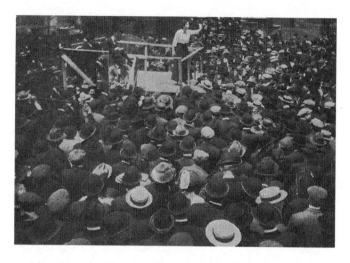

*The left's heroic tradition. Industrial Workers of the World organizers rally workers to fight for the eight-hour day at decent pay during the Paterson silk strike of 1913.*

It was thus very disturbing to many American leftists when people started showing up at their meetings in the late 1960s insisting that they take up the cause of population control. This was a complete break from the left's traditions and commitments. Since the days of Henry George and Friedrich Engels, American leftists had always been vehemently opposed to Malthusianism, which they correctly understood as a reactionary racist doctrine conceived for the purpose of denying the just aspirations of working people. But now, descending upon the meetings of the Students for a Democratic Society (the grab-bag organization for Sixties campus radicals) came the acolytes of Paul Ehrlich. Instead of *The Grapes of Wrath,* they carried copies of *The Population Bomb.* Instead of voting rights for minorities, they wanted to give them abortions. Instead of "Stop the War," their buttons read "Stop at Two"; instead of "Power to the people," their slogan was "People pollute."

At first they met resistance. The Marxists rushed reprints of their founding fathers' anti-Malthusian tracts back into publication.[2] The Black Panther Party expressed itself rather more plainly, saying, "What pollutes our air is not industrial smog but exclusion from the industrial benefits of racist, imperialist Amerika."[3] The Christian radical Richard Neuhaus, pastor of the Lutheran Church of St. John the Evangelist in Brooklyn and founder of National Clergy and Laymen Concerned About Vietnam, wrote an entire book blasting Ehrlich and the ecology movement for their flagrant antihumanism. Entitled *In Defense of People: Ecology and the Seduction of Radicalism*, the book makes poignant reading today, recalling as it does the waning moments of the era when the left stood up for human beings.

"The project of greening America is obscene so long as vast areas of the world are parched by war and famine," Neuhaus wrote.

The self-satisfaction of groupings in culturally liberated zones mocks the babies who die of lead poisoning and play with rats in Brooklyn tenements. The delight in achieving an organically pure eco-diet is frivolous in a world where twelve thousand brothers and sisters die from starvation each day. . . .

If one takes seriously, for example, the triage proposal of forced starvation [advanced by Ehrlich and fellow Malthusian Garrett Hardin] it readily becomes apparent how difficult it would be to implement. . . . Having classified India as "hopeless" (no doubt Orwellian euphemisms will be substituted), the United States declares a blockade. . . . After the blockade, armed forces (U.S. or those of a U.N. in which the Third World members had been effectively silenced) would patrol the borders of East and West Pakistan, Nepal, China, and the Soviet Union to hold back the hordes seeking to escape from the great hunger. In the United States and other developed countries the press and other media would be rigidly censored so that the islands of survival will not be exposed to pictures and written accounts of suffering and thus provoke that do-gooder sentimentality that Paul Ehrlich so despises. . . . It is not clear whether Ehrlich wants all 540 million Indians dead before the embargo is lifted. That would seem most sensible, however, since any survivors of several years' rampant cannibalism and total absence of social order would be unlikely candidates for the "quality environment" which we desire. Naturally, many people in the United States and other countries would have protested this whole course from the beginning, but their protest would be futile (and probably forbidden) since by this time the developed countries will have recognized the wisdom of those eco-enthusiasts who argue that democratic processes and values simply are not able to cope with the enormity of the crisis we face.[4]

But neither the Marxist catechism, the elegant polemics of Neuhaus, nor even the cries of outrage from the left's own Black Panther heroes could hold the line against a massive public-relations campaign that was transforming the entirety of America's intellectual atmosphere. In 1969, *Ramparts* magazine, the flagship high-gloss mass-circulation gold standard for radical politics, devoted an entire issue to ecology, including as its cover story "Eco-Catastrophe!," the article (described in Chapter Eight) by Paul Ehrlich predicting the death of the ocean and even *the exhaustion of the Earth's oxygen supply* unless forceful measures were taken immediately to suppress population and industrial growth.[5] In parallel with such promotions of the Ehrlich cult, Hugh Moore and William Draper stepped up the work of their Campaign to Check the Population Explosion, distributing hundreds of thousands of pamphlets and placing dozens of full-page ads in major newspapers signed by lists of Nobel Prize recipients and liberal luminaries demanding immediate action to stop the "population explosion."[6]

Building on this, Moore and his media consultants conceived the project of launching population control as a mass movement by making it the central plank of a "National Environmental Teach-In,"

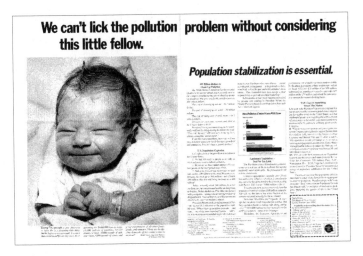

*Hugh Moore's Campaign to Check the Population Explosion warns that babies threaten the Earth's environment.*

or "Earth Day" nationwide rally on April 22, 1970, orchestrated by Wisconsin Senator Gaylord Nelson and coinciding with the hundredth anniversary of the birthday of Russian revolutionary Vladimir Lenin. No expense was spared on this coming-out party for the new antihuman movement. Lawrence Lader, an associate of Ehrlich working with Moore's organizing committee, subsequently recounted how they pulled it off:

> First, a third of a million leaflets, folders, and pamphlets (in-cluding a new pictorial edition of the venerable *Population Bomb*) were produced for campus and community distribution. Next, three efforts stressed the intimate relation between over-population and a degraded environment. One was the free distribution to 300-odd college radio stations of a taped program featuring Paul Ehrlich and David Brower. The second was provision, for reproduction free by college newspapers, of a score of editorial cartoons highlighting the population crisis. The third was a contest, conducted on over 200 campuses,

that awarded prizes for slogans relating environmental problems to "popullution."[7]

This was just the beginning. Large corporate donations flowed in to help the organizing effort, which was seen in some establishment circles —including that of President Nixon—as an excellent way to divert radicals from less convenient activity.[8] As Earth Day approached, it became apparent that it was going to be a very big affair. Rather than be left on the sidelines of the new radicalization, leaders of the various left-wing organizations decided to "go to where the people are at" and jump on the bandwagon.

In the *Communist Manifesto*, Marx and Engels had called upon the working class to take power—not to stop the industrial revolution unleashed by capitalism, but to carry it further. But now, embracing the Malthusian cause, America's leftist leaders offered the services of socialism as the most efficient agent for imposing zero-growth. In his 1941 classic, "Roll On, Columbia, Roll On," leftist balladeer Woody Guthrie had sung the praises of hydroelectric dams whose "power is turning our darkness to dawn." No more. Henceforth the role of the peoples' tribunes would be to tell their clients that the time had come to turn out the lights.

Many on the left were appalled by the betrayal. One of these dismayed individuals was Allan Chase, an old-school left-wing journalist who had cut his teeth exposing Axis operations in Latin America during the 1940s. In his magisterial book, *The Legacy of Malthus: The Social Costs of the New Scientific Racism*, written a few years later, Chase gives some sense of the disgust he and others like him felt as they watched the travesty unfold:

By 1970, thousands of earnest and idealistic Americans of all ages were swapping their "End the Killing in Vietnam" buttons for more modish buttons bearing the words "People Pollute."

The greatest peace movement ever created in America, a coalition of young people powerful enough to have driven

*The old and new left in contrast, for and against human dignity. Top, civil rights protestors participating in Rev. Martin Luther King's March on Washington in 1963. Later, in 1968, they would carry signs reading "I AM A MAN." Bottom, environmentalist radicals in Boston say that humans are a pollutant, on Earth Day in 1970.*

Lyndon Johnson out of public life in 1968, now committed hara-kiri on national network television in the name of the Moore revival of Malthusianism. . . .

What the might of the Johnson and Nixon administrations had been unable to do with all of their propaganda agencies and secret police powers, the new Malthusian population-bombers did with taped radio programs, syndicated editorial cartoons, brainwashing prize contests, and some 330,000 folders, leaflets, and pamphlets.

In a holy fervor of opportunism and righteousness, let alone profound relief to find the angry campus generation mesmerizing itself into abandoning the cause of peace in Indochina, President Nixon and various of his high officials joined in the orgies of well-televised oratory and *Kraft durch Freude*[9] fiestas that marked Earth Day, 1970: the day the young people switched goals from the quest for peace to the crusade for Zero Population Growth and Clean Cars. From that point forward, Nixon embraced the new Malthusian "environmentalism" with public passion.[10]

But Chase's *cri de cœur* was of little avail. The left had sold out. Henceforth its legions of writers, organizers, and demonstrators would be at the disposal of the Malthusians.

Henceforth genocide would be "progressive."

## CHAPTER ELEVEN

# The Anti-Nuclear Crusade

*Except in special circumstances, all construction of power gen-*
*erating facilities should cease immediately.... Power is much*
*too cheap. It should certainly be made more expensive and per-*
*haps rationed, in order to reduce its frivolous use.*

PAUL EHRLICH and RICHARD HARRIMAN
*How to Be a Survivor, 1971* [1]

WITH THE BANNING of DDT in 1972, the antihuman movement lost its sharpest agitational issue. The radical left was now on board, but if recruitment and fundraising were to be maintained, a new target capable of being used to generate public hysteria needed to be designated. Fortunately for the movement, such a target was available: the young commercial nuclear power industry.

When considered as an effort in defense of the environment, the anti-nuclear campaign that was launched worldwide in the early 1970s made no sense whatsoever. Mining coal requires the displacement of five thousand times more soil than what is required to mine its energy equivalent in uranium; transporting coal requires hundreds of thousands of times the energy. [2] Since 1968, over thirty thousand Americans have died from coal workers' pneumoconiosis, also known as black lung disease, and many more continue to suffer from other hazards involved in mining coal. [3] Mining uranium presents roughly the same risk of accidents as mining coal, and evidence that uranium miners are at higher risk than coal miners for cancer is inconclusive or negative, particularly for operations employing modern safety

133

measures, while the risk of black lung and other diseases is unique to coal miners.[4] The major difference in overall safety is that it takes far less uranium, and so less uranium mining, to generate a given amount of energy, meaning that uranium is far safer to mine per megawatt-hour of energy generated.[5]

When it comes to the health of the general public, the negative effects of fossil fuel pollution are clear, real, and profound. Counter-intuitively, the amount of *radiological* pollution released by a coal-fired power plant is a hundred times higher than that from a nuclear plant per amount of energy produced, due to radioactive elements present in coal being concentrated and released, while nuclear waste is contained.[6] Meanwhile, the amount of solid toxic waste generated by coal-fired plants, particularly the older plants still widely operating in America, is *hundreds of thousands* of times greater than that created by nuclear reactors—and unlike waste created by nuclear power plants, which is contained and decays to a harmless condition over time (with 99.9 percent of it gone in ten years),[7] the toxic chemicals from coal plants (like heavy metals) are emitted into the environment where they can last forever.[8]

In the early 1970s, an estimated ten to fifty thousand Americans died every year from carcinogenic air pollution released from fossil fuel-fired power plants.[9] In terms of public safety, massive death tolls from fossil fuel combustion fumes trapped over cities during atmospheric inversions remain a demonstrated threat. Over 3,900 people perished from asphyxiation by air pollution in London in December 1952, and there have been many smaller events since—and much larger near-misses—including several during the very period that the anti-nuclear movement was launched.[10]

On January 6, 1973, for example, oil storage tanks in Bayonne, New Jersey went up in flames, releasing a thick toxic smoke cloud that was far deadlier than the London smog of 1952. Only a favorable wind saved Manhattan from disaster.[11] Three years later, a storage facility in south Brooklyn that housed 90,000 barrels of oil caught fire, exploded, and burned out of control for four days, sending a giant

*In December 1952, a cold-air inversion caused fumes
from coal-fired power plants to settle on London for four
days. Nearly four thousand people died immediately,
with another eight thousand expiring from respiratory
problems over the following weeks.*

plume of toxic smoke into the sky.[12] Again, it was only the lucky circumstance of a fortunate breeze blowing out to sea that prevented a massive loss of life. In contrast, there have never been any environmental or public health effects caused by any radiological release from a nuclear power plant in the United States, and each new nuclear power plant, by replacing its equivalent in coal, is estimated to save hundreds of lives and cut emissions of greenhouse gases and air pollutants by millions of tons per year.[13]

In their anti-DDT campaign, the environmental groups claimed that they were concerned about a new, artificial, and—for certain kinds of life at least—toxic substance being introduced into nature. But in launching its assault on nuclear power, the movement attacked a technology that released almost nothing, and in fact acted materially to *eliminate* existing pollution already tangibly affecting man and nature. Engineers working in the nuclear industry at the time, many of whom considered themselves environmental white knights, were dumbfounded.

Their confusion is understandable. Why attack nuclear power in the early 1970s, rather than the millionfold dirtier coal- and oil-fired power plants that it threatened to replace? The answer is simple: attacking coal was pointless, because coal-fired power plants had been around for nearly a century. While the environmental and safety hazards presented by coal were real, they were accepted, and had little value for the purpose of creating panic. In contrast, nuclear power, while non-polluting, was novel, and had particular qualities—notably its association with nuclear weapons—that made it an ideal target for the generation of hysteria.

Realizing this, professional demagogues like Ralph Nader seized upon the issue. Observing the successful recruitment and fundraising that followed from his efforts, environmental groups wasted little time in adopting the new strategy. Spreading the lie that nuclear power plants could explode like bombs—a physical impossibility—the panic-mongers achieved truly impressive results.[14] Between 1970 and 1974, 115 orders for nuclear power plants had been placed in the United States, for an average of 23 per year. But following the birth of the anti-nuclear movement, this fell to an average of less than 3 orders per year between 1975 and 1979—and nearly all of these orders were subsequently canceled.[15] No construction permits for new reactors have been issued in the United States since 1979.[16] Had the American nuclear power industry been allowed to continue to grow at the rate it was achieving in the early 1970s, it would have replaced nearly all fossil fuel use for power generation in the United States by 1990. Instead, the industry was aborted, and with it the promise of cheap, clean, and unlimited electricity for all.

But the more profound effect of the anti-nuclear agitation was, as intended, the further growth of the antihuman movement. In the

*Anti-nuclear demonstrations swept the globe. Here,*
*members of the Clamshell Alliance protest against the*
*construction of a nuclear power plant at Seabrook,*
*New Hampshire, during the 1970s.*

United States, this movement now became capable of deploying shock troops in mass demonstrations, lawyers in litigation without limit, and millions of votes in support or opposition to candidates of its choice. In Europe, things went still further, with old fascist elements uniting with a new generation of idealistic youth to form powerful new "Green" political parties whose principle basis was antihuman ideology itself.

## FOCUS SECTION: THE TRUTH ABOUT NUCLEAR POWER

The most important thing there is to know about nuclear power is that it is by far the greatest resource available to humanity today.

Energy is the most basic physical resource. With sufficient energy, you can make anything. Without it, you can do nothing. In arguing for limits to growth, the Malthusians always inevitably end up pointing to energy. There is only so much to go around, they say, so human aspirations must be crushed. Lest we run out of energy, they claim, people in advanced countries must accept lower living standards and the poor nations must stay poor forever.

But nuclear power completely upends this rationale for putting chains on humanity. This is shown in Table 11.1, which presents both the size and per capita cash value of the Earth's energy resources. Table 11.1 is divided into two sections, the first dealing with resources that can be used today, the second showing additional resources that could become available in the future provided human technology continues to advance. It can be seen that nuclear resources vastly outclass fossil energy sources in both the current and future categories.

Focusing on the resources that are usable today, we see that our known fossil fuel reserves are sufficient to provide 1,197 terawatt-years (TW-years) of electricity. (A watt-year is an amount of energy, and a terawatt-year is a trillion watt-years. For example, a 100-watt light bulb burned for a year uses 100 watt-years of energy. United States energy usage per capita was roughly 11,000 watt-years in 2010.[17]) Since humanity is currently using about 15 TW-years annually, fossil fuel reserves would represent enough energy to power the globe at current rates for eighty years.[18] (This figure is meant only to provide scale, and implies no prediction of a time to fuel exhaustion, as usage rates will change and new fuel reserves will likely be discovered.) By contrast, our presently known reserves of uranium and thorium fuel comprise at least 250,000 TW-years of energy, over two hundred times as much as fossil fuels, sufficient to power the globe at current rates for over 16,000 years.

There are those who argue that the Earth's natural resources should be considered "the common heritage of mankind."[19] This is a debatable proposition, but it has some merit, since they are in fact a natural gift of great value to everyone. So, if we were to divide our

TABLE 11.1

*The Earth's Energy Resources*[20]

| CURRENTLY USABLE RESOURCES | ENERGY (TW-YEARS) | VALUE PER CAPITA (1000S OF DOLLARS) |
|---|---|---|
| Oil  (known reserves) | 202 | 18 |
| Coal  (known reserves) | 790 | 69 |
| Natural Gas (known conventional reserves) | 205 | 18 |
| Nuclear Fission (Uranium fuel, without reprocessing) | 685 | 60 |
| Nuclear Fission (Uranium fuel, with reprocessing) | 50,000 | 4,400 |
| Nuclear Fission (Thorium fuel, with reprocessing) | 200,000 | 17,500 |
| RESOURCES POTENTIALLY USABLE IN THE FUTURE | | |
| Natural Gas (including sub-sea methane hydrates) | 24,000 | 2,100 |
| Nuclear Fusion | 100,000,000,000 | 8,800,000,000 |

planet's energy largesse equally, how much would your share of it be worth? The answer is shown in the second column of Table 11.1, showing the cash value of these resources. These figures come from taking the total worth of each resource if converted into electricity at a price of 7 cents per kilowatt-hour, and dividing it among the globe's current population of around 7 billion people.[21] Figured this way, the share of the world's common heritage of oil fairly due to you and your heirs would be worth about $17,700 each, while your coal and natural gas assets would be worth another $87,200 combined. In contrast, the value of your nuclear reactor fuel would come to some $22 million.

Of course, you and your kids only get your $22 million if we *have* nuclear reactors. Without them, all of your uranium and thorium is just so much dirt. I put it this way because it is important that people understand exactly what they are giving up should we be forced to forgo nuclear power.

## TECHNICAL CONCERNS OVER NUCLEAR POWER

Now that we have established what the stakes of nuclear power are, let's discuss the technical issues, beginning at the beginning. There are two kinds of nuclear power: fission and fusion. Fission works by using a neutron as a kind of projectile to split the nuclei of very heavy atoms such as uranium and plutonium into middle-weight elements, thereby releasing energy, as well as several more neutrons which can be used to continue to process in a "chain reaction." Fusion, which is the reaction that powers the sun and all the stars, works by fusing the nuclei of hydrogen isotopes into helium, in the process releasing even more energy than fission. Fission reactors have been a practical means of generating electricity at commercially competitive rates since the 1950s. Controlled fusion is still experimental.

Despite its lack of air pollution or greenhouse emissions, nuclear fission has provoked much opposition due to alarm raised by environmentalists over the possibility of nuclear accidents. Other key issues in the anti-nuclear catechism include the problem of disposing of radioactive waste products, exposure of the public to radioactivity through radioactive emissions during routine power plant operations, and the possibility of proliferation of nuclear weapons. We address each of these areas of concern in turn.

## NUCLEAR ACCIDENTS

Nuclear accidents are certainly possible, but rare. Over the course of its entire history, the world's commercial nuclear industry has had three major accidents: one at Three Mile Island in Pennsylvania in 1979; one in Fukushima, Japan, in March 2011; and the other at Chernobyl in the Ukraine in 1986. The Three Mile Island event was a core meltdown caused by a failure of the cooling system. A billion-dollar reactor was lost, but the containment system worked. As a result, there were no human fatalities, nor was there any significant environmental impact.[22]

The 2011 Japanese accident was much more serious. Caused by a powerful undersea earthquake and resulting tsunami that buffeted the facility with waves nearly fifty feet high, the power plant flooded, eventually leading to full meltdown of three of the six reactors.[23] Nevertheless, if anything, the Fukushima event proved the safety of nuclear power. In the midst of a devastating disaster which killed some 20,000 people by drowning, falling buildings, fire, suffocation, exposure, disease, and many other causes, not a single person was killed by radiation. There may have been substantial nuclear-related casualties, however—but these were caused by Gregory Jaczko, the chairman of the Obama administration's Nuclear Regulatory Commission. Following the Fukushima incident, Jaczko spread panic by warning all American citizens to stay at least fifty miles away from the Fukushima power plants.[24] The resulting climate of fear and panic hampered rescue efforts. United States Navy forces steaming toward the rescue were ordered to stay 100 miles away[25]—leaving unknown numbers of victims trapped under buildings or stranded at sea within the fifty-mile zone to die, despite a complete lack of evidence for any actually dangerous levels of radiation outside of the plant gate.

(Jaczko may well be the most anti-nuclear chairman that the Nuclear Regulatory Commission has ever had. A former aide to the very anti-nuclear Representative Ed Markey [D.-Mass.] and to Senate

Majority Leader Harry Reid [D.-Nev.], Jaczko has been responsible for the extraordinary efforts of the Obama administration to prevent the establishment of a permanent nuclear waste repository at Yucca Mountain, Nevada. In doing so, he not only broke his word to Congress—which, concerned about bias stemming from his work for Harry Reid, asked him at his confirmation hearing to recuse himself from Yucca Mountain matters—but violated the fundamental purpose of his office. Instead of trying to make nuclear power as safe as possible, Jaczko's effort to stop safe nuclear waste storage far away from populated areas represented an attempt to make the industry as dangerous as possible, in order to shut it down.[26])

From the point of view of radiation release, Chernobyl was the most serious nuclear-plant disaster of all time. At Chernobyl, the reactor actually had a runaway chain reaction and disassembled, breaching all containment. Approximately fifty people were killed during the event itself and the fire-fighting efforts that followed immediately thereafter. Furthermore, radioactive material comparable to that produced by an atomic bomb was released into the environment. According to an authoritative twenty-year study by the International Atomic Energy Agency and World Health Organization, over time this fallout will most likely be responsible for four thousand deaths among the surrounding population.[27] So Chernobyl was really about as bad as a nuclear accident can be. Yet in comparison to all the deaths caused *every year* as a result of the pollution emitted from coal-fired power plants, its impact was minor. Chernobyl-like catastrophes would have to occur *every day* to approach the toll on humanity currently inflicted by coal. By replacing a substantial fraction of the electricity that would otherwise have to be generated by fossil fuels, the nuclear industry has actually saved countless lives.

Still, Chernobyl events need to be prevented, and they can be, by proper reactor engineering. The key is to design the reactor in such a way that as its temperature increases, its power level will go *down*. In technical parlance, this is known as having a "negative temperature coefficient of reactivity." As early as 1950, Captain Hyman Rickover,

the leader of the U.S. Navy's effort to create the first nuclear submarine, realized that having such negative feedback against power spikes
was fundamental to ensuring safe operation of a nuclear reactor.
Accordingly, the reactor of the submarine *Nautilus* was designed in
such a way that a chain reaction could not be sustained unless liquid
water was present in the cooling channels throughout its core. Water
is necessary for a sustained nuclear reaction because it serves to slow
down, or "moderate," the fast neutrons born of fission events enough
for them to interact with surrounding nuclei to continue the reaction.
(Just like an asteroid passing by the Earth, a neutron is more likely to
be pulled in to collide with a nucleus if it is going slow than if it is
going fast.) It is physically impossible for such a water-moderated
reactor to have a runaway chain reaction, because as soon as the reactor heats beyond a certain point, the water starts to boil. This reduces
the water's effectiveness as a moderator, and without moderation,
fewer and fewer neutrons strike their target, causing the reactor's
power level to drop. The system is thus intrinsically stable, and there
is no way to make it unstable. No matter how incompetent, crazy, or
malicious the operators of a water-moderated reactor might be, they
can't make it go Chernobyl. It was on this principle that Rickover
designed both the *Nautilus* and the subsequent first civilian nuclear
reactor at Shippingport, Pennsylvania, and these have served to set
the pattern for nearly all American reactors ever since.[28]

In contrast, the reactor that exploded at Chernobyl—a Soviet
RBMK reactor—was moderated not by water, but by graphite, which
does not boil. It therefore did not have the strong negative temperature reactivity feedback of a water-moderated system, and in fact, due
to various other design features, it actually had a *positive* temperature
coefficient of reactivity. It was thus an unstable system, and could
lead to a runaway reaction when its operators decided to do some
really dumb experiments. No such system could ever be licensed in
the United States.

However, it is physically impossible for any nuclear power reactor,
including even the kind used at Chernobyl, to explode in the manner

of an atomic bomb.[29] This is because a functional atomic bomb requires a system that can bring together a critical mass of fissionable material so suddenly that the heat generated as the chain reaction begins does not have time to blow the device apart before the chain reaction can run to substantial completion. This is a very hard thing to do. It requires not only the use of nuclear fuel that is enriched to 90 percent fissionable material (natural uranium is 0.7 percent fissionable, while commercial reactor fuel is 3 percent fissionable), but exquisite engineering design. In fact, it took the concerted efforts of some of the world's greatest scientists working at Los Alamos to design and implement such a controlled "implosion" system during World War II. The idea that such precisely-designed conditions could arise spontaneously in a reactor (whose fuel is insufficiently enriched to allow for a fast chain reaction in any case) is preposterous.

So the claim that nuclear reactors can go off like Hiroshima bombs is simply false. But certainly nuclear reactors can fail, just as airplanes can crash, and bridges and apartment buildings can collapse, if they are poorly designed or maintained. In this sense, nuclear power is no different from any other complex engineering system; it needs to be done right. If it is not, significant financial losses and human casualties can result. But these limited consequences and their probabilities need to be put in perspective and compared to the massive harm to human life and health and the loss of the wherewithal to support human existence that are necessarily entailed by the rejection or delay of atomic power. If such a rational comparison is done, it becomes clear that the real menace comes not from nuclear reactors, but from those who seek to prevent humanity from enjoying their benefits.

## NUCLEAR WASTE DISPOSAL

The hazards of nuclear waste disposal have also been wildly exaggerated by environmentalists, with the openly stated purpose of seeking to create a showstopper for the nuclear industry. They claim to be interested in public safety and ecological preservation. Yet it must perplex the rational mind that anyone can agitate, litigate, and argue with a straight face that it is better that nuclear waste be stored in hundreds of cooling ponds adjacent to reactors located near metropolitan areas all across the country than that they be gathered up and laid to rest in a government-supervised desert depository deep under Nevada's Yucca Mountain. The Department of Energy's Yucca Mountain plan has been exhaustively and thoroughly vetted, and it meets even the most stringent standards of public safety. (Among others, the public dosage would be required to stay below 15 millirems of radiation per year for at least 10,000 years.[30] The best estimates, though, show that the average public dosage would be far, far less: under 0.0001 mrem/year for 10,000 years.[31]) Those who oppose its usage seem to be more interested in manufacturing a problem than in solving one.

It is true, however, that Yucca Mountain is expensive. A more cost-effective solution would be to simply glassify the waste into a water-insoluble form, put it in stainless steel cans, take it out in a ship, and drop it into mid-ocean sub-seabed sediments that have been, and will be, geologically stable for tens of millions of years. Falling down through several thousand meters of water, such canisters can readily reach velocities that will allow them to bury themselves deep under the mud. After that, the waste is not going anywhere, and no one, by accident or design, will ever stumble upon it. This solution has been well-known for years.[32] Unfortunately, it has been shunned by Energy Department bureaucrats who seemingly prefer a large land-based facility because it involves a much bigger budget, and by antihumanists who wish to prevent the problem of nuclear waste disposal from being solved.

Nevertheless, the Yucca Mountain plan will work. And even though the project has been thoroughly analyzed—the site has been called "the most studied real estate on the planet"[33]—environmentalist opposition has caused the Obama administration and many lawmakers to oppose the project, and in 2011 federal funding for it was revoked. The Government Accountability Office noted that no technical or safety reasons were provided for shutting down the project.[34] Meanwhile, even with funding revoked, the government faces a liability of $11 billion, growing by another billion every two years, for failing to meet its contractual obligations to produce a nuclear waste repository.[35]

## ROUTINE NUCLEAR POWER PLANT
## RADIOLOGICAL EMISSIONS

Radiation doses are measured in units called rems, or, more often, thousandths of a rem (millirems, abbreviated mrem). While high doses of radiation delivered over short periods of time can cause radiation poisoning or cancer, there is, according to the U.S. Nuclear Regulatory Commission, "no data to establish unequivocally the occurrence of cancer following exposure to low doses and dose rates—below 10,000 mrem."[36] The annual radiation doses that each American can expect to receive from both natural and artificial radiation sources are given in Table 11.2.[37]

TABLE 11.2

*Radiation Doses from Natural and Artificial Sources*

| | |
|---|---|
| Blood | 20 mrem/year |
| Building Materials | 35 mrem/year |
| Food | 25 mrem/year |
| Soil | 11 mrem/year |
| Cosmic Rays (sea level) | 35 mrem/year |
| Cosmic Rays (Denver altitude) | 70 mrem/year |
| Medical X-Rays | 100 mrem/year |
| Air travel (New York to LA round trip) | 5 mrem |
| Nuclear power plant (limit, at property line) | 5 mrem/year |
| **Nuclear power plants (dose to general public)** | **0.01 mrem/year** |
| Average annual dose (general public) | 270 mrem/year |

Examining Table 11.2, we see that the amount of radiation dose that the public receives from nuclear power plants is insignificant compared to what they receive from their own blood (which contains radioactive potassium-40), from the homes they live in, from the food they eat, from the medical care and air travel they enjoy, from the planet on which they reside, and from the universe in which their planet resides.

In fact, far from increasing the radiological exposure of the public, nuclear power plants reduce it. Coal contains radioactive constituents. Worldwide, coal-fired electricity stations release some 30,000 tons of radioactive uranium and thorium into the atmosphere every year (as well as millions of tons of toxic chemical ash).[38] By replacing coal, nuclear power serves to eliminate these emissions.

## NUCLEAR PROLIFERATION

The final concern regarding nuclear power is that it might facilitate the proliferation of nuclear weapons. Natural uranium contains 0.7 percent uranium-235 ($^{235}$U), which is capable of fission, and 99.3 percent uranium-238 ($^{238}$U), which is not. In order to be useful in a commercial nuclear reactor, the uranium is typically enriched to a 3 percent concentration of $^{235}$U. The same enrichment facilities could also be used, with some difficulty, to further concentrate the uranium to 93 percent $^{235}$U, which would make it bomb-grade. Additionally, once the controlled reaction begins, some of the $^{238}$U will absorb neutrons, transforming it into plutonium-239 ($^{239}$Pu), which is fissile. Such plutonium can be reprocessed out of the spent fuel and mixed with natural uranium to turn it into reactor-grade material; but it could also be used to make bombs instead. Thus, the technical infrastructure required to support an end-to-end nuclear industry fuel cycle could also be used to make weapons.

This, however, does not mean that the construction of nuclear power plants should be avoided. It is the enrichment and reprocessing facilities that actually present the weapons-making danger, and such capabilities should certainly be forbidden to terrorist states like Iran. But the power stations themselves are not the threat. If plutonium is desired, much better material for weapons purposes can be made in standalone atomic piles than can be made in commercial power stations.[39] Both the United States and the Soviet Union had thousands of atomic weapons before either had a single nuclear power plant, and others desirous of obtaining atomic bombs can proceed the same way today.

That said, nuclear power is not for every country—yet. Nuclear power plants are very expensive. They require an educated workforce, a responsible government, and a safe security environment. It would be insane, for example, to build a nuclear power plant today in the Congo or Somalia. But of course, the largest consumers of electricity worldwide are well-organized countries to begin with. Nuclear power could someday meet most of the needs of an advancing world. As for those nations that are not yet ready for nuclear power, the task of our age is to help transform them so that they are. The issue is not one of "inappropriate technology," but of inappropriate social conditions. Backwardness, savagery, and anarchy are the things that are inappropriate. For many reasons that go well beyond energy policy, we need to make the world safe for nuclear power.

That means that instead of trying to keep Third World nations down, we need to do everything we can to raise them up—exactly the opposite of the antihuman policy recommended by the Malthusians.

## THE POWER THAT LIGHTS THE STARS

While nuclear fission has radically expanded humanity's potential energy resources, the achievement of controlled nuclear fusion will make them virtually infinite. The basic fuel for fusion is deuterium, an isotope of hydrogen that is called "heavy" because, in addition to having the proton in its nucleus that all hydrogen atoms have, it also has a neutron, which doubles its weight. Deuterium is found naturally on Earth; one hydrogen atom out of every 6,000 is deuterium. This number might not seem like much, but because of the enormous energy released when a fusion reaction occurs, it's enough to endow each and every gallon of water on Earth, fresh or salt, with a fusion energy content equivalent to that obtained by burning 350 gallons of gasoline.[40] To understand what this means for the human future, take a look at the final entry in Table 11.1. The Earth's fusion resources are half a million times greater than its fission resources, and a hundred million times greater than its known fossil-fuel resources. Even at ten times our current rate of consumption, there is enough fusion fuel on this planet (alone) to power our civilization for nearly a billion years.

Furthermore, fusion produces no greenhouse gases, and if done correctly, need not produce significant radioactive waste. When they collide, the deuterium nuclei fuse to form tritium or helium-3 ($^3$He) nuclei, plus some neutrons. The tritium and $^3$He will then react with other deuterium nuclei to produce ordinary helium ($^4$He) and common hydrogen ($^1$H), plus a few more neutrons. If the reactor is made of conventional materials, like stainless steel, the neutrons can produce some activation, resulting in the production of about 0.1 percent the radioactive waste of a fission reactor. However, if specially chosen structural materials like carbon-carbon graphite are used, there will be no activation, and the system can produce endless amounts of energy without radiation or pollution of any kind.[41]

Once we have fusion, we will be able to make as much liquid chemical fuel as we desire. For example, methanol, an excellent vehicle fuel, can readily be manufactured inorganically, simply by reacting carbon dioxide with electrolysis-produced hydrogen over copper on zinc oxide catalyst.[42] Under such circumstances, the OPEC nations' possession of the world's oil reserves would give them as much influence over the human future as they currently derive from their monopoly of camel milk.

But fusion is not just a plentiful source of energy; it is a new *kind* of energy. Fusion offers the potential to do things that are simply impossible without it. If we can get fusion, we will be able to use the superhot plasma that fusion reactors create as a torch to flash any kind of rock, scrap, or waste into its constituent elements, which could then be separated and turned into useful materials. Such technology would eliminate any possibility of exhausting Earth's resources. And using fusion power, we will be able to create space propulsion systems with exhaust velocities hundreds or thousands of times greater than the best possible chemical rocket engines. With such technology, the stars would be within our reach.[43]

So the fusion game is really worth the candle. It's a tough game, though, because while fusion occurs naturally in the stars, creating the conditions on Earth to allow it to proceed in a controlled way, in a human-engineered machine, is quite a challenge.

All atomic nuclei are positively charged, and therefore repel each other. In order to overcome this repulsion and get nuclei to fuse, they must be made to move very fast while being held in a confined area where they will have a high probability of colliding at high speed. Superheating fusion fuel to temperatures of about 100 million degrees Celsius gets the nuclei racing about at enormous speed. This is much too hot to confine the fuel with a solid chamber wall—any known or conceivable solid material would vaporize instantly if brought to such a temperature. However, at such temperatures, matter exists in a fourth state, known as plasma, in which the electrons and nuclei of atoms move independently of each other. (In school we are taught that there are three states of matter: solid, liquid, and gas. These dominate on Earth, where plasma exists only in transient forms in flames and lightning. However, most matter in the universe is plasma, which constitutes the substance of the sun and all the stars.) Because the particles of plasma are electrically charged, their motion can be affected by magnetic fields. Magnetic traps such as the toroidal or "doughnut-shaped" tokamak (as well as a variety of alternative concepts like stellarators, magnetic mirrors, and so on) have been designed to contain fusion plasmas without ever letting them touch the chamber wall.

At least, that is how it is supposed to work in principle. In practice, all magnetic fusion confinement traps are leaky, allowing the plasma to gradually escape by diffusion. When the plasma particles escape, they quickly hit the wall and are cooled to its (by fusion standards) very low temperature, thereby causing the plasma to lose energy. However, if the plasma is producing energy through fusion reactions faster than it is losing it through leakage, it can keep itself hot and maintain itself as a standing, energy-producing fusion "fire" for as long as additional fuel is fed into the system. The more dense a plasma is, and the higher its temperature, the faster it will produce fusion

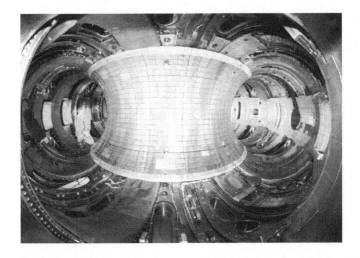

*Interior of the TFTR tokamak at the Princeton Plasma*
*Physics Lab. Built in 1980, it approached breakeven, pro-*
*ducing a world-record 10.7 megawatts of fusion power in*
*1994. It was shut down in 1997. No subsequent large*
*American tokamak has been built.*
(Courtesy Princeton Plasma Physics Laboratory.)

reactions, while the longer the individual particles remain trapped, the slower will be the rate of energy leakage. The critical parameter affecting the performance of fusion systems is the product of the plasma density, the temperature, and the average particle confinement time achieved in a given machine. The progress that the world's fusion programs have had in raising this triple product, known as the Lawson parameter, is shown in Figure 11.1.

The crucial trait of a useful fusion reaction is that it produces more power than the amount of external power applied to heat the plasma (via microwave heaters or other means). In other words, a fusion reactor becomes viable only at the point that it produces as much power as it uses—a condition known as "breakeven." The fusion reaction in which this condition is most easily achieved is the deuterium-tritium (D-T) reaction, which for breakeven requires a

Lawson parameter of $9 \times 10^{20}$ keV-s/m$^3$ (where the units are kilo-electronvolt-seconds per cubic meter). This point was nearly reached at the European JET tokamak in 1995.[44] A further crucial condition, known as "ignition," occurs when the reaction becomes so powerful that it heats itself, and external heating is no longer required. For D-T, this requires a Lawson parameter of $4 \times 10^{21}$ keV-s/m$^3$. Ignition is the final, major physics milestone that needs to be achieved before actual energy-producing fusion reactors can be engineered.

A fusion reactor could be operated as a D-T system, obtaining its tritium by reacting the neutrons it emits with a lithium blanket surrounding the reactor vessel. (When a lithium nuclei absorbs a neutron, it splits into a helium and a tritium atom, and sometimes emits a neutron, which allows yet another tritium atom to be produced.)

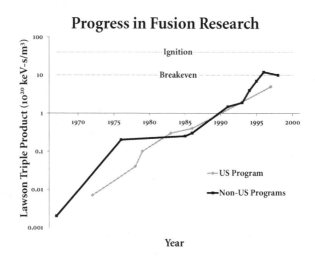

### Progress in Fusion Research

FIGURE 11.1: *Progress in controlled fusion. Since 1965, the world's fusion programs have advanced the achieved Lawson parameter by a factor of 10,000. A further increase of a factor of 6 will take us to ignition. Note the logarithmic scale.*

(Adapted from data provided by the European Fusion Development Agreement.)

First-generation fusion reactors may be designed along these lines.[45] However, with a little further progress in improved magnetic confinement, this will become unnecessary. Instead, once ignition is reached, we will be able to use the plasma's own power to increase its temperature to the point at which the deuterium and its byproducts will burn by themselves.[46]

As can be seen in Figure 11.1, the world's fusion programs have made enormous strides over the past thirty years, raising the achieved Lawson parameter by a factor of almost ten thousand to reach breakeven. Another factor of six, which I expect can be accomplished *if* funds are provided to build the next generation of experimental tokamaks, would take us to ignition.

Fusion can be developed, and when it is, it will eliminate the specter of energy shortages for millions of years to come. It is therefore the greatest nightmare of the Malthusians.[47] The technological challenges of fusion are significant, but provided that human ingenuity remains free, there can be little doubt that it can, and will, solve them all. There need be no limits to human aspirations, because fundamentally our wherewithal does not come from the Earth, but from ourselves. We are the ultimate resource.

CHAPTER TWELVE

# Population Control: Preparing the Holocaust

*Pharaoh said to his subjects, "Look how numerous and powerful the Israelite people are growing, more so than ourselves! Come, let us deal shrewdly with them to stop their increase; otherwise in time of war they too may join our enemies to fight against us, and so leave our country." Accordingly, taskmasters were set up over the Israelites to oppress them with forced labor.... Yet the more they were oppressed, the more they multiplied and spread. The Egyptians, then, dreaded the Israelites and reduced them to cruel slavery, making life bitter for them with hard work.... [Still] the people ... increased and grew strong. Pharaoh then commanded all his subjects, "Throw into the river every boy that is born to the Hebrews."*

EXODUS 1:9–22[1]

*Five dollars invested in population control is worth a hundred dollars invested in economic growth.*

PRESIDENT LYNDON B. JOHNSON, 1965[2]

UNTIL THE MID-1960S, American population control programs, both at home and abroad, were largely funded and implemented by private organizations such as the Population Council and Planned Parenthood. While disposing of millions of dollars provided to them by the Rockefeller, Ford, and Milbank Foundations,[3] among others, the resources available to support their work were meager in comparison with their vast ambitions. This situation changed radically in the mid–1960s when the U.S. Congress, responding to public opinion organized by Moore, Draper, Osborn, Rockefeller, and other overpopulation ideologues, finally appropriated federal funds to underwrite first domestic and then foreign population control programs.[4] Suddenly, instead of mere millions, there were hundreds of millions and eventually billions of dollars available to fund global campaigns of mass abortion and forced sterilization. The result would be human catastrophe on a worldwide scale.

Among the first to be targeted were America's own Third World

*Hugh Moore's Campaign to Check the Population Explosion warns that Third World people are a threat to peace.*

population at home—the American Indians. Starting in 1966, Secretary of the Interior Stuart Udall began to make use of newly available Medicaid money to set up sterilization programs at federally-funded Indian Health Services (IHS) hospitals. As reported by Angela Franks in her 2005 book *Margaret Sanger's Eugenic Legacy*:

> The Native American population was quickly subjected to a sterilization campaign that must be described, given the breathtaking percentage of Native American women of childbearing age involved, as effectively genocidal. These sterilizations were frequently performed without adequate informed consent.... In 1976 the General Accounting Office, in an audit examining one-third of the IHS districts, revealed that 3,406 Native American women, who were given consent forms "not in compliance with regulations," were sterilized from 1973 to 1976. Based on these figures and her own research, Native American physician Constance Redbird Uri estimated that up to one-quarter of Indian women of childbearing age had been sterilized by 1977; in one hospital in Oklahoma, one-fourth of the women admitted (for any reason) left sterilized.... She also gathered evidence that all the pureblood women of the Kaw tribe in Oklahoma were sterilized in the 1970s—a truly genocidal process....
>
> Unfortunately, and amazingly, problems with the Indian Health Service seem to persist . . . recently [in the early 1990s], in South Dakota, IHS was again accused of not following informed-consent procedures, this time for Norplant, and apparently promoted the long-acting contraceptive to Native American women who should not use it due to contraindicating, preexisting medical conditions. The Native American Women's Health Education Resource Center reports that one woman was recently told by her doctors that they would remove the implant only if she would agree to a tubal ligation. The genocidal dreams of bureaucrats still cast their shadow on American soil.[5]

Programs of a comparable character were also set up in clinics funded by the U.S. Office Economic Opportunity in low-income (predominantly black) neighborhoods in the United States.[6] On the U.S. territory of Puerto Rico, a mass sterilization program was instigated by the Draper Fund/Population Crisis Committee and implemented with federal funds from the Department of Health, Education, and Welfare through the island's major hospitals as well as a host of smaller clinics. According to the report of a medical fact-finding mission conducted in 1975, the effort was successful in sterilizing close to one-third of Puerto Rican women of child-bearing age.[7]

## BETTER DEAD THAN RED

However, it was not at home but abroad that the heaviest artillery of the population control onslaught was directed. During the Cold War, anything from the Apollo program to public-education funding could be sold to the federal government if it could be justified as part of the global struggle against communism. Accordingly, Draper and Moore, together with the large contingent of Population Crisis Committee members and supporters infesting the senior levels of the Johnson administration, formulated a party line that the population of the world's poor nations needed to be drastically cut in order to reduce the potential recruitment pool available to the communist cause. (Averell Harriman, Defense Secretary Robert McNamara, George Ball, General Maxwell Taylor, General William Westmoreland, Ambassador Ellsworth Bunker, and National Security Council deputy director Robert W. Komer all were or eventually became members; National Security Council director McGeorge Bundy and Secretary of State Dean Rusk were supporters.)

To get President Johnson on board, Komer provided Bundy with a fraudulent study by a RAND Corporation economist to show the president; the study used cooked calculations to prove that Third World children actually had *negative economic value*. This was so, the study declared, because *assuming a discount rate of 15 percent*, the funds used to care for them as minors could never be paid back by their earnings as adults, no matter how long they lived.[8] Thus, by allowing excessive numbers of children to be born, Asian, African, and Latin American governments were deepening the poverty of their populations, while multiplying the masses of angry proletarians ready to be led against America by the organizers of the coming World Revolution. In passing the study on to Bundy, Komer commented: "Here's a little flank attack that I think might just penetrate LBJ's defenses. . . . It might score."[9]

It did. Johnson bought the claptrap, including the phony mathematical results. Two months later, he declared to the United Nations that "five dollars invested in population control is worth a hundred dollars invested in economic growth." Having succeeded in this policy coup, "Blowtorch" Komer was promoted to become chief of the pacification program in Vietnam, a position in which his desire to reduce Third World peasant populations found ample scope for implementation.[10]

With the Johnson administration now backing population control, Congress passed the Foreign Assistance Act in 1966, including a Title X provision earmarking USAID funds for population control programs to be implemented abroad. The legislation further directed that *all* U.S. economic aid to foreign nations be made contingent upon their governments' willingness to cooperate with State Department desires for the establishment of such initiatives within their own borders.[11] In other words, for those Third World rulers willing to help sterilize their poorer subjects, there would be carrots. For the uncooperative types, there would be the stick. Given the nature of most Third World governments, such elegant simplicity of approach practically guaranteed success. The population control establishment was delighted.

An Office of Population was set up within USAID, and Dr. Reimert Thorolf Ravenholt was appointed its first director in 1966. He would hold the post until 1979, using it to create a global empire of interlocking population control organizations operating with billion-dollar budgets to suppress the existence of people considered undesirable by the U.S. State Department.[12]

lifestyle, staying in the best hotels, eating the best foods, and flying first class as they jetted around the world to set up programs to eliminate the poor.[15]

Ravenholt also had no compunction about buying up huge quantities of unproven, unapproved, defective, or banned contraceptive drugs and intrauterine devices (IUDs) and distributing them for use by his population control movement subcontractors on millions of unsuspecting Third World women, many of whom suffered or died in consequence. For example, he bought a huge supply of discounted birth control pills from the Syntex company after the pill was declared unsafe by the FDA.[16] (Its higher estrogen content caused needless vitamin depletion, and thus was even *more* dangerous to already-malnourished women on the other side of the world than to relatively healthy Americans.) Another deal involved the defective Dalkon Shield IUD, which Ravenholt purchased in large lots at half price after its manufacturer was hit by class-action lawsuits.[17] (When sterilized, the "Shield" was already known to put women at risk for complications ranging from blood poisoning to uterine rupture. Ravenholt distributed the device *un*sterilized.[18]) He also bought and sent out shipments of the hormonal contraceptive Depo-Provera, even though the drug was deemed "not approvable" by the FDA for use in America.[19] These practices delighted the manufacturers of such equipment.

Having thus secured the unqualified support of both the population control establishment and several major pharmaceutical companies, Ravenholt was able to lobby Congress to secure ever increasing appropriations to further expand his growing empire.

His success was remarkable. Before Ravenholt took over, USAID expenditures on population control amounted to less than 3 percent of what the agency spent on health programs in Third World nations. By 1968, Ravenholt had a budget of $36 million, compared to the USAID health programs budget of $130 million. By 1972, Ravenholt's population control funding had grown to $120 million per year, with funds taken directly at the expense of USAID's disease prevention and other health care initiatives, which shrank to $38 million in consequence.[20] In just five short years, the U.S. non-military foreign aid program was transformed from a mission of mercy to an agency for human elimination.

In 1968, Robert McNamara resigned his post as Secretary of Defense to assume the presidency of the World Bank in Washington, D.C. From this position he was able to dictate a new policy, making World Bank loans to Third World countries contingent upon their governments' submission to population control, with yearly sterilization quotas set for them by World Bank experts. Cash-short and heavily in debt, many poor nations found this pressure very difficult to withstand. This strengthened Ravenholt's hand immeasurably.

## DESTROYING THE VILLAGE

Upon coming into office in January 1969, the new Nixon administration not only fully embraced but actively sought to further advance the population control agenda. Responding to lobbying by the ever-persistent General Draper, Nixon approved U.S. government support for the establishment of the U.N. Fund for Population Activities (UNFPA). With this organization as a vehicle, vast additional American funds would be poured into the global population control effort, with their source disguised so as to ease acceptance by governments whose leaders needed to maintain a populist pose in opposition to "Yankee Imperialism." While the United States was its primary backer, the UNFPA also served as a channel for significant additional population control funds from European nations, Canada, and Japan, collectively equal to about half the American effort.[21]

Going still further, President Nixon in 1970 set up a special blue-ribbon Commission on Population Growth and the American Future, with none other than longtime population control kingpin John D. Rockefeller III as its chairman. Reporting back in 1972, Rockefeller predictably cited the menace of U.S. population growth with alarm, and called for a large variety of population control measures to avert the putative threat of welfare-dependent, criminalistic, or other financially burdensome populations multiplying out of control. Just as predictably, the report generated scores of newspaper headlines and feature magazine articles serving to cement the population control consensus. Nixon's politically-driven rejection of one of the commission's recommendations—government-funded abortion on demand—only served to make Rockefeller's Malthusian committee seem all the more "progressive."[22]

President Nixon also appointed William Ruckelshaus to be the administrator of the newly established Environmental Protection Agency (EPA). As we saw in Chapter Eight, Ruckelshaus used his powers as head of the EPA to ban DDT, an action which would cost the lives of millions of poor people, especially children, in Africa and Asia. Subsequent to his government service, Ruckelshaus joined the Draper Fund.

But for the Nixon administration, the supposed potential value of population control as a Cold War weapon held the greatest interest. The president charged his National Security Advisor (and Secretary of State) Henry Kissinger with conducting a secret study on the role of population control measures in the fight against global communism. Kissinger pulled together a group of experts drawn from the National Security Council (NSC), CIA, Department of Defense, Department of State, USAID, and other governmental agencies to study the question. The result was issued on December 10, 1974 in the form of the classified NSC document titled "Implications of Worldwide Population Growth for U.S. Security and Overseas Interests." The document—known as National Security Study Memorandum 200 (NSSM 200), or simply as the Kissinger Report—represented the encoding of Malthusian dogma as the strategic doctrine of the United States.

NSSM 200 was leaked in 1990 and consequently declassified, so it is now available for scrutiny. Examining the document, what is apparent is the Nietzschean mindset on the part of its authors, who (implicitly embracing the communist line) clearly regarded the newborn masses of the world as America's likely enemies, rather than her friends, and as potential obstacles to the exploitation of the world's wealth, rather than as customers, workers, and business partners participating together with America in a grand global team effort to grow and advance the world economy.

Wading through the report's obscure bureaucratese, one finds the following:

*"The political consequences of current population factors in the LDCs [less developed countries] . . . are damaging to the internal stability and international relations of countries in whose advancement the U.S. is interested, thus creating political or even national security problems for the U.S. . . . Adverse socio-economic conditions generated by these and related factors may contribute to . . . revolutionary actions."*[23] Translation: Population growth provides recruits and opportunities for the Reds.

*"If these conditions result in expropriation of foreign interests, such action, from an economic viewpoint, is not in the best interests of either the investing country or the host government."*[24] Translation: We don't want uppity wogs seizing back control of their nations' assets.

*"Assistance for population moderation should give primary emphasis to the largest and fastest growing developing countries where there is special U.S. political and strategic interest. Those countries are: India, Bangladesh, Pakistan, Nigeria, Mexico, Indonesia, Brazil, the Philippines, Thailand, Egypt, Turkey, Ethiopia and Colombia."*[25] Translation: Let's cut the big ones down to size first.

*"Growing numbers of experts believe that the population situation is already more serious and less amenable to solution through voluntary measures than is generally accepted. . . . In view of the seriousness of these issues, explicit consideration of them should begin in the Executive Branch, the Congress, and the U.N. soon."*[26] Translation: If we can't obtain compliance through other means, we should prepare ourselves to use force.

*"Where population pressures lead to endemic famine, food riot, and breakdown of social order, those conditions are scarcely conducive to systematic exploration for mineral deposits or the long-term investment required for their exploitation. . . . Foreign companies are likely to be expropriated or subjected to arbitrary intervention. . . . The smooth*

*flow of needed materials will be jeopardized.*"[27] Translation: We want their gold. We want their cobalt. We want their oil. They could get in the way. So let's get rid of them.

"*Although the scope for raising agricultural activity is very great in many of these areas, the available technologies for doing so require much higher capital costs per acre and much larger foreign exchange outlays for 'modern' inputs. . . . Thus the population growth problem can be seen as an important long-run, or structural, contributor to current LDC balance of payments problems.*"[28] Translation: We want our money. They should be forced to repay their loans before they are allowed to spend money on agricultural development, schools, or raising children.

"*In developing countries, the burden of population factors, added to others, will weaken unstable governments. . . . Countries suffering under such burdens will be more susceptible to radicalization.*"[29] Translation: They might join the Reds, so we don't want them born.

"*Within the overall array of U.S. foreign assistance programs, preferential treatment in allocation of funds and manpower should be given to cost-effective programs to reduce population growth. . . . There are many opportunities, bilaterally and multilaterally, for U.S. representations to discuss and urge the need for stronger family planning programs. There is also some established precedent for taking account of family planning performance in appraisal of assistance requirements by AID.*"[30] Translation: Money talks. We can use the leverage offered by control of our foreign-aid funds to make LDC governments fall in line.

"*In these sensitive relationships, however, it is important in style as well as substance to avoid the appearance of coercion.*"[31] Translation: Be sure to provide a little something for the leaders of these developing countries to steal for themselves. A spoonful of sugar helps the medicine go down.

"*We must take care that our activities should not give the appearance to the LDCs of an industrialized country policy directed against the LDCs. . . . 'Third World' leaders should be in the forefront and obtain the credit for successful programs.*"[32] Translation: Our role in pushing this stuff needs to be disguised.

*"It is vital that the effort to develop and strengthen a commitment on the part of the LDC leaders not be seen by them as an industrialized country policy to keep their strength down or to reserve resources for use by the 'rich' countries. Development of such a perception could create a serious backlash adverse to the cause of population stability."* [33] Translation: Don't let them find out our plan.

On November 26, 1975, NSSM 200 was formally adopted as U.S. foreign policy by National Security Decision Memorandum 314, which was signed on behalf of President Gerald Ford by Kissinger's successor as National Security Advisor, Lt. General Brent Scowcroft. [34] A follow-up memo issued in 1976 by the NSC (which now included CIA director George H. W. Bush) called for the United States to use control of food supplies to impose population control on a global scale. It further noted the value of using dictatorial power and military force as means to coerce Third World peoples into submission to population control measures:

> Population programs have been particularly successful where leaders have made their positions clear, unequivocal, and public, while maintaining discipline down the line from national to village levels, marshalling governmental workers (including police and military), doctors, and motivators to see that population policies are well administered and executed. . . . In some cases, strong direction has involved incentives such as payment to acceptors for sterilization, or disincentives such as giving low priorities in the allocation of housing or schooling to those with larger families. Such direction is the *sine qua non* of an effective program. [35]

Without a shred of justification, but with impeccable organization, generous funding, aggressive leadership, and backing by a phalanx of established respectable opinion, the population control movement was now doctrinally enshrined as representing the core strategic interest of the world's leading superpower. It was now positioned to wreak havoc on a global scale.

In the next chapter we will see how it proceeded to do so.

## CHAPTER THIRTEEN

# Population Control: Implementing the Holocaust

*The degree of coercive policy brought into play [in a population control program] should be proportional to the degree of seriousness of the present problem and should be introduced only after less coercive means have been exhausted. Thus, overt violence or other potentially injurious coercion is not to be used before noninjurious coercion has been exhausted.*

BERNARD BERELSON
(President, Population Council)
and JONATHAN LIEBERSON, 1979[1]

SINCE THE MID-1960S, the United States government has served as the leading funder of a global empire of population control slaughterhouses. Of the billions of dollars expended on such work, a portion has been directly spent by the U.S. Agency for International Development (USAID) on its own field activities. But the majority of the taxpayer cash has been laundered through either the U.N. Fund for Population Activities (UNFPA), the World Bank, various foreign governments, or a host of private non-governmental organizations (NGOs) and foundations notably led by the International Planned Parenthood Federation (IPPF) and the Population Council. As a result of this indirect funding scheme, all attempts to compel the population control empire to conform its activities to accepted medical, ethical, safety, or human rights norms have proven completely futile.

Rather, in direct defiance of laws enacted by Congress to try to correct the situation, what has and continues to be perpetrated at public expense is an atrocity on a scale so vast and varied as to almost defy description.[2] Nevertheless, in this chapter I shall attempt to convey to readers some sense of the evil that is being done with their money.

The population control agenda has now been implemented in well over a hundred countries. Limitations of space preclude the possibility of providing detailed accounts of the efforts in each of them here. Rather, we shall confine ourselves to descriptions of several important national case studies. But by way of preface, let us consider the primary characteristics manifested by nearly all the campaigns.

First, they are **top-down dictatorial**. In selling the effort to Americans, USAID and its beneficiaries claim that they are providing Third World women with "choice" regarding childbirth. There is no truth whatsoever to this claim. As Betsy Hartmann, a (genuine) liberal feminist critic of these programs, has trenchantly pointed out, "a woman's right to choose" must necessarily include the option of *having* children—precisely what the population control campaigns deny her.[3] Rather than providing "choice" to individuals, the purpose of the campaigns is to strip entire populations of their ability to reproduce. This is done by national governments, themselves under USAID or World Bank pressure, setting quotas for sterilizations, intrauterine device (IUD) insertions, or similar procedures to be imposed by their own civil service upon the subject population. Those government employees who meet or exceed their quotas of "acceptors" are rewarded; those who fail to do so are disciplined.

Second, the programs are **dishonest**. It is a regular practice for government civil servants employed in population control programs to lie to their prospective targets for quota-meeting about the consequences of the operations that will be performed upon them. For example, Third World peasants are frequently told by government population control personnel that sterilization operations are reversible, when in fact they are not.

Third, the programs are **coercive**. As a regular practice, population control programs provide "incentives" and/or "disincentives" to compel "acceptors" into accepting their "assistance." Among the "incentives" frequently employed is the provision or denial of cash or food aid to starving people or their children. Among the "disincentives" employed are personal harassment, dismissal from employment, destruction of homes, and denial of schooling, public housing, or medical assistance to the recalcitrant.

Fourth, the programs are **medically irresponsible and negligent**. As a regular practice, the programs use defective, unproven, unsafe, experimental, or unapproved gear, including equipment whose use has been banned outright in the United States. They also employ large numbers of inadequately trained personnel to perform potentially life-endangering operations, or to maintain medical equipment in a supposedly sterile or otherwise safe condition. In consequence, millions of people subjected to the ministrations of such irresponsibly run population control operations have been killed. This is particularly true in Africa, where improper reuse of hypodermic needles without sterilization in population control clinics has contributed to the rapid spread of deadly infectious diseases, including AIDS.[4]

Fifth, the programs are **cruel, callous, and abusive of human dignity and human rights**. A frequent practice is the sterilization of women without their knowledge or consent, typically while they are weakened in the aftermath of childbirth. This is tantamount to government-organized rape. Forced abortions are also typical. These and other human rights abuses of the population control campaign have been widely documented, with subject populations victimized in Australia, Bangladesh, China, Guatemala, Haiti, Honduras, India, Indonesia, Kenya, Kosovo, South Africa, Sri Lanka, Thailand, Tibet, the United States, Venezuela, and Vietnam.[5]

Sixth, the programs are **racist**. Just as the global population control program itself represents an attempt by the (white-led) governments of the United States and the former imperial powers of Europe to cut nonwhite populations in the Third World, so, within each targeted nation, the local ruling group has typically made use of the population control program to attempt to eliminate the people they despise. In India, for example, the ruling upper-caste Hindus have focused the population control effort on getting rid of lower-caste untouchables and Muslims. In Sri Lanka, the ruling Singhalese have targeted the Hindu Tamils for extermination.[6] In Peru, the Spanish-speaking descendants of the conquistadors have directed the country's population control program toward the goal of stemming the reproduction of the darker non-Hispanic natives. In Kosovo, the Serbs used population control against the Albanians,[7] while in Vietnam the Communist government has targeted the population control effort against the Hmong ethnic minority, America's former wartime allies.[8] In China, the Tibetan and Uyghur minorities have become special targets of the government's population control effort, with multitudes of the latter rounded up for forced abortions and sterilizations.[9] In South Africa under apartheid, the purpose of the government-run population control program went without saying. In various black African states, whichever tribe holds the reins of power regularly directs the population campaign towards the elimination of their traditional tribal rivals.[10] There should be nothing surprising in any of this. Malthusianism has always been closely linked to racism, because the desire for population control has as its foundation the hatred of others.

Let us now turn to examine several important population control campaign case studies.

## INDIA

Since the time of Malthus, India has always been a prime target in the eyes of would-be population controllers. Both the British colonial administrators and the high-caste Brahmins who succeeded them in power following independence in 1947 looked upon the "teeming masses" of that nation's lower classes with fear and disdain. Jawaharlal Nehru's Congress Party (which controlled India's national government for its first three decades without interruption) had been significantly influenced by pre-independence contacts with the pro-Malthusian British Fabian Society. Notable members of the native elite, such as the influential and formidable Lady Rama Rau, had found Margaret Sanger and her ideas quite appealing.[11] Thus during the 1950s and early 1960s, the Indian government allowed organizations like the Population Council, the Ford Foundation, and the IPPF to set up shop within the country's borders, where they could set about curbing the reproduction of the nation's Dalits, or "untouchables." The government did not, however, allocate public funds to these organizations, so their programs remained relatively small.

Things changed radically in 1965, when war with Pakistan threw the country's economy into disarray, causing harvest failure and loss of revenue. When Prime Minister Indira Gandhi—Nehru's daughter—assumed office in January 1966, India was short twenty million tons of grain and lacked money to buy replacement stock on the world market. She was left with no choice but to go to the United States, hat in hand, to beg for food aid.

There was a lot that the United States could have asked for in return from India, such as support for the Western side in the Cold War (India was non-aligned), and particularly for the war effort in nearby Vietnam, which was heating up rapidly. One of President Lyndon Johnson's aides, Joseph Califano, suggested in a memo to the president that the United States move rapidly to commit food aid in order to secure such a pro-American tilt. In reply he got a call from Johnson that very afternoon. "Are you out of your fucking mind?" the president exploded. He declared in no uncertain terms that he was not going to "piss away foreign aid in nations where they refuse to deal with their own population problems." Population control initiative architect Bob Komer, who had recently been promoted to the post of National Security Advisor, was delighted. "We finally have the Indians where you've wanted them ever since last April," he wrote to President Johnson. "From now on we hinge aid to performance."[12]

Indira Gandhi arrived in Washington in late March and met first with Secretary of State Dean Rusk, who handed her a memo requiring "a massive effort to control population growth" as a condition for food aid. Then on March 28, 1966, she met privately with the president. There is no record of their conversation, but it is evident that she capitulated completely. Two days later, President Johnson sent a message to Congress requesting food aid for India, noting with approval: "The Indian government believes that there can be no effective solution of the Indian food problem that does not include population control."[13]

In accordance with the agreement, sterilization and IUD-insertion quotas were set for each Indian state, and then within each state for each local administrative district. Every hospital in the country had a large portion of its facilities commandeered for sterilization and IUD-insertion activities. (The IUDs, which were provided to the Indian government by the Population Council, were non-sterile.[14] In Maharashtra province, 58 percent of women surveyed who received them experienced pain, 24 percent severe pain, and 43 percent severe and excessive bleeding.[15]) But hospitals alone did not have the capacity to meet the quotas, so hundreds of sterilization camps were set up in rural areas, manned and operated by paramedical personnel who had as little as two days of training. Minimum quotas were set for the state-salaried camp medics—they had to perform 150 vasectomies or 300 IUD insertions per month each, or their pay would be docked. Private practitioners were also recruited to assist, with pay via piecework: 10 rupees per vasectomy and 5 rupees per IUD insertion.[16]

To acquire subjects for these ministrations, the Indian government provided each province with 11 rupees for every IUD insertion, 30 per vasectomy, and 40 per tubectomy. These funds could be divided according to the particular population control plan of each provincial government, with some going to program personnel, some spent as commission money to freelance "motivators," some paid as incentives to the "acceptors," and some grafted for other governmental or private use by the administrators. Typical incentives for subjects ranged from 3 to 7 rupees for an IUD insertion and 12 to 25 rupees for a sterilization. These sums may seem trivial—a 1966 rupee is equivalent to

65 cents today—but at that time, 2 to 3 rupees was a day's pay for an Indian laborer. When these pittances did not induce enough subjects to meet the quotas, some states adopted additional "incentives": Madhya Pradesh, for example, denied irrigation water to villages that failed to meet their quotas.[17] Faced with starvation, millions of impoverished people had no alternative but to submit to sterilization. As the forms of coercion employed worked most effectively on the poorest, the system also provided the eugenic bonus of doing away preferentially with untouchables.[18]

The results were impressive. In 1961, the total number of sterilizations (vasectomies and tubectomies combined) performed in India was 105,000. In 1966–67, the yearly total shot up to 887,000, growing further to more than 1.8 million in 1967–68.[19] No doubt, LBJ was proud.

But while ruining the lives of millions of people, the steep rise in sterilization figures had little impact on the overall trajectory of India's population growth. In 1968, Paul Ehrlich wrote in *The Population Bomb*, "I have yet to meet anyone familiar with the situation who thinks India will be self sufficient in food by 1971, if ever,"[20] thus justifying his explicitly antihuman call that we "must allow [India] to slip down the drain."[21] As in so many other things, Ehrlich was wrong; India did achieve self-sufficiency in food in 1971—not through population control, but through the improved agricultural techniques of the Green Revolution. It did not matter. The holders of the purse-strings at USAID demanded even higher quotas. They got them. By 1972–73, the number of sterilizations in India reached three million per year.[22]

Then, in the fall of 1973, OPEC launched its oil embargo, quintupling petroleum prices virtually overnight. For rich nations like the United States, the resulting financial blow was severe. For poor countries like India, it was devastating. In 1975, conditions in India became so bad that Prime Minister Gandhi declared a state of national emergency and assumed dictatorial power. Driven once again to desperation, she found herself at the mercy of the World Bank, led by arch-Malthusian Robert S. McNamara.

McNamara made it clear: if India wanted more loans, Gandhi needed to use her powers to deal more definitively with India's supposed population problem. She agreed. Instead of incentives, force would now be used to obtain compliance. "Some personal rights have to be kept in abeyance," she said, "for the human rights of the nation, the right to live, the right to progress."[23]

Gandhi put her son Sanjay personally in charge of the new population offensive. He took to his job with gusto. Overt coercion became

*Mass sterilization camp in India.*

the rule: sterilization was a condition for land allotments, water, electricity, ration cards, medical care, pay raises, and rickshaw licenses. Policemen were given quotas to nab individuals for sterilization. Demolition squads were sent into slums to bulldoze houses—sometimes whole neighborhoods—so that armed police platoons could drag off their flushed-out occupants to forced-sterilization camps. In Delhi alone, 700,000 people were driven from their homes. Many of those who escaped the immediate roundup were denied new housing until they accepted sterilization.[24]

These attacks provoked resistance, with thousands being killed in battles with the police, who used live ammunition to deal with protesters.[25] When it became clear that Muslim villages were also being selectively targeted, the level of violence increased still further.[26] The village of Pipli was only brought into submission when government officials threatened locals with aerial bombardment. As the director of family planning in Maharashtra explained, "You must consider it something like a war.... Whether you like it or not, there will be a few dead people."[27]

The measures served their purpose. During 1976, eight million Indians were sterilized. Far from being dismayed by the massive violation of human rights committed by the campaign, its foreign sponsors expressed full support. Sweden increased its funding for Indian population control by $17 million. USAID population czar Reimert Ravenholt ordered 64 advanced laparoscope machines—altogether sufficient to sterilize 12,800 people per day—rushed to India to help the effort.[28] World Bank president McNamara was absolutely delighted. In November 1976, he traveled to India to congratulate Indira Gandhi's government for its excellent work. "At long last," he said, "India is moving effectively to address its population problem."[29]

Prime Minister Gandhi got her loans. She also got the boot in 1977, when in the largest democratic election in history, the people of India defied three decades of precedent and voted her Congress Party out of power in a landslide.[30]

Unfortunately, in most Third World countries, people lack such an option to protect themselves against population control. Equally unfortunately, despite the fall of the Gandhi government, the financial pressure on India from the World Bank and USAID to implement population control continued.[31] By the early 1980s, four million sterilizations were being performed every year on India's underclasses as part of a coercive two-child-per-family policy.[32]

Since in rural India sons are considered essential to continue the family line and provide support for parents in their old age, this limit caused many families to seek means of disposing of infant daughters, frequently through drowning, asphyxiation, abandonment in sewers or garbage dumps, or incineration on funeral pyres.[33] More recently the primary means of eliminating the less-desirable sex has become sex-selective abortion, skewing the ratio of the sexes so that 1 1 2 boys are born for every hundred girls in India (far beyond the natural ratio of 1 0 3 to 1 06).[34] A sense of the scale on which these murders were and are practiced, even just in the aspect of gendercide, can be gleaned from the fact that in India today there are 3 7 million more men than women.[35]

## INDONESIA

Indonesia's first president, the independent nationalist Sukarno, was strongly pro-natalist, and resisted all attempts to impose population control on his country. In 1 9 6 6, however, Sukarno was overthrown in a CIA-backed military coup that left millions dead. Having massacred Sukarno's political base, the new ruler, General Suharto, proceeded to implement the population control dictates of his sponsors in the U.S. national security establishment and the World Bank.[36]

In 1 9 7 0, Suharto set up the National Family Planning Coordinating Board (BKBBN) to implement a population control program, and with backing from USAID, UNFPA, the Population Council, and IPPF, by the mid–1 9 7 0s this bureaucracy had established local Village Contraceptive Distribution Centers and corresponding Acceptor Clubs in tens of thousands of hamlets across the nation.[37] While some of the contraceptives distributed were pills, government staffers preferred that the "acceptors" submit to more effective barriers to pregnancy, including Norplant contraceptive injections, IUD insertions, and sterilizations. Initially, membership in the Acceptor Clubs was encouraged by denying credit, government jobs, and health care to non-members. As the program developed, it became even more coercive.

In her book *Reproductive Rights and Wrongs: the Global Politics of Population Control*, feminist writer Betsy Hartmann describes the Indonesian program:

> In the early 1 9 8 0s, as part of an intensification of population control efforts, the BKBBN launched a mass IUD insertion

campaign. There was little concern for the fact that the IUD is an inappropriate form of contraception for many women, because of side effects such as heavy bleeding and the risk of infertility, or that mass insertions could easily lead to infection. The campaign included mass IUD "safaris" where thousands of women were brought together, often under pressure from local officials, to have IUDs inserted in a "picniclike" atmosphere.[38]

Hartmann cites a 1990 internal Population Council report to the effect that, by that point, almost half a million Indonesian women had received Norplant, noting that by 1995 that number was approaching 1.5 million. These procedures were taking place "often without counseling on the side effects . . . or proper sterilization of equipment. Many were not even told that the implant had to be removed after five years to avoid the risk of life-threatening ectopic pregnancy."[39]

Hartmann also reports that, according to USAID, "the most ready explanation given for the success of the Indonesian family planning program is the strong hierarchical power structure, by which central commands produce compliant behavior all down the administrative line to the individual peasant."[40] She continues:

> In 1990, reports of coercion in the Indonesian vasectomy program hit both the national and international press. . . . Coercion of women is still much more common, however. A case study of Kembangwangi Subdistrict in West Java reveals the role of the military in threatening villagers. . . . In one safari in 1990 family planning workers accompanied by the police and army went from house to house and took men and women to a site where IUDs were being inserted. Women who refused had IUDs inserted at gunpoint.[41]

In addition to denying millions of people their fundamental human right to have children, the Indonesian population control program had a major detrimental impact on public health by sapping funding and personnel badly needed to provide basic medical care. In 1984, for example, the Ministry of Health budget provided $1.30 worth of health care per capita to the nation's people. Out of this cruelly small allotment, $0.75 per capita—58 percent—went to support the population control programs of the BKBBN. As a consequence of this horrible misallocation, Indonesia's infant mortality rate remains double that of neighboring Malaysia and Thailand.[42]

## PERU

Because of their proximity to the United States, Central and South America have long been in the sights of population controllers from the American national security establishment. Since the 1960s, on the urging of USAID, brutal population control programs have been implemented in nearly every country from Mexico to Chile. In this section we shall focus on just one of them, that of Peru, because the criminal investigation of its leading perpetrators has provided some of the best documentation of the systematic abuses that have been and continue to be carried out under the cloak of population control across Central and South America.

Mountainous Peru features some of the most thinly populated regions on the planet. This fact, however, in no way deterred USAID planners from deeming these rural areas to be overpopulated, nor from funding programs designed to eliminate their people. Begun in 1966, these efforts proceeded on a comparatively low level until the 1990s, when strongman Alberto Fujimori assumed nearly dictatorial powers in the country.[43]

In 1995, President Fujimori launched a nationwide sterilization campaign. Mobile sterilization teams were assembled in Lima and then deployed to move through the countryside to conduct week-long "ligation festivals" in one village after another. Prior to the arrival of the sterilization teams, Ministry of Health employees were sent in to harass local women into submission. Women who resisted were subjected to repeated home visits and severe verbal abuse by the government workers, who chided the native women and girls that they were no better than "cats" or "dogs" for wanting to have children. If this did not suffice, mothers were told that unless they submitted to ligation, their children would be made ineligible for government food aid.[44]

Both the government harassment squads and the members of the sterilization units themselves operated under a quota system, striving to meet the nationwide target of 100,000 tubal ligations per year. They were paid if they met their quotas but punished if they failed to capture the designated number of women for sterilization. As a result, many women entering clinics for childbirth were sterilized without any pretext of gaining their permission. Given the limited training of the sterilization personnel (provided in many cases by imported Chinese population control experts), the unsanitary conditions prevailing during the village "ligation festivals," and the complete lack of post-operation care, it is not surprising that many suffered severe complications and more than a few died subsequent to their mutilations.[45]

While the government personnel performing the mass sterilizations were urbanites of Spanish derivation, the overwhelming majority of the victims were rural Quechua-speaking natives of Inca descent. This, of course, was no coincidence. When Fujimori was booted out in 2000, the new president, Alejandro Toledo, asked the Peruvian Congress to authorize an investigation into the population control campaign. Accordingly, an investigative commission known as the AQV was formed under the direction of Dr. Hector Chavez Chuchon. The AQV submitted its report to the Human Rights Commission of the Peruvian Congress on June 10, 2003.

According to the report, in the course of a five-year effort the Fujimori government had sterilized 314,605 women. Furthermore, Fujimori's population control campaign had "carried out massive sterilizations on designated ethnic groups, benefiting other ethnic or social groups which did not suffer the scourge with the same intensity ... the action fits the definition of the crime of Genocide." The report

went on to make a "Constitutional Indictment against Alberto Fujimori, [former Health Minister] Marino Costa Bauer . . . [former Presidential Health Advisor] Eduardo Yong Motta, [and others] for the
alleged commission of crimes against Individual Liberty, against Life,
Body, and Health, of Criminal Conspiracy, and Genocide."[46]

The primary funders of Fujimori's genocide campaign were USAID
(which ignored U.S. law and a 1998 congressional investigation to
continue its financial support for the effort), UNFPA, and IPPF.[47]

*In a May 2011 rally, Peruvian victims of forced steriliza-
tion demand that Fujimori and his associates
be brought to justice.*

## CHINA

In June 1978, Song Jian, a top-level manager in charge of developing
control systems for the Chinese guided-missile program, traveled to
Helsinki for an international conference on control system theory
and design. While in Finland, he picked up copies of the Club of Rome

publications *The Limits to Growth* and *Blueprint for Survival*, and made the acquaintance of several Europeans who were promoting the reports' method of using computerized "systems analysis" to predict and design the human future.

Fascinated by the possibilities, Song returned to China and republished the Club's analysis under his own name (without attribution), establishing his reputation for brilliant and original thinking.[48] Indeed, while Club of Rome computer projections of impending resources shortages, graphs showing the shortening of population-increase times, and discussions of "carrying capacities," "natural limits," mass extinctions, and the isolated "spaceship Earth" were all clichés in the West by 1978, in China they were fresh and striking ideas. In no time at all, Song became a scientific superstar. Seizing the moment to grasp for greater power and importance, he pulled together an elite group of mathematicians from within his department, and with the help of a powerful computer to provide the necessary special effects, issued the profoundly calculated judgment that China's correct population size was 650 to 700 million people—which is to say some 280 to 330 million less than its actual 1978 population.[49] Song's analysis quickly found favor at top levels of the Chinese Communist Party because it purported to prove that the reason for China's continued poverty was not thirty years of disastrous misrule, but the very existence of the Chinese people. (To make the utter falsity of Song's argument clear, it is sufficient to note that in 1980, neighboring South Korea, with four times China's population density, had a per capita gross national product seven times greater.[50]) Paramount Leader Deng Xiaoping and his fellows in the Central Committee were also very impressed by the pseudo-scientific computer babble Song used to dress up his theory—which, unlike its Club of Rome source documents in the West, ran unopposed in the state-controlled Chinese technical and popular media.

However, even the heirs of Mao were unprepared to adjust China's population by 300 million through blatant slaughter. Instead, Song prepared a hundred-year plan whereby the goal could be attained by the year 2080. Basing himself on his home ground of missile guidance theory, Song proposed that the nation's population be considered a mathematical entity, like the position of a missile in flight, whose trajectory could be optimized by the input of a correctly calculated series of directives. Viewed thus, Song saw just one answer: China must impose a limit of one child per family, effective immediately.[51]

Deng Xiaoping liked what Song had to say, so those who might have had the power to resist the one-child policy were quick to protect themselves by lining up in support. At the critical Chengdu population conference in December 1979, only one brave man, Liang Zhongtang, a teacher of Marxism at the Shaanxi Provincial Party School, dared to offer open opposition. Like the White Rose crying out against the evils of Nazism, Liang called upon his party comrades to consider the brutality they were about to inflict. "This approach is not right," he cried. "We have made the peasants' suffering bitter enough in the economic realm. We cannot make them suffer further."[52]

Liang also tried to argue from a practical standpoint. If we implement this policy, he said, every working Chinese married couple will need to support four elderly grandparents, one child, and themselves. That means that each two will need to work to support seven—a clear impossibility. None of the children will have any brothers or sisters, or uncles or aunts. None of the parents will have any relatives of their own generation to help out in time of need. The social fabric of village life will break down completely. There will be no one to serve in the Army.

But such common-sense objections were of no avail. Liang was a high school graduate, a peasant's son who spoke in a rustic Shaanxi provincial accent. Song had a Ph.D. from Moscow University, sophisticated jet-set *savoir faire*, a huge mass of computer-generated scientific abracadabra to throw around, and most importantly, a network of powerful friends at the highest levels of the Communist Party in Beijing. By the conclusion of the conference, he had crushed Liang completely. Within a few months the word came down from the top. One child per family was now the policy of the infallible Party leadership itself, and no further disagreements would be tolerated.

Thus began the most forceful population control program since Nazi Germany. No more would the population controllers need to depend on tricks, bribes, denial of benefits, traveling ligation festivals, or slum demolition platoons to obtain their victims. They now had the organized and unrelenting power of a totalitarian state to enforce their will, holding sway over not only a massive bureaucracy but gigantic police and military forces, secret police, vast prison facilities, total media control, and tens of millions of informers. In his 1968 book, *The Population Bomb*, Paul Ehrlich had called for state control of human reproduction, with "compulsory birth regulation."[53] Now, just twelve years later, Ehrlich's utopian dream had become a nightmare reality for one-fifth of the human race.[54]

Qian Xinzhong, a Soviet-trained former major general in the People's Liberation Army, was placed in charge of the campaign. He ordered that all women with one child were to have a stainless-steel IUD inserted, and to be inspected regularly to make sure that they had not tampered with it. To remove the device was deemed a criminal act. All parents with two or more children were to be sterilized. No pregnancies were legal for anyone under 23, whether married or not, and all unauthorized pregnancies were to be aborted. "Under no circumstances is the birth of a third child allowed," Qian said.[55]

Women who defied these injunctions were taken and sterilized by force. Babies would be aborted right through the ninth month of pregnancy, with many crying as they were being stabbed to death at the moment of birth. Those women who fled to try to save their children were hunted, and if they could not be caught, their houses were torn down and their parents thrown in prison, there to linger until a ransom of 20,000 yuan—about three years' income for a peasant— was paid for their release. Babies born to such fugitives were declared to be "black children," illegal non-persons in the eyes of the state, without any right to employment, public schooling, health care, or reproduction.[56]

The leaders of the UNFPA and the IPPF were delighted, and rushed to send money (provided to them primarily by the U.S. State

*Law enforcement in China.*

Department) and personnel to help support the campaign. China was so openly brutal in its methods that IPPF's own information officer, Penny Kane, expressed alarm—not at what was being done to millions of Chinese women, girls, and infants, but at the possible public-relations disaster that could mar the IPPF's image if Americans found out what it was doing. "Very strong measures are being taken to reduce population," Kane wrote from China, "including abortion up to *eight* months. I think that in the not-too-distant future this will blow up into a major press story as it contains all the ingredients for sensationalism—Communism, forced family planning, murder of viable fetuses, parallels with India, etc. When it does blow up, it is going to be very difficult to defend. . . . We might find it extremely difficult to handle the press and the public if there were a major fuss about the Chinese methods."[57]

Disregarding Kane's worries, the IPPF stepped up its support for the campaign. True to her predictions, however, the story did begin to break in the West. On November 30, 1981, the *Wall Street Journal* ran an eyewitness story by Michele Vink reporting women being "hand-cuffed, tied with ropes, or placed in pig's baskets" as they were being hauled off for forced abortions. According to Vink, vehicles transporting

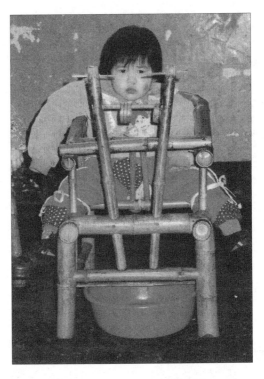

*Babies born in China in spite of the one-child policy are declared "black children" and have no right to food, health care, or education. If female, they are frequently killed, either at birth, or if apprehended later, at orphanages where they are gathered. Shown above is Mei Ming, a two-year-old girl tied to a chair in a "dying room." The bucket below her is to catch her urine and feces as she dies over the next several days from starvation and neglect. The above photo was taken by a British TV crew during their filming of the 1995 documentary exposé* The Dying Rooms. *The Chinese government denies the existence of dying rooms.*

women to hospitals in Canton were "filled with wailing noises," while unauthorized infants were being killed en masse. "Every day hundreds of fetuses arrive at the morgue," one of Vink's sources said.[58]

On May 15, 1982, *New York Times* foreign correspondent Christopher Wren offered an even more devastating exposé. He reported on stories of thousands of Chinese women being "rounded up and forced to have abortions," and tales of women "locked in detention cells or hauled before mass rallies and harangued into consenting to abortion," as well as "vigilantes [who] abducted pregnant women on the streets and hauled them off, sometimes handcuffed or trussed, to abortion clinics." He quoted one Chinese reporter who described "aborted babies which were actually crying when they were born."[59] The horror became so open that it could not be denied. By 1983, even Chinese newspapers themselves were running stories about the "butchering, drowning, and leaving to die of female infants and the maltreating of women who had given birth to girls."[60]

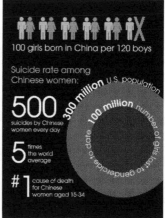

*Chai Ling (left, in 1990) was a leader of the 1989 Tiananmen Square protests, denounced by the Chinese government as the second-most-wanted "culprit" of those events. Since her escape from China, she has founded an organization called All Girls Allowed to fight against the government's policy of "gendercide." At right is one of her posters.*

Unfazed by the press coverage, Qian redoubled the effort. Local Communist Party officials were given quotas for sterilizations, abortions, and IUD insertions. If they exceeded them, they could be promoted. If they failed to meet them, they would be expelled from the Party in disgrace. These measures guaranteed results. In 1983, 16 million women and 4 million men were sterilized, 18 million women had IUDs inserted, and over 14 million infants were aborted. Going forward, these figures were sustained, with combined total coerced abortions, IUD implantations, and sterilizations exceeding *30 million per year* through 1985.[61]

In celebration of his achievements, in 1983 the UNFPA gave Qian (together with Indira Gandhi) the first United Nations Population Award, complete with diploma, gold medal, and $25,000 cash. In a congratulatory speech at the award ceremony in New York, U.N. Secretary General Javier Pérez de Cuéllar said: "Considering the fact that China and India contain over 40 per cent of humanity, we must all record our deep appreciation of the way in which their governments have marshaled the resources necessary to implement population policies on a massive scale." Qian stood up and promised to continue "controlling population quantity and raising population quality."[62] The U.N. was not alone in expressing its appreciation. The World Bank signaled its thanks in the sincerest way possible—that is to say, with cash, providing China with $22 billion in loans by 1996.[63]

Given the supreme importance to rural Chinese families of having a son, both to take care of aging parents and to continue the line and honor family ancestors, many peasants simply could not accept a daughter as their only child. The resultant spike in female infanticide was perhaps not especially concerning to the authorities in itself, given their attitude toward related matters, but the total social breakdown it betokened was. Facing this reality, in 1988 the government in some provinces compromised just a little and agreed that couples who had a daughter as their first child would be allowed one more try to have a son—provided that there were no unauthorized births or other violations of the population policy by anyone in the couple's village during that year. While giving a bit on the population front, this "reform" had the salutary effect—from the totalitarian point of view—of destroying peasant solidarity, which previously had acted to shield local women giving birth in hiding. Instead, hysterical group pressure was mobilized against such rebels, with everyone in the village transformed into government snoops to police their neighbors against possible infractions.[64]

The killing of daughters, however, continued apace. During the period from 2000 to 2004, almost 1.25 boys were born for every girl born—indicating that one-fifth of all baby girls in China were either being aborted or murdered. In some provinces the fraction eliminated was as high as one-half.[65]

In 1991, UNFPA head Nafis Sadik went to China to congratulate the oligarchs of the People's Republic for their excellent program, which by that time had already sterilized, implanted IUDs in, or performed abortions on some 300 million people. "China has every reason to feel proud of and pleased with its remarkable achievements made in its family planning policy and control of its population growth over the past ten years," she said. "Now the country could offer its experiences and special experts to help other countries. . . . UNFPA is going to employ some of [China's family planning experts] to work in other countries and popularize China's experience in population growth control and family planning." Sadik made good on her promise. With the help of the UNFPA, the Chinese model of population control was implemented virtually in its entirety in Vietnam, and used to enhance the brutal effectiveness of the antihuman efforts in many other countries, from Bangladesh, Sri Lanka, and Indonesia to Mexico and Peru.[66]

Around the world, billions of people have paid, and are continuing to pay, with ruined lives for the fraudulent writings of the Club of Rome.

\* \* \*

## SUB-SAHARAN AFRICA

Sub-Saharan Africa is largely composed of very poor countries ruled by governments which in many cases are little more than tribal or criminal gangs. Such regimes have been easy prey for the population controllers, as it generally takes little more than an easily graftable World Bank loan, or UNFPA or USAID grant, to obtain the cooperation of their leadership. As a result, the population controllers have been able to run riot, going well beyond even the regular arsenal of sterility-dealing tricks, incentives, and coercive tactics they have used in the countries already discussed. In Africa, for example, the population establishment pays a pittance to outbid other health care programs to take away from them the services of the precious few qualified local doctors and the equipment of local hospitals, thereby depriving millions of people of critically needed treatment for malaria and other deadly diseases. As Dr. Stephen Karanja, former secretary of the Kenyan Medical Association, wrote in 1997:

> Our health sector is collapsed. Thousands of the Kenyan people will die of malaria, the treatment of which costs a few cents, in health facilities whose shelves are stocked to the ceiling with millions of dollars' worth of pills, IUDs, Norplant, Depo-Provera, and so on, most of which are supplied with American money.... Special operating theaters fully serviced and not lacking in instruments are opened in hospitals for the sterilization of women. While in the same hospitals, emergency surgery cannot be done for lack of basic operating instruments and supplies.[67]

In a 2000 interview, he continued, "You can't perform operations because there is no equipment, no materials. The operation theater isn't working. But if it is for a sterilization, the theater is equipped."[68]

Across Africa, health care clinics have been converted into "family planning" stations where there are no antibiotics, no vitamins, no anti-malarial drugs—in fact, no medical care of any kind except abortions, IUD insertions, anti-fertility injections, and sterilizations.[69] Even worse, invasive procedures are generally performed by unqualified personnel in unsanitary conditions. This network of "family planning" clinics has thus become a major threat to public health. In his essential 2008 book *Population Control: Real Costs, Illusory Benefits*, author Steven Mosher has assembled an impressive body of evidence indicating that the population control operation in Africa may be the major cause behind that continent's horrific AIDS epidemic. I will attempt to present an outline of his most salient points here. Those who require further proof should read Mosher's book.[70]

Sub-Saharan Africa has a population of 863 million people; it contains 12 percent of humanity as a whole.[71] Yet by 2009, it was home to 68 percent of the world's HIV cases, including more than 90 percent of the world's HIV-infected children.[72] Of the 30 countries classified by the U.N. Program on HIV/AIDS in 2010 as "most severely affected by HIV," 25 were in sub-Saharan Africa.[73] In many of these countries, over 13 percent of the adult population (between the ages of 15 and 49) is infected; in some countries, a quarter of that age cohort has HIV.[74] Since the 1990s, each year has seen more than a million new AIDS deaths across the region, and each year more than 1.5 million people are newly infected with HIV.[75] Outside of sub-Saharan Africa, fewer than two out of every thousand people are HIV-positive. Inside the region, 27 out of every thousand are infected.[76]

It is obvious from these figures that AIDS is being transmitted in Africa under very different circumstances than those prevailing in the rest of the world. In most areas of the world, especially in the West, the leading vector of HIV transmission is unprotected homosexual male intercourse—as can be confirmed by the much higher incidence of new cases of HIV among homosexuals than among heterosexuals.[77] But inside Africa, HIV and AIDS disproportionately affect women: while outside sub-Saharan Africa only 35 percent of people with HIV are women, inside sub-Saharan Africa the figure is 54 percent.[78]

How, then, is AIDS in Africa being transmitted? The population control establishment clearly believes it to be via rampant sexual,

# Prevalence of AIDS in Africa

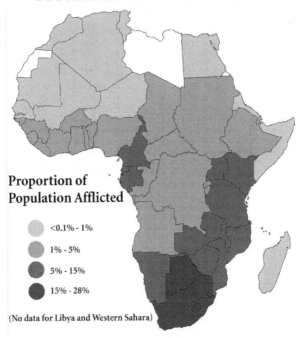

**Proportion of Population Afflicted**

- <0.1% - 1%
- 1% - 5%
- 5% - 15%
- 15% - 28%

(No data for Libya and Western Sahara)

*United Nations statistics showing 2009 prevalence of AIDS.*

especially heterosexual, activity—despite the fact that the latter activity is not in any way unique to Africa—and has rallied to the cause by plastering the continent with condoms (generously funded by Western governments and agencies, of course), thereby fighting AIDS and childbirth at the same time.[79] The racist stereotype underlying these programs is undermined by the fact that the programs had no effect in slowing the spread of HIV, with the number infected quadrupling between 1995 and 2008 even as spending on those programs was skyrocketing.[80] And the reason for their failure is clear: the data do not support the prejudiced belief in the "promiscuous African." On the contrary, as noted in a 2003 article in the *International Journal of STD and AIDS*, "Levels of sexual activity reported in a dozen general population surveys in Africa are comparable to those reported elsewhere, especially in North America and Europe."[81]

There is another explanation for the rapid spread of HIV in sub-Saharan Africa. Condoms are not the only items that population control clinics are distributing in sub-Saharan Africa; they are also giving out hypodermic needles in very large numbers. For reasons that remain unclear, the dominant method of long-term contraception pursued by the population controllers in Africa is not sterilization via tubal ligations or vasectomies, as is their practice elsewhere, but Depo-Provera (also known under its British name, Megastron), a contraceptive drug which needs to be injected by hypodermic needle every three months. Between 1994 and 2006, USAID shipped over 140 million Depo-Provera kits worldwide, mostly to Africa. The needles from these kits are used and *re*used by meagerly trained personnel employed in African government or IPPF clinics. Moreover, they are *given out over the counter* in huge numbers to completely uneducated African women to use at home.[82] It is estimated that since the 1990s at least 100 million hypodermic needles have been put into public circulation in sub-Saharan Africa through these programs. It is true that in many cases the packages are marked that their needles are not for reuse, or not for reuse without sterilization. Plastic syringes, however, are very difficult to sterilize, and neither the knowledge nor the facilities required to do so properly are generally available in clinics, let alone among the women "patients." As for package instructions to discard needles after one use, the idea that a poor African girl, unaware of the germ theory of disease, would simply throw away a perfectly serviceable hypodermic syringe worth a day's wages stretches credibility. Indeed, even if she did, the most likely fate of a discarded syringe would be recovery from the trash by rag-pickers for resale on the black market.[83]

The threat to African public health posed by the population controllers' syringe distribution system is not obscure. It has been recognized publicly by the U.N.'s own World Health Organization (WHO), which warns: "Reuse of syringes and needles in the absence of sterilization exposes millions of people to infection ... syringes and needles are often just rinsed in a pot of tepid water between injections ... in some countries this proportion [of injections given with syringes or needles reused without sterilization] is as high as 70 percent."[84] WHO also notes that "in developing countries, additional hazards occur from scavenging on waste disposal sites and manual sorting of the waste recuperated at the back doors of health-care establishments."[85]

Analysis by Mosher and others suggests strongly that the career of a typical "single-use" needle in Africa may not be just a few reuses, but perhaps scores. Mosher estimates that about 4 billion injections (of all types, perhaps half for population control) are given per year in sub-Saharan Africa.[86] If up to 70 percent of these are non-sterile, as WHO estimates, then as many as 3 billion unsafe injections may be performed in the region annually. If only a tiny fraction of these is

*Patients wait in line at an AIDS clinic in Uganda.*
*According to the International Monetary Fund, in Zambia,*
*as a result of HIV/AIDS, less than 30 percent of people who*
*reach the age of 20 are expected to survive to the age of 60.*

tainted with AIDS, the result would be sufficient to spread disease on an epidemic scale.

There is a point at which gross irresponsibility becomes criminal. Over thirty million people now face death from AIDS in sub-Saharan Africa, and nearly two million more will be doomed this year, and next, and for years more to come, by the spreading epidemic.[87] The population controllers will probably never be brought to the dock for prosecution for what they have done in Africa. But if history is the world's court, then someday there will most assuredly be judgment.

## CHAPTER FOURTEEN

# Better Dead than Fed: Green Police
# for World Hunger

> *To deny desperate, hungry people the means to control their*
> *futures by presuming to know what is best for them is not only*
> *paternalistic but morally wrong. . . . We want to have the oppor-*
> *tunity to save the lives of millions of people and change the course*
> *of history in many nations. . . . The harsh reality is that, without*
> *the help of agricultural biotechnology, many will not live.*
>
> HASSAN ADAMU
> Nigerian minister of agricultural
> and rural development, 2000[1]

THE FIRST AND MOST important of the Green Parties was founded in Germany in 1980 under the leadership of August Haussleiter.[2] A former officer in the Nazi SS, Haussleiter had a long history in fascist politics, going back to standing beside Adolf Hitler during the Beer Hall Putsch of 1923.[3]

After the war, Haussleiter continued his efforts by joining the *Bruderschaft*, or "brotherhood," of former SS men active within the German military and political worlds. His colleagues in this network included General Gert Bastian, Colonel Otto Skorzeny (the rescuer of Mussolini), and General Otto Ernst Remer (the turncoat responsible for crushing the German officers' July 1944 plot to overthrow Hitler).[4] In the late 1960s, Haussleiter saw an opportunity to recruit radicalized students around ecological and anti-nuclear causes. Beginning with an organization he founded, Action Community of Independent Germans, Haussleiter drew together other environmental groups, many of which were growing rapidly during the 1970s through anti-nuclear agitation, to create the Green Party, with himself as its first chairman, and Ludwig Klages's 1913 proto-Nazi German youth-movement tract *Man and Earth* as its founding manifesto.[5] The new movement thus solidly launched, the old Nazi warhorse then stepped aside to allow its leadership to assume a much more appealing face in the form of Gert Bastian's youthful mistress, the fervent anti-nuclear advocate Petra Kelly. Attractive and vivacious, Kelly was able to use her powerful charisma to grow the Greens into a major political party, with a share of the vote and parliamentary representation exceeding ten percent. She was, however, apparently too interested in human rights and, pushed out of the Party leadership, she was murdered by Bastian in 1992.[6]

That Nazis were involved in the founding of the German Green Party should not be surprising, since the Nazi Party itself was to a large extent an outgrowth of a pre-existing German green movement

*August Haussleiter (second from left), a member of the Nazi Party since the 1920s, founded the Green Party and served as its first chairman. Petra Kelly is speaking beside him.*

with roots dating back to the early nineteenth century. As historian George Mosse has shown in his seminal book *The Crisis of German Ideology: Intellectual Origins of the Third Reich*,[7] starting with Ernst Moritz Arndt's 1815 essay, "On the Care and Conservation of Forests," a succession of nationalistic German nature worshippers developed and popularized a cult ideology celebrating the natural "authentic" qualities of the good old-fashioned German country people, or *Volk*—including Arndt's student Wilhelm Riehl; Darwinian exponent Ernst Haeckel (who, as we have seen, coined the word "ecology"); writers Paul de Lagarde, Julius Langbehn, Eugen During, and Ludwig Klages; publisher Eugen Diederichs; *The Third Reich* author Arthur Moeller van den Bruck; and Hitler's own mentor Dietrich Eckhart. According to these writers, the *Volk* (literally "folk," but also carrying the meaning of "tribe") derived their deep and "genuine" souls from their "rootedness" in the land, shared ancestral kinship, and connection to nature. Jews, by contrast, representing corrupt urban modernity and lacking in landed rootedness, were soulless and thus could never be part of the German *Volk*. Christianity, science, technology, industry, progress, "mechanical and materialistic civilization," and all else that proposed to raise man above nature were also to be abhorred. Popularized widely in prose works, fiction, and drama, these ideas formed the basis of the huge back-to-nature *Völkisch* and related Youth movements that arose in Germany during the late nineteenth century. When in the 1920s the new Nazi Party raised the pagan swastika flag celebrating the power of irrational animal nature over civilization and reason, the *Völkisch* greens flocked to the cause.

One of the more peculiar sensibilities that the modern German Greens inherited from their *Völkisch* and Nazi predecessors was a form of food fetishism, which the Nazis had themselves imbibed from the early twentieth century teachings of Rudolf Steiner. Steiner was an Austrian mystic who combined the ideas of Nietzsche, Haeckel, the mystic Madame Blavatsky, and Field Marshall Helmuth von Moltke (whom he channeled) to create a popular cult promoting Aryan racial superiority. This "Anthroposophy" movement also included extensive strictures extolling the virtues of "biodynamic" or organic farming, vegetarianism, and natural foods.[8] These teachings were embraced by many leading Nazis, including Minister of Agriculture Richard Walther Darré. In his 1931 book *A New Nobility Out of Blood and Soil*, Darré had originated the Nazis' famous "Blood and Soil" slogan based on the Steinerite ideal of a pure race on pure soil; to realize this ideal, he developed the plan to depopulate eastern Europe of impure Slavs and Jews.[9] Deputy Führer Rudolf Hess was himself a practicing anthroposophist, while Hitler and Himmler both believed firmly in Steiner's dietary prescriptions—Himmler going so far as to arrange for the creation of biodynamic gardens at Auschwitz and Dachau so that his SS exterminators could enjoy the benefits of organically grown vegetables while they set about their work.[10] Anthroposophic dietary ideas were accordingly taught to all the boys and girls of the Hitler Youth and the League of German Maidens, and continued to be taught to German children (down to the present day) after the war in the hundreds of Waldorf Schools that Steiner and his followers had established across the Reich.[11] Many of those so instructed, including practicing anthroposophists like future German Interior Minister (from 1998 to 2005) Otto Schily, were founding members of the Green Party.[12]

Thus when the new technology of genetically modified crops

Völkisch *youth in pre-Hitler Germany. Note the pagan headbands on the girls at left.*

appeared in the early 1990s, the German Green Party was uniquely prepared to launch a campaign of opposition. Observing the ease with which the German Greens were able to promote hysteria (and thus garner funds, recruits, and votes) on this issue, other European Green organizations rushed to join the fray as well.

It was like the anti-nuclear campaign all over again. Far from representing a threat to the environment, genetically modified crops offer tremendous environmental benefits, allowing more food to be grown with much less land clearance, tillage, irrigation, fertilizer, and pesticides. By making crops more productive, less land is needed to meet humanity's demand for food. By providing plants with precisely selected spliced-in genes, crops could be made more drought-resistant, thereby reducing the need for irrigation, or be given the ability to produce their own nitrates or pesticides, thereby eliminating the need for chemical fertilizers or insect sprays. In other words, essentially *all* the agricultural issues that the environmental movement had been screaming about for decades could be addressed by the genetic engineering of crop varieties.[13]

Again, as in the case of the anti-nuclear campaign, the fearmongering propaganda of the putative environmentalists was essentially baseless. Far from representing a more dangerous type of food than traditional varieties, genetically modified crops are actually far safer, precisely because their content can be controlled. Except for fish and game, humans today actually eat no "natural" foods. All of our domestic plants and animals are the product of thousands of years of artificial breeding, radically altered from their natural state. That is very fortunate, because wild plants and animals are frequently quite dangerous, as it behooves them to be if they are to survive in the wild. It is not genetically modified tomatoes that represent a threat to the consumer, but wild tomatoes, which are loaded with toxins and allergens—so much so that in early nineteenth-century America daredevils could sometimes make themselves a hatful of cash by eating a tomato in front of a crowd on a bet. A traditional plant breeder seeking tougher survival traits for agricultural tomatoes might try to cross-breed them with a wild variety, but in doing so he would risk importing genes into the crop that could produce potentially lethal substances at random. In contrast, the genetic engineer can act with precision and select only the traits desired. But not only that, the genetic engineer also has the freedom to import beneficial traits from other species too distantly related to allow combination through conventional breeding techniques.[14]

The benefits following from this ability are enormous. For example, genetic engineers have already found ways to put bacterial genes in cotton that produce a substance deadly to insects that eat it, thereby protecting the crop from insects without the need for chemical pesticides. Such "Bt cotton" strains (named for the inserted bacteria gene) are now widely in use around the globe, saving farmers and their customers money while reducing environmental impact.[15] Currently, 40 percent of all crops grown in Africa and Asia (which cannot afford much pesticide use) are lost to insects.[15] Creating Bt varieties of food staples would thus do much to save these vitally needed crops. The yield per acre of American corn growers has been radically improved through the use of genetically modified strains, so much so that in 2007 the state of Iowa alone produced more corn than the entire United States did in 1947, when the total number of harvested acres was comparable; the yield of corn bushels per acre has risen nationwide from 28.6 bushels to 152.8 bushels over that same time period.[16] As the best farms are now achieving harvests approaching 300 bushels per acre, continuation of this progress may allow yet another doubling of yield within the decade.[17] Not only that, experiments are now underway with corn varieties containing genes that give them the power to fix their own nitrates—an improvement which, once implemented, will radically reduce the amount of chemical fertilizer needed to grow corn worldwide, save energy, and greatly increase yields in Third World countries that are too impoverished to currently use fertilizer. Drought-resistant varieties of cassava and several other staple crops essential to Africa have been developed, which promise to do much to ease the threat of famine to the poorest of the world's poor.[18]

And far from being less nutritious than "natural" (conventionally bred) crops, the new varieties are more nutritious—in some instances, radically more so. To take one important example, by placing beta-carotene-producing genes from daffodils into rice, genetic engineers have created a new strain called "golden rice" rich in vitamin A.[19] Around the world, 250 million children suffer from vitamin A deficiency, with perhaps 500,000 of them going blind every year, and as many as 2.5 million children dying each year as a result of the deficiency.[20] The planting of golden rice in place of conventional rice could end that horror. Another variety of genetically engineered rice has been developed which is rich in iron, offering the prospect of ameliorating the anemia that impairs the lives of over half a billion women worldwide, mostly in poor countries.[21]

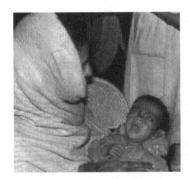 

*Vitamin A deficiency causes blindness in millions of Third World children every year. Golden rice can prevent it.*

## THE GREEN BIOTECH BLOCKADE

As a technology holding potential for uplifting the human condition, the genetic modification of crops is unmatched by any development of the modern age except for antibiotics and electricity. It seems incredible that any group of people could be so lacking in compassion as to strive to prevent its implementation. Yet that is the cause that the German Greens and their European followers, collaborators, and appeasers have chosen to embrace. Justifying this crusade, the Greens have proclaimed a radical new antihuman idea, the *Vorsorgeprinzip* ("Precautionary Principle"). According to this concept, no innovation can be permitted which cannot be proven *in advance* to be completely harmless.[22] If accepted, this idea would make all technological progress impossible. Indeed, it is difficult to think of any form of human freedom or creative activity, ranging from entrepreneurship to childbirth, which would not require severe restriction under the Precautionary Principle.

If the *Vorsorgeprinzip* were just some more crazy German philosophical claptrap, it would be of limited interest. After all, the Germans already have Hegel, Riehl, Haeckel, Nietzsche, Klages, Spengler, Steiner, and Heidegger to muse upon; how much worse can it get? But the Greens have not put the *Vorsorgeprinzip* forward as (merely) a basis for faculty lounge discussions, but as a strict guideline for state policy—demanded by a political party with sufficient clout to make or break coalition governments. Responding to their pressure, European politicians have accordingly passed measures that not only ban the planting of genetically modified crops within Europe, but even the *importation of the products of such agriculture* for sale.[23] Since in recent years roughly 70 percent of processed food made in the United States has been derived from genetically modified species,[24] these regulations have been perceived by many to be a form of protectionism directed against American farmers, and were protested as such by the Bush administration in litigation brought to the World Trade Organization in 2003.[25] However, as significant as the damage to the interests of U.S. farmers and European consumers might be, the people harmed most by the Green trade embargo are the hungry poor of the Third World.

In the face of the threat of the exclusion of their farm exports from the European market, most African and many other Third World countries have been forced to shun the benefits offered to them by genetically modified crops. Indeed, several African governments have even capitulated to the extent of refusing to distribute American food aid under famine conditions, willfully starving their own people rather than displease the European Greens.[26] Across a malnourished continent, drought-resistant cassava is not planted, vitamin-enriched golden rice is not grown, and millions of anemia-weakened women must continue to watch sadly as their emaciated children sicken and go blind.

But as its attempt to enshrine the Precautionary Principle makes clear, the ultimate target threatened by the anti-advanced crop crusade is not *just* the life and health of millions, but the liberty of all mankind. The *Vorsorgeprinzip* is nothing less than the pure crystallized philosophy of smothering bureaucratic dictatorship. In our next chapter, we shall see how its advocates are now seeking to expand its purview far beyond the domain of biotechnology, creating thereby a new world order in which all human decisions and actions will be subject to review, and control, by their own higher authority.

## *FOCUS SECTION: BIOTECHNOLOGY AND AGRICULTURAL PROGRESS*

Agriculture is the art of improving nature. As such, it is not only the most essential human activity, but the most emblematic. It is through agriculture that man continues the work of creation, quite literally *changing the world* to make it a better place in which to live.

We have done this since our earliest days, both by altering the environment through irrigation and fertilization, and by creating new life forms more supportive of human existence than those that preceded them.

One of our first living inventions was the dog. By transforming wolves into dogs, our ancestors turned some of our deadliest of enemies into our best of friends. To grasp how critical a step this was, think of a small tribe of early humans, poorly nourished, and armed only with stones and pointed sticks, being stalked by a pack of wolves. The wolves are stronger, faster, better armed, and far better equipped to detect and track their prey. Taking advantage of surprise, they might attack at night and massacre the entire tribe. Certainly they would have no difficulty hiding in the vicinity, waiting for the moment when the men leave to hunt, the women go to fetch water, or some children wander off to play or pick berries, to strike. If there were game in the area, they could find it and get to it first, leaving the humans to starve. But with the aid of dogs, humans could match wolves and other predators sense for sense, thereby securing the two essentials of food and safety.

Other inventions followed. Starting with wild animals, we created chickens, sheep, goats, and cattle to provide us with eggs, meat, milk, fertilizer, and clothing. We created oxen, donkeys, and horses to supply us with muscle power and mobility.

In the case of plants, our creativity has been even more extravagant. Over time, we have used breeding to create varieties that from the point of view of design for the wild are simply ludicrous, featuring as they do gigantic fruits or seeds loaded with nutritious sugars, starches, vegetable oils, and proteins.

None of these many species of domesticated animals and plants exist in nature, or ever existed in nature, in the forms we know them today. All of them are the product of deliberate artificial genetic alteration, done with cruder means, but in many cases far more radical effect, than anything contemplated by modern-day bioengineers.

*The first bioengineered organism was the dog.*

Wheat was first cultivated in the Levant around 10000 B.C., but the wheat now grown in 90 percent of the world, called "hexaploid," is not a naturally occurring wheat. Hexaploid does not grow in the wild, and only came about by selective cross-breeding of the many varieties that had been developed over the millennia. The wheat cultivated in 10000 B.C. was eventually merged with a grass (*Aegilops tauschii*) developed near the Caspian Sea around 2000 B.C., ultimately giving us what we refer to as "bread wheat." Modern wheat has three pairs of chromosomes from three plant genera, and has never been found in the wild. That's right, our wholesome daily bread—even the stuff sold by all-natural, organic, free range, biodynamic, macrobiotic, etc., etc., Whole Foods-type companies—is a "Frankenplant," a monstrosity if you will, created by the devious genius of ancient bioengineers. Bread wheat is thus "unnatural," and yet is a staple for most of the world, and has been since near the dawn of civilization. Bioengineering defines human life.[27]

These genetic advances occurred in parallel with human mastery of irrigation and fertilization techniques. In the case of irrigation, technology has moved forward from hand-carried water, to irrigation systems driven by downhill flow, to windmills, and ultimately to combustion engines. Simultaneously we have made the soil much more fertile through the application of animal manure, crop rotation, and chemical fertilizers produced on an industrial scale. More recently, we have even been making the air more fertile by adding carbon dioxide; one study has shown a 14 percent increase in plant growth in the United States in the second half of the twentieth century, with increased carbon dioxide levels as a contributing factor.[28] Based upon lab experiments assessing the effects of carbon dioxide enrichment on plant growth, we can expect that similar increases have occurred around the world.

Now, we can imagine extraterrestrial tourists who might bemoan the loss of an Earth where they could find amusement watching human children being torn apart by wolves, but for the rest of us, a world with dogs in it is a better world than one without. Similarly, a world with orchards in it, and vineyards, and wheat fields, and yes, even such manifest (because recent) artificialities as nectarines, is a better place than it would be if it were lacking in these genetically engineered and other improvements upon nature.

A point requires emphasis, because of the hysteria aroused against bioengineering by demagogues who claim that we are "playing God" through indulgence in such activity. (The fact that most of those engaged in such agitation generally don't believe in God adds a peculiar element of hypocrisy to their appeals, but that is another issue.) *All* forms of agriculture are unnatural. Watering a plant is *unnatural*, because it involves putting water in a place where Nature did not put it, thus allowing a plant to grow where Nature would forbid. Engaging in three-field crop rotation puts far more nitrates in the soil than Nature would prescribe. And again, all of our domesticated plant and animal allies are unnatural, intelligently contrived products of an age-old effort by many generations of people to improve upon what Nature had to offer.

All evolution, whether accomplished by Nature, Bronze Age farmers, or twenty-first-century bioengineers, occurs through fundamentally the same process. New genetic traits are created by mutation, which can be caused by radiation, chemical effects, bacteria or virus-induced interspecies genetic transfer,[29] or other cellular accidents. Organisms containing these modified genes are then bred with existing stock to produce offspring, which may, as a result, manifest new traits. These novel traits in turn may sometimes find favor by Nature, farmers, or engineers, and if so may spread to become a new characteristic feature of the species.

In Nature, the mutations are caused by random accident, and so are the cross-breeds that follow. Early farmers were stuck with random mutation as the source of potential new traits, but were able to greatly improve upon the natural evolutionary process by using their intelligence to direct the subsequent breeding program. This intelligence became increasingly effective as human understanding of the rules of plant and animal breeding, and ultimately, the science of genetics, advanced over time. In the mid-twentieth century, artificial radiation sources became available, thus allowing researchers to sharply accelerate matters by inducing mutations in experimental seed stock at a much faster rate than that caused by cosmic rays. While providing scientific breeders much more novelty to choose from, however, the mutations themselves were still accidental and unpredictable in character. Nevertheless, over 2,250 such artificially mutated plant varieties have been grown and bred in more than fifty countries, including Europe and the United States, since the 1950s.[30]

Bioengineering differs from the preceding methods in one important respect. Instead of attempting to exploit random mutations and gene transfers, it makes use of changes initiated by design—specifically designed, that is, to be *safer* and *more* nutritious than "natural" varieties. Nature's products do not come tested and approved by the Food and Drug Administration, and many of them—ranging from wild berries to polar bear meat—can be outright poisonous. Agricultural goods are better, having been made and proven safe (though not to FDA standards) through their willful breeding and consumption by millions of people over time.

That said, traditional crops have plenty of room for improvement, in that they lack many essential vitamins and nutrients. This is entirely understandable, since they were bred by people who had a very incomplete knowledge of the science of nutrition, and who, moreover, lacked the tools required to effectively correct the problem in any case. Thus those dependent on such foods face the possibility of nutritional deficiency ailments, as well as stunted growth, strength, energy, and intelligence, and increased vulnerability to all manner of disease. Through biotechnology, however, these defects can be remedied, and foods created that are *far healthier* than any that exist today.

## THE GREEN REVOLUTION

Starting in the 1950s, plant geneticists created a series of new crop varieties that have made possible a vast improvement in the human condition worldwide. The most famous achievement of this justly-named "Green Revolution" was the development of "miracle" varieties of wheat and rice by the team led by American scientist Norman Borlaug.

Borlaug's project was made possible by the work of Cecil Salmon, a scientist accompanying the American occupation forces in postwar Japan. Salmon noticed that the Japanese were growing a mutant dwarf variety of wheat, known as "Norin 10," and sent it back with other wheat samples to the United States. In 1952, Borlaug, a young researcher working on a joint project of the Rockefeller Foundation and the Mexican government, began crossing some Norin 10 samples with a variety that he had spent ten years developing to be especially rust-resistant.[31] In fact, it was Borlaug's interest in rust—a category of plant diseases caused by fungi—that led him to change the course of his scientific career in forestry towards wheat breeding.[32] What made his new hybrid diminutive strain especially valuable was that its stalks could bear a heavy load of grain without bending and breaking. Borlaug's stalks were straighter, sturdier, and had three times the ordinary yield; all while being resistant to crop-devastating rust. By 1963 Mexico's wheat harvest—consisting nearly entirely (95 percent) of Borlaug dwarf hybrids—had increased sixfold over what it had been in 1944.[33]

With this success under his belt, Borlaug set out to spread his work internationally. After waging a tenacious struggle for several years, he managed to overcome resistance from protectionists and bureaucrats in India and Pakistan, with the first large shipments of the Mexican dwarf seed reaching those countries in 1968. The results were immediate. In the very same year that Paul Ehrlich called for starving the "hopeless" subcontinent whose people he found so repellent, Pakistan became a self-sufficient wheat producer. India, meanwhile, produced a harvest so far beyond any previous record that it lacked facilities to store the grain. Overjoyed, the Indian government struck a stamp commemorating the event. By 1971, India was self-sufficient in grain, and by 1974, with its wheat production tripled, the nation was a significant net grain *exporter*.[34]

This entire Green Revolution was made possible by taking advantage of a single accidental mutant gene, known as Rht1, which caused the dwarfism in Norin 10. As a result, Asian agriculture was completely transformed, and the specter of famine banished from the world's largest continent.[35] With the aid of bioengineering, we will be able to design and implement such enormously valuable gene alterations at will, creating not one, but an endless series of Green Revolutions, offering unlimited benefits for the human future.

As for Borlaug, in 1970 he was awarded the Nobel Peace Prize and then continued his efforts, creating new varieties of miracle dwarf rice and other crops as well. Actually, Borlaug is a fascinating case study, as even he had been influenced by "green" thinking early on in his career but later was to undergo a complete reversal. His Nobel acceptance speech reveals that at the time, he did not understand the implications of his own achievement:

> Science, invention, and technology have given [man] materials and methods for increasing his food supplies substantially and sometimes spectacularly. . . . But he is not yet using adequately his potential for decreasing the rate of human reproduction. The result is that the rate of population increase exceeds the rate of increase in food production in some areas. There can be no permanent progress in the battle against hunger until the agencies that fight for increased food production and those that fight for population control unite in a common effort. Fighting alone, they may win temporary skirmishes, but united they can win a decisive and lasting victory to provide food and other amenities of a progressive civilization for the benefit of all mankind.[36]

It is terribly sad, though not entirely surprising, that the pervasive population control ideology had managed to affect even someone *whose very work is evidence* that the scarcity of resources is a problem to be overcome by innovation, not oppression. He was financed by the Rockefeller Foundation, after all, a known funding source for the

Population Council and other eugenic causes. But Norman Borlaug, the "father of the Green Revolution" whose efforts have saved the lives of a billion people so far, was not an antihumanist at heart—far from it. At the age of 86, three decades after winning the Nobel, he had a very different perspective:

> Thirty years ago, in my acceptance speech for the Nobel Peace Price, I said that the Green Revolution had won a temporary success in man's war against hunger, which if fully implemented, could provide sufficient for humankind through the end of the twentieth century. But I warned that unless the frightening power of human reproduction was curbed, the success of the

*Norman Borlaug (center), father of the Green Revolution. Of the revolution's environmentalist critics, Borlaug said in a 1997 interview: "They've never experienced the physical sensation of hunger. They do their lobbying from comfortable office suites in Washington or Brussels. If they lived just one month amid the misery of the developing world, as I have for fifty years, they'd be crying out for tractors and fertilizer and irrigation canals and be outraged that fashionable elitists back home were trying to deny them these things."*

Green Revolution would only be ephemeral. I now say that the world has the technology to feed a population of 10 billion people. The more pertinent question today is: Will farmers and ranchers be permitted to use this new technology?[37]

That is the question indeed.

## BIOTECHNOLOGY CASE STUDIES

Here are a few case studies illustrating the incredible untapped potential of biotechnology.

### BT CROPS

There is a wild bacterium known by its scientific name as *Bacillus thuringiensis*, or Bt for short. In nature, Bt reproduces by being ingested along with plant material by foraging insects. Once inside the bug's stomach, the bacteria produce tiny crystals that cut the insect's guts, killing it, and thereby turning it into a food supply to support the growth and multiplication of Bt. These crystals only form in the alkaline stomach of insects, not in the acidic stomachs of vertebrates. As a result, Bt is harmless to fish, amphibians, reptiles, birds, and mammals, and has been used safely as a pesticide (under the name Sporeine) by *organic* gardeners in both Europe and the United States since the 1930s. Bioengineers have now found a way to put Bt genes into some crops, allowing them to produce their own natural pesticide that only operates against those insects that try to eat them. Thus crops can be protected at very low cost without the need for chemical pesticides and without harming innocent and useful insects, like honeybees, that are just flying through or pollinating.[38]

In *Silent Spring*, Rachel Carson called for replacing chemical pesticides with organic alternatives. Bioengineering Bt into plants actually allows this to be done for the purpose of crop protection, which is by far the largest insecticide application. But the Greens have rejected the technology.

## ROUNDUP RESISTANCE

The most widely used herbicide in the world is glyphosphate, more generally known by its Monsanto trade name Roundup. Glyphosphate is the herbicide of choice (by both the USDA and the environmentalist Pesticide Action Network) because it is non-toxic to humans and animals, cheap, and disappears from the environment within days of application. Unfortunately, many of the most important food crops are vulnerable to it, making the use of long-lasting toxic or carcinogenic chemicals necessary if they are to be protected from weeds. However, through bioengineering, scientists have found a way to engineer Roundup resistance into soybeans, a very important protein crop.[39] This offers a path towards increased food production with greatly reduced herbicide pollution and soil tillage as well. But of course, the Greens have rejected it.

## CROP IMMUNIZATION

Bioengineers have been able to insert traits into crops to immunize them against diseases caused by viruses and bacteria. For example, a bioengineered papaya has been created which is immune to the papaya mosaic virus which wiped out Hawaii's orchards in the 1990s. As a result, Hawaii's papaya farmers are back in business, and the new variety is being offered to Third World countries to protect their plantations as well.[40] Nearly half of Africa's vital cassava crop was destroyed by cassava mosaic virus a few years ago. Bioengineers working at the Danforth Plant Science Center in St. Louis will soon have a virus-immune cassava variety ready.[41] But will the European Greens allow starving Africans to grow it?

The question is not rhetorical. In 2001, Kenyan agronomist Dr. Florence Wambugu announced that she had bioengineered a virus-resistant variety of sweet potato. In response, Green terrorists invaded her lab, destroying it, her records, and all of her test crops, thereby setting back her work for years. This was done despite the fact that the sweet potato was intended only for local consumption. Denouncing the attack, Wambugu said, "This is not a question of export to Europe or America. If they don't want it, they don't have to have it. We have local demand. We're dying. So can we eat first?"[42]

## ENVIRONMENTALLY ROBUST CROPS

Bioengineered crops have been created that can grow well in acidic soils, such as those common in the tropics, whose aluminum toxicity can otherwise reduce harvest yields by as much as 80 percent. Bioengineered plants tolerant of salinity are also being created. Drought resistance can also be engineered into plants. For example, Cornell researchers Ajay Garg and Ray Wu have identified genes in South African "resurrection plants" which allow them to produce a sugar known as trehalose which gives them the ability to survive and then resume growing after droughts. Taking advantage of this insight, Garg and Wu have successfully added the resurrection genes to rice, thereby giving it the same drought-resistant powers.[43] Endowing plants with the ability to endure dry spells by going dormant, instead of dying, could prevent enormous losses to farmers worldwide.

Going even further, bioengineers are now closing in on the ability to transfer genes enabling nitrogen fixation from legumes to grains. This will allow plants to grow their own nitrates, thereby making productive agriculture possible in the poorest of soils without the need for chemical fertilizer.

## NUTRITION ENHANCEMENT OF CROPS

Many essential vitamins and other nutrients are not found in today's cereal grains. Instead they must be obtained from more expensive foods, such as meat, fruits, and vegetables. As a result, the world's poor, who cannot afford such costly forms of sustenance in sufficient quantities, frequently suffer from vitamin deficiency diseases, as well as from general weakness and excessive vulnerability to contagious ailments caused by their defective diets.

Bioengineering can remedy this tragic situation by installing the genes for vitamin manufacture in the cheap grain plants that constitute the basic diet of the poor. A leading example of such an innovation is the "golden rice" mentioned above. By inserting daffodil and bacteria genes enabling beta-carotene production into rice, researchers at the Swiss Federal Institute have created a new strain rich in vitamin A; it is called "golden rice" because of its color.[44] It bears repeating that worldwide, about 250 million children under the age of five suffer from vitamin A deficiency, with half a million of them going blind every year, and as many as 2.5 million dying each year.[45] Golden rice, in combination with similar innovations, is an important step toward truly providing the world's poor with affordable nutritious food. Already, bioengineered rice strains have been developed that are rich in iron, and thereby can serve to prevent anemia, a disease that afflicts hundreds of millions of Third World women. Well on the way are additional crops that include higher and better protein content; more antioxidants; lower levels of saturated fat, toxins, anti-nutrients, and allergens; and increased amounts of numerous necessary vitamins and minerals.

But none of these products will do anybody any good if the poor are not allowed to grow and eat them. So long as the European Greens deny worldwide access to all but "natural" vitamin-deficient rice varieties, the global horror of malnutrition will go on.

## DISEASE-PREVENTING CROPS

Bioengineered crops can also be created that can immunize people against diseases. For example, Cornell University researchers have transferred genes into potatoes that offer protection against the Norwalk virus, which causes diarrhea. In another project, the same group reports success in preliminary tests of bioengineered potatoes conferring immunity against hepatitis B, a disease afflicting 2 billion people. Bioengineering can also develop medicine-producing plants, which can synthesize human antibodies to treat cancer, arthritis, and many other diseases. Preliminary studies indicate that such technology could potentially cut the cost of drug manufacture by an order of magnitude—since planting more crops is cheaper than retooling a chemistry lab—thereby radically reducing health care costs worldwide.[46]

## BIOTECH FORESTS

Biotechnology can also be used to produce genetically enhanced trees, which grow faster and straighter than unimproved varieties, thereby allowing them to produce much more useful high-quality lumber on a given amount of land. According to forestry genetics professor Steve Strauss of Oregon State University, "you could get all the wood the world needs pretty much from five, ten, or twenty percent of the land used now" from plantations of such trees, allowing the remaining 80-plus percent of the world's forests to be left in their natural state.[47] Trees can also be engineered to contain less lignin, making them better for paper production. Of particular interest is the creation of tree varieties resistant to blight. During the twentieth century, America's grand populations of chestnut and Dutch elm trees were devastated by fungal diseases. Chinese chestnuts, however, are resistant. With the aid of bioengineering, researchers at the University of Georgia and the State University of New York are well on their way to transferring the genetic resistance of the Chinese chestnut to the American variety.[48] Restoring the Dutch elm could come next. Currently the trees of the American west are under severe attack by pine beetles, which threaten to turn tens of millions of acres of living mountain woodlands into kindling for the largest forest fire in history. Bioengineering beetle-resistant or -repellent trees could save the day.

## NON-DISEASE-CARRYING INSECTS

Worldwide, over 80 percent of contagious diseases are transferred by insects. Using bioengineering, we can modify insects to make such transmission impossible. For example, bioengineers have been able to genetically modify mosquitoes so that they cannot harbor a number of disease-carrying organisms, including the malaria parasite and the viruses that cause dengue and yellow fever. Other researchers have bioengineered bacteria that kill the trypanosome parasites within insects, including the "kissing bugs" that transmit Chagas disease in South America and the tsetse flies that carry sleeping sickness in Africa.[49]

Human beings, however, are not the only victims of insect-borne diseases. They afflict every animal, whether tame or wild, that walks upon the Earth or flies in its skies. They kill plants by the billion as well. By replacing disease-transporting insects with non-contagion-carrying counterparts we can confer an incalculable blessing on the entire community of life of this planet. Bioengineering provides a way to do it.

## BIOTECH AQUACULTURE

Nearly every major source of food that supports human existence today derives from a plant or an animal created by human ingenuity and multiplied through human effort. There is, however, one important exception: seafood. While our techniques of collecting it have advanced in parallel with all our other technological achievements, the actual development and production of fish, shrimp, lobsters, clams, oysters, and the rest has remained largely the province of the bounty of nature. As a result, the saltwater fish we eat today are virtually identical to those that were gathered when Neolithic man made his first catch, while the ocean that provides them is no more productive.[50] This is unfortunate, because in the meantime, the human population has increased a thousandfold. If we are going to be able to continue to enjoy food from the sea, we will need to take action to multiply it, just as we have done so well with food from the land.

This process has already begun, as anyone can see by visiting the seafood section of the local supermarket, where "farm-raised" fish can frequently be seen on display. While the yield of the world's capture fisheries (oceans and inland bodies of water) has remained static at about 90 million tons per year since the mid–1990s, annual aquaculture yields have increased steadily from less than 1 million tons in the 1950s to 52.5 million tons in 2009, with a continued projected annual growth of 8.3 percent (based on 1970–2008 increases). The world population has grown at a 1.6 percent average rate in that same time span. Biotechnology can play a critical role in helping to ensure that this harvest keeps increasing by producing healthier and faster-growing varieties of fish. The fact that this is possible is shown by the success of the AquaBounty Technologies company, which has bioengineered a variety of salmon that produces growth hormone all year long, instead of just the warmer seasons. As a result, the Aqua-Bounty salmon grow to full size twice as fast as other salmon. Such farmed salmon need only one and a half pounds of feed to produce one pound of high-protein fish, a sixfold improvement over cattle, which need ten pounds of feed to yield one pound of beef.[51]

But why stop there? With bioengineering, we could create faster-growing and healthier varieties of wild fish as well, thereby multiplying the bounty not just of fish farms, but of the vast ocean itself.

There need be no shortage of either loaves or fishes, and much sickness can indeed be driven from this Earth. Such is the promise of biotechnology.

*Comparison of AquaBounty genetically modified salmon with non-modified salmon at 18 months.*
(Photo courtesy of AquaBounty Technologies.)

## CHAPTER FIFTEEN

# Quenching Humanity's Fire: Global Warming and the Madness of Crowds

*No matter if the science is all phony, there are collateral environmental benefits. . . . Climate change [provides] the greatest chance to bring about justice and equality in the world.*

CHRISTINE STEWART
Canadian Minister of the Environment,
December 1998[1]

*The Book of Revelation [says] God will destroy those who destroy his creation. . . . Noah was commanded to preserve biodiversity. . . . Politics falls short of the minimum necessary to really address this crisis. . . . If you believe, if you accept the reality that we may have less than ten years before we cross a point of no return—if you believe that, this is a time for action.*

Former Vice President AL GORE
New York City town meeting
May 23, 2006[2]

NUCLEAR POWER represents unlimited resources for the future. Biotechnology is a tremendous enhancement of our ability to improve nature. Yet, as harmful as the loss of these technologies might be, human society could survive it. But there is one technology that civilization cannot do without: fire.

Since the dawn of mankind, the control of combustion has been

219

central to human life. According to the ancient Greek tale of Prometheus, it was fire, stolen from heaven, that uniquely enabled mankind to rise above the beasts. There is plenty of truth in this story. It was the use of fire by our proto-human ancestors to cook that allowed them to develop into beings with smaller digestive systems and bigger brains, literally becoming human in the process.[3] Fire allowed early humans to migrate out of their warm habitat in the Kenyan Rift Valley to settle the cold wilds of Ice Age Europe, Asia, and America, thereby transforming humanity from an East African biological curiosity into a global species. Fire allowed Neolithic farmers to turn grain into bread and clay into ceramic pots, and gave their Bronze and Iron Age successors the metal tools they needed to build houses, ships, and civilizations. Then, with the coming of the Industrial Revolution, fire-driven machines liberated mankind from the slavery of brute toil, replacing poverty with plenty, isolation with mobility, darkness with light, and ignorance with knowledge.

Without fire, there can be no human existence worthy of the name. Control access to fire, and you control humanity.

It is in this context that one must understand the campaign to stop global warming.

## THE GREENHOUSE EFFECT

Venus is a planet of steaming jungles. Or so it was speculated until 1962, when NASA's Mariner 2 probe reported that instead of boasting a tropical climate, Venus baked like an oven. Based simply on its distance from the Sun, scientists had anticipated an average temperature of $64°C$ ($147°F$)[4]; Mariner's instruments measured $330°C$.[5] As the astronomer Carl Sagan put it: "Venus is hell."

The disparity was astonishing, but it didn't take scientists long to explain it. The planet named for the Goddess of Love is in fact surrounded by a very thick atmosphere of carbon dioxide ($CO_2$).[6] Carbon dioxide molecules strongly absorb infrared radiation, which is the type of radiation given off by hot objects. A thick $CO_2$ atmos-

phere would thus act as a kind of greenhouse roof over the planet, letting sunlight in to warm the surface, but then trapping the heat below
before it could escape back into space. Thus was born, in popular
parlance, the "greenhouse effect."[7]

Fortunately, the discovery did not immediately start a panic.
While it was well-known in the 1960s that our industrial society was
producing increasing amounts of $CO_2$ emissions,[8] the atmosphere of
Venus contains 300,000 times as much $CO_2$ as Earth's.[9] It was clear
that no disaster could transform our planet into anything comparable
to the Venusian greenhouse. Furthermore, the Earth at that time was
actually undergoing a cooling trend, so the climate doomsayers of the
day were predicting global freezing.[10] In their book *Global Ecoscience*
(1971), John Holdren and Paul Ehrlich warned that particulate pollution from "overdeveloped countries" like the United States could
cause "another ice age," and it was for *this* reason that industrial
growth needed to be stopped.[11] So while taking fire away from human
beings was already on the antihumanists' agenda, global warming
was not the chosen pretext.

In the late 1970s, however, worldwide temperature measurements started to *increase*, and by the next decade some climatologists
began warning of a threat to society posed by a man-made greenhouse effect.[12]

Arriving at a time when the resource-depletion predictions of the
Club of Rome were all coming due but proving false, this new cause
was a godsend to the antihuman movement, allegedly providing clear
and damning proof that humanity's aspirations must be constrained
lest we destroy Nature. In contrast to industrial smoke, which can
be—and was—dealt with using pollution-control technology, $CO_2$
emissions cannot be stopped without radical restrictions on modern
civilization. Since coordination of efforts to counter the greenhouse
effect would require a massive expansion of government powers,
those favoring greater state control of economic life were quick to
jump on the global warming bandwagon as well. Thus, since the
1980s, the view that global warming is a real danger has become

increasingly popular among policymakers, leading to the signing of an international treaty in Kyoto in 1997 that would impose drastic anti-greenhouse countermeasures upon all its signatories.

On the other hand, precisely because of its implications for human freedom, some with more libertarian leanings have dismissed the global warming threat as little more than a hoax.[13] But is it?

The stakes in this debate are high. For example, it has been claimed that a sharp temperature increase could melt the glaciers of Greenland and Antarctica, resulting in a rise in the sea level of as much as 70 meters (230 feet).[14] Low-lying coastal areas would be flooded, and massive economic damage would result. On the other hand, government regulations in accordance with the Kyoto Protocol that would force the reduction of $CO_2$ emissions could stifle worldwide economic growth, causing millions of deaths and continued widespread misery through the perpetuation of global poverty.

The threat of catastrophic global warming is not an "issue" on which policymakers may choose a position that comports with their private beliefs. Either it is real, or it isn't. With the potential consequences of a mistaken response so serious, and with the antihuman movement's leading figures relying on global warming as a foundation of their argument, it behooves us to examine the matter in some detail. So let's have a careful look at the facts.

## IS GLOBAL WARMING REAL?

It can be difficult to measure the "global temperature," since the actual temperature differs from place to place, and the average temperature derived from a large number of stations can be severely skewed by the choice of location of the measuring stations. Nevertheless, serious efforts to provide an estimate of average global temperature through systematic worldwide thermometer readings have been made since about 1858. The data since 1880 from this research program is summarized in Figure 15.1. This is the best historical climate-change data set that there is, and it forms the basis of all the official analysis and policy documents issued by the U.N. Intergovernmental Panel on Climate Change (IPCC) and similar bodies. It can be seen that there has been an increase in global temperature of about 0.8 °C (1.4 °F) over the period in question.

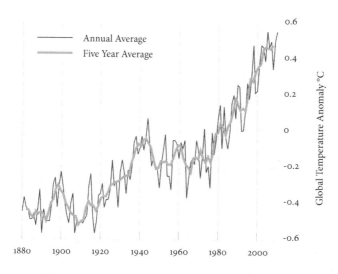

FIGURE 15.1: *Global average temperatures.*
*(Data from NASA's Goddard Institute for Space Studies.)*

So, as measured empirically since the mid-nineteenth century, global warming is certainly real. A temperature increase of 0.8 °C over 130 years works out to a rate of just over 0.06 °C (0.1 °F) per decade—not particularly alarming. It may be noted, however, that over the past thirty years the pace seems to have picked up. Measured over that time, the rate of increase is 0.17 °C (0.3 °F) per decade, or 1.7 °C (3 °F) per century.

And sea levels are rising, too. This is confirmed both by tidal gauges positioned all over the world and by altimetry data taken by NASA's TOPEX-Poseidon Satellite. The data from both sources is shown in Figure 15.2. It can be seen that world sea levels are currently rising at a rate of about 3 mm per year, or 30 cm (12 inches) per century.

So, if continued through the year 2100, the more rapid warming

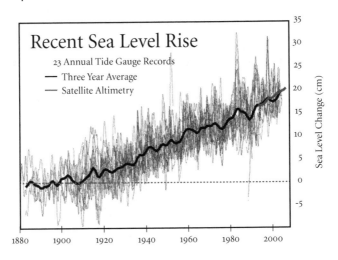

FIGURE 15.2: *Sea Level, 1880 to present.*
*(Source: Bruce Douglas, "Global Sea Rise: A Redetermination,"*
Surveys in Geophysics, 18:279–272, 1997.
*Updated graph courtesy of GlobalWarmingArt.com.)*

rate would have moderate effects, but these measurements give no support to alarmist assertions, like Al Gore's pronouncement that we only have ten years to stop global warming. After ten years at the current rate, global temperatures will increase less than 0.2 °C, and sea levels will rise 3 cm (1.2 inches). Neither of these outcomes would be catastrophic, or noticeable for that matter.

The next question is whether this warming trend is actually being caused by an increased concentration of $CO_2$ in the atmosphere. This question is hard to answer, because there are many other factors that affect climate. As shown in Figure 15.3, however, there is no doubt that global atmospheric $CO_2$ concentration is increasing, and has risen about 20 percent since 1958.[15]

The record shown in Figure 15.3 looks like saw teeth because atmospheric $CO_2$ concentration changes over the course of a year. Green plants absorb $CO_2$ during the spring and summer when they are actively growing. There is more land area in the Northern Hemi-

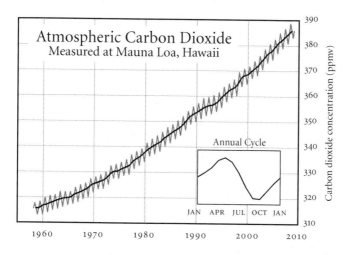

FIGURE 15.3: *Record of the CO2 in the atmosphere from 1958 to 2002.*

(*Source: Data from Mauna Loa Observatory.*
*Graph courtesy GlobalWarmingArt.com.*)

sphere than the Southern Hemisphere, so $CO_2$ concentration increases and decreases in accord with the Northern seasonal cycle, and these concentrations peak each year in March, just before the growing season starts in the North.[16]

Taking the data from Figures 15.1 and 15.3 together, we see that we have an approximately 20 percent increase in $CO_2$ over the same period that we observe a 0.4°C increase in global temperature. Could one have caused the other? Quite possibly. According to the mathematical models used by climatologists, each doubling of atmospheric $CO_2$ concentration should lead to a temperature increase on the order of 1.5 to 5°C.[17] If that's the case, then a $CO_2$ increase of 20 percent should cause a temperature increase of between 0.39 and 1.32°C.[18] Thus, the observed 0.4°C increase is a fair match for the low end of the theoretical predictions.

If we extend the rate of $CO_2$ concentration increase shown in Figure 15.3 forward another century, we get a prediction of about 575 parts per million (ppm) for the year 2100, which is half again today's level, and roughly double the pre-industrial level of 280 ppm.[19] Using the middle of the theoretical range—a temperature increase of 3.2°C per doubling of $CO_2$ concentration—we expect a temperature increase of 1.8°C (3.2°F) by 2100, close to our previous estimate of 2°C. Alternatively, if we assume a low-end temperature increase of 1.5°C per doubling of $CO_2$ concentration—as appears to be justified by the data so far—the result would be a 0.84°C (1.5°F) temperature rise by 2100.

In going from 315 ppm of atmospheric $CO_2$ in 1958 to 375 ppm today, we increased the total mass of carbon in the atmosphere from 630 gigatonnes (Gt) to 750 Gt (note that these figures count only the carbon, not the oxygen, in carbon dioxide).[20] Since coal is composed almost entirely of carbon, and natural gas and oil are 75 to 87 percent carbon, blaming humanity alone for this increase assumes that we burned at least 120 Gt of fossil fuels between 1958 and today. In fact, the actual amount of fossil fuels used worldwide over that period was around 250 Gt, so it is plausible that we are responsible for the observed increase in atmospheric carbon.[21] Further, the current climate models lead us to conclude that we would have caused an even bigger increase, if it weren't for the ability of the biosphere to take in our $CO_2$ emissions and turn them into plant material. So, as well as such things can be argued, the basic case is strong: human beings may well be changing the climate of the Earth.

But before you go enlist with Al Gore, you should stop and take a look at the data presented in Figures 15.4, 15.5, and 15.6. Here we see a much broader history of temperature data than that measured by the thermometers deployed since 1858.

Let's start with Figure 15.4, which shows the temperature of the Sargasso Sea, a region of the middle North Atlantic Ocean, as determined by isotope ratios of marine organism remains.[22] Preserved in sediment on the sea floor, these fossils provide us with a temperature record that covers not 150 years, but 3,000 years. These data, which comport with paleoclimatological data collected in other studies at

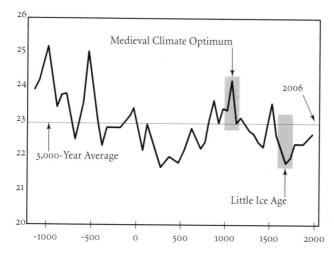

FIGURE 15.4: *Surface temperatures in the Sargasso Sea.*
*(Graph courtesy* Journal of American Physicians and Surgeons.*)*

various locations, show a period of higher temperatures 1,000 years
ago ("Medieval Climate Optimum") and lower temperatures 300
years ago ("Little Ice Age"). The horizontal line is the average temperature for the 3,000-year period.

It may be true that the world today is warming up; but it is a fact
that a thousand years ago it was significantly warmer. A millennium
ago, the snow line in the Rockies was a thousand feet higher than it is
now, and Canadian forests flourished tens of kilometers further
north. Oats and barley were grown in Iceland, wheat in Norway, hay
in Greenland. As far north as York, the vineyards of England produced fine wines.[23] These warm temperatures were no disaster. On
the contrary, they are believed by historians to have contributed
materially to the growth of population and prosperity in Europe during the High Middle Ages (roughly the years from 1000 to 1300).

In Figure 15.5, we show global temperature for the past 420,000
years, estimated from ice core data.[24] Here we see that the temperature rose about 8°C from the end of the last Ice Age, 18,000 years
ago, to the dawn of civilization, several thousand years later.

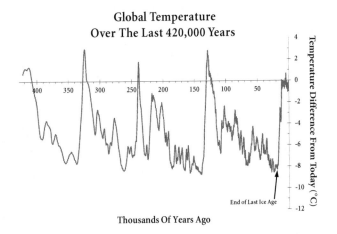

**FIGURE 15.5:** *Global Temperature over the Past 420,000 years.*

*(Data from Vostok Ice Core, NOAA/NGDC Paleoclimatology Program.)*

In Figure 15.6, the history of the Earth's climate since the end of the age of dinosaurs is shown, based on data derived from examining oxygen isotopic ratios in sea-floor material.[25] Clearly the overall trend has been a cooling one, with average temperature dropping 19°C (34°F) over the past 50 million years.

If we consider Figures 15.4, 15.5, and 15.6 together, two remarkable generalizations stand out. In the first place, the natural variations in Earth's temperature exceed possible man-made warming effects to date by a long shot. Second, despite these significant natural temperature wanderings, in the largest scheme of things, Earth's temperature does not change very much. This can only imply that, considered as a system, the Earth's climate is *stable*.

Stable systems are those that, when perturbed by outside influences, tend to return to their original condition. Unstable systems, in contrast, respond to perturbations by increasing the disturbance. By way of analogy, think of a ball in a crater as representing a stable system, and a ball on a hill as an unstable one: kick a ball around in the

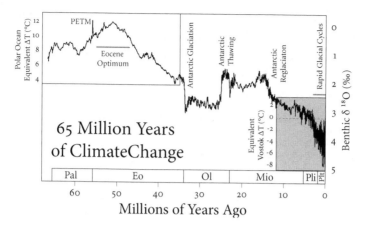

FIGURE 15.6: *Deep ocean temperatures over the last 65 million years.*
(*Graph courtesy GlobalWarmingArt.com.*)

crater and it will roll back roughly to the center; kick the unstable ball even a little off the summit and it will roll completely off the hill.

Earth's climate may get kicked out of place from time to time, but it always rolls back. This is a fundamental feature of the biosphere; it acts to regulate climate to ensure that it always stays within parameters acceptable for life. For example, let's say $CO_2$ concentrations were to increase due to some natural event such as volcanic activity. The increased $CO_2$ level would cause some global warming to occur, which in turn would cause increased water evaporation from the surface, and thus increased rainfall. Both $CO_2$ and water availability are limiting constraints on plant growth, and with more of each, photosynthetic activity would be increased on a global scale. As a result, the plants would both grow more leaf area, and consume more carbon dioxide per unit of leaf area per day, until the carbon dioxide addition to the atmosphere was devoured and the warming trend reversed. The increased tree cover would not go away instantly when things returned to "normal," however, and so $CO_2$ levels would generally be pushed below their original level. This would go on until the resulting global cooling decreased vegetative activity until carbon dioxide levels, and thus temperature, had a chance to rebound. For the past several hundred million years, this built-in negative feedback against climate change, along with other similar negative feedback effects, has served to keep global temperatures within limits acceptable to life, regardless of many strong temperature perturbations introduced into the system by outside forces. This built-in stability proves that all claims that anthropogenic global warming could trigger a runaway greenhouse effect are nonsensical.

Thus the system can oscillate, like the ball rolling around the basin of the crater, but always stays within fairly well-confined parameters. There is some change, however, over eons of geologic time. This is because the biosphere is evolving. For example, looking at Figure 15.6, we see the basic trend over the past 65 million years is one involving significant global cooling since the time of the Paleocene-Eocene Thermal Maximum (PETM), whose atmosphere of about 2,000 ppm of $CO_2$ supported a global climate that was 12 °C warmer than our own.[26] During the same period, new types of plants appeared, capable of using carbon dioxide more efficiently. The most important of these were the grasses, which, originating at the end of the Paleocene about 58 million years ago, drove temperatures sharply down from that point on. Things then stabilized in the Oligocene, until the mid-Miocene, about 15 million years ago, when new types of grasses appeared.[27] These more advanced grasses, dubbed $C_4$ as compared to the previous $C_3$ varieties, were much more efficient at utilizing $CO_2$, and, as they replaced their predecessors, they drove atmospheric carbon dioxide levels below 300 ppm for the first time in Earth's history. In the process, they sent the planet's climate plunging into a glacial age that has continued to the present day.

The fact that the Earth's atmospheric $CO_2$ concentration was about 280 ppm shortly before the Industrial Revolution implies that this value is close to the equilibrium level for the modern biosphere. As human industrial activity raises $CO_2$ concentration, plant productivity will increase, causing the biosphere to push back like a spring, with the force of its push becoming stronger the further the system is displaced from equilibrium.

This brings us to the heart of the matter. Human industrial $CO_2$ emissions may be having a modest effect on climate, but they are having a *positive* effect on plant growth worldwide; one study has shown a 14 percent increase in plant growth in the United States in the second half of the twentieth century, with increased carbon dioxide levels as a contributing factor.[28] Studies done at Oak Ridge National Laboratory on forest trees have shown that increasing the concentration of $CO_2$ to 550 ppm, the level projected for the end of the twenty-first century, will likely increase photosynthetic productivity for both agricultural and wild plants by at least a further 24 percent.[29] Furthermore, to the extent that this concentration causes any increase in temperature—and thus evaporation rate—of the oceans, global warming will increase worldwide rainfall. Finally, by lengthening the growing season, global warming promises to increase still further the bounties of both agriculture and nature.

In other words, from any rational point of view, global warming is a very *good* thing. By enriching the carbon dioxide content of the atmosphere from its impoverished pre-industrial levels, *human beings have increased the productivity of the entire biosphere*—so much so that as many as one out of every seven plants on the planet owes its sustenance to the marvelous improvement in nature that humans have effected.[30] *Through our $CO_2$ emissions we are making the Earth a more fertile world.*

The global-cooling doomsayers of the 1970s may have been wrong, but they denounced something that, had it been real, would have been bad. Leading as it would to a drier, colder, more sterile planet, global cooling could indeed have been a disaster. Had the threat of another ice age actually been valid, a forceful government effort to avert catastrophe might have been justified. But as the blame for global cooling could not conclusively be assigned to humanity, the case did not hold the interest of humanity's prosecutors.

In contrast, the role of humanity in raising global $CO_2$ levels is more or less clear, and the empowerment of authority legitimized by the alleged need to suppress it is enormous. The fact that such alteration of atmospheric composition is constructive and highly beneficial to both mankind and the natural world is ignored. Rather, for those seeking cause to oppress humanity, any change in nature effected by humans is criminal on its face. Since all human activity must perforce release $CO_2$, all human existence is a crime against nature. Therefore nothing we can do is right—and so, in the name of the Higher Good, we must be constrained to do as little as possible.

*We have only ten years left to stop global warming, says Al Gore in his sensational 2006 movie* An Inconvenient Truth, *predicting total destruction unless human aspirations are curbed. Above, Gore blames global warming for Hurricane Katrina. Gore also warns of floods, droughts, plagues, and a runaway greenhouse effect that could cause the Earth to become another Venus.*

Thus, the global warming argument recasts the basic Malthusian line in a novel form, but with the equivalent end result. Instead of claiming that human activity must be limited because there are not enough resources, it is said that what is limited is not resources, but the right to use resources. It all amounts to the same thing: there isn't enough to go around, therefore human aspirations must be crushed, and authorities must be constituted that are capable of doing the crushing. Q.E.D. Tyranny is necessary.

## HUMAN SACRIFICE FOR WEATHER CONTROL

The cure of choice for global warming is human sacrifice. Of course, as with all such programs, it would be uncomfortable for those seeking to curb the appetites of others to endure the same constraints themselves. Therefore, the partisans of global warming governance have conceived of an opportunity-limiting concept called "cap and trade." Under this approach, those wishing to commit the sin of carbon use would be allowed to purchase an indulgence provided by the Regulatory Bureaucracy of the Church of the Climatic Apocalypse. In this way people of quality would be freed from carbon sin, and allowed to consume as desired without unnecessary limitations— such inconvenience being reserved for the rabble of lost souls, too improvident, alas, to pay for their salvation. As an added benefit, some of the revenue acquired by First World governments through the sale of such indulgences could be used to reward those virtuous leaders of underdeveloped nations who nobly prevent their subjects from increasingly using carbon. In other words, under cap and trade, advanced-sector nations will impose highly regressive carbon taxation domestically, and transfer some of the take to Third World despots to pay them to keep their people poor.

The economic burden of the proposed cap-and-trade scheme would be great. Today, the United States produces about 5.5 billion tonnes of $CO_2$ per year.[31] Under the most recent cap-and-trade proposal, the Waxman-Markey bill (passed by the U.S. House of Representatives in 2009 and later killed in the Senate), the federal government would sell to the public permits for the emission of $CO_2$, allowing a number of permits near current emissions levels and falling off over time. The Congressional Budget Office (CBO) notes that estimates for the cost of these permits range from $18 per tonne to nearly $50 per tonne in 2020, and $70–160 by 2050.[32] As the number of permits issued falls, the cost per permit steeply increases. So, billed to the U.S. economy as a whole, under any of these estimates, cap and trade would cost the public hundreds of billions of dollars.

The Heritage Foundation estimates that Waxman-Markey would have cost the U.S. economy $161 billion in 2020—or $1,870 for a family of four, rising to $6,800 by 2035. The costs would be stratified so as to be borne more by those with higher incomes; even so, this represents a substantial economic burden. As a result of the markup of carbon costs, businesses would be burdened as well, meaning that many working families would be out of work and unable to pay their existing bills, let alone new ones.[33]

Consider that burning one tonne of coal produces about 2.5 tonnes of $CO_2$. So a tax of even $20 per tonne of $CO_2$ emitted (a *low-end* estimate for the Waxman-Markey bill's cost by 2020) would be the equivalent to a tax of $50 per tonne on coal. The price of anthracite coal runs in the neighborhood of $57 per ton, so under the proposed system, such coal would be taxed at a rate of nearly 100 percent.[34] The price of Western bituminous coal is about $14 per ton. This coal would therefore be taxed at a rate of over 300 percent. Coal provides almost half of America's electricity, so such extraordinary levies could easily double the electric bills paid by consumers and businesses across half the nation. In addition, many businesses, such as the metals and chemical industries, use a great deal of coal directly. By doubling or potentially even quadrupling the cost of their most basic feedstock, the cap-and-trade system's indulgence fees could make many such businesses uncompetitive and ultimately throw millions of working men and women into the unemployment lines.

Similarly, the CBO estimates that, under cap and trade, gasoline prices would increase by 40 cents per gallon by 2018, and up to $1.70 per gallon over the next forty years.[35] This would not only hit consumers' pockets, but increase transportation costs throughout the economy, hobbling businesses and further increasing unemployment. While harming the economy, such a gas tax would do nothing material toward the truly essential goal of decreasing America's dependence on foreign oil. Indeed, the bill's dramatic hikes in electricity costs would have the opposite effect, since, by forcefully increasing electric power costs, the bill would actually be likely to discourage adoption of electric means of transportation in many areas, including mass-transit systems today and potentially plug-in hybrid cars in the future.

There is another danger even worse than the implicit taxes that would result from passing into law a cap-and-trade scheme like the one outlined in the Waxman-Markey Bill: *tax farming*. A bit of history is useful here. When ancient Near Eastern potentates wanted ready cash to fund their wars, human-sacrifice community centers, or other worthy projects, they sold the right to loot various districts within their kingdoms to wealthy gangsters, known as tax farmers.[36] In this win-win arrangement, the rulers got the gold they needed without any fuss or bother, while the tax farmers secured themselves a handsome return on their investment by deploying thugs to mercilessly loot the peasants within their jurisdiction. Everybody who mattered was happy.[37]

Cap-and-trade carbon-permit tax farming would work similarly. When the carbon emission permits are offered by the government for sale, most of them could be bought by speculators with sufficient ready cash to snatch them up. By doing so, these speculators could secure for themselves *the power to tax without limit* anyone who needed to use combustion to stay in business. Since the entire purpose of the cap-and-trade system is to fix the total amount of society's carbon-emitting activities—with the stated aim, in the Waxman-Markey Bill, of reducing U.S. carbon emissions by over 80 percent by the year 2050—the price of the permits would soar, allowing the carbon-tax farmers to strangle and loot the productive sectors of the economy at will.[38] Opportunities for paid employment would become increasingly hard to find. Monopolies would persist, but with their costs vastly inflated by their need to pay tribute to the carbon tax farmers. These costs would then be passed on to consumers, with the poor being hurt the most.

The most alarming potential for tragedy from cap and trade, however, is not domestic, but in the possible impact on the world's food supply. Modern agriculture is one of the greatest success stories in human history. In 1930, hunger still stalked the entire globe. Not just in Africa, India, and China, but even in Europe and America, the struggle to simply get enough food to live on still preoccupied billions of people. Since 1930, the world population has tripled. But instead of going hungrier, people nearly everywhere are now eating much better. This miracle depends upon the availability of cheap fertilizer and pesticides, which in turn require carbon-based energy to produce. If you tax carbon, you tax fertilizer and pesticides—and, in turn, you tax food, and by no small amount. A tax of $20 per tonne of $CO_2$ would directly increase fertilizer production costs by roughly $50 per tonne, with the cap-and-trade bill's increased transport costs inflating the burden still more.[39] That's enough to make many farmers use less fertilizer, and less fertilizer means less food.

To get a sense of what it would mean for farmers to abandon fertilizer, it is only necessary to go to the supermarket and compare the price of the "organic" produce, grown without chemical fertilizer, to the regular produce, which typically costs less than half as much. It is one matter for wealthy organic food buffs to choose to pay such high prices for their food—that is their right. But to impose such costs for basic groceries on everyone else, and particularly the poor, as part of a largely symbolic effort to try to change the weather, is arrogant in the extreme. Forcing the abandonment of fertilizer worldwide could starve billions.

These are just a few examples of the likely destructive effects of cap and trade. The $20 per tonne $CO_2$ tax is just the government's cut. Carbon tax farmers will charge a lot more. As a result, the prices of not only electricity, fertilizer, and food but all products requiring energy to produce or transport are certain to soar. The effects would seep through the entire global economy, with disastrous consequences.

Yet this is the program that has been embraced by nearly all advanced-sector political parties claiming to represent the plebeian interest.

## ENERGY STARVATION THROUGH CARTEL ACTION

The antihuman movement does not need to wait for a cap-and-trade regime to be established in order to deny the world the power it needs to grow. They possess a potent weapon to enforce an energy starvation program: the OPEC oil cartel. In fact, this effort has already begun.

From the end of World War II through 1973, the global economy grew at unprecedented rates. Europe and Japan were rebuilt, and then radically advanced. The United States was transformed from Depression America, hoping to provide a chicken for each family pot, to Suburban America, with color TVs, two cars for every family, and the majority of middle-class kids going to college. Many new countries, such as South Korea and Taiwan, began rapid industrialization. Had this rate of growth been allowed to continue, there might be no mass privation in the world today.

But in 1973, OPEC slammed on the brakes. The postwar global economic boom was enabled by cheap oil prices, which was ensured by the international oil companies—the "Seven Sisters": British Petroleum, Shell, Chevron, Exxon, Gulf, Texaco, and Mobil—who planned ahead and expanded oil production to match growing global demand.[40] World oil prices, adjusted for inflation, were thus flat from 1947 to 1972. But in 1972, Egyptian president Anwar Sadat threw the Soviets out of Egypt. This freed the Saudis of the need for American bayonets for protection against the Communist menace. Thus emboldened, they proceeded to use the 1973 Arab-Israeli War as a pretext to lead OPEC in launching a global embargo that quadrupled the price of oil virtually overnight. This action, along with other actions taken at the time, resulted in the effective seizure of control of the international oil business. In place of the Seven Sisters, the cartel of state-run petroleum companies operated by the OPEC governments was now running the show, and the new management had a new policy: instead of increasing production to facilitate growth of the market, they would constrict production in order to loot the world economy.

Proof of OPEC's *modus operandi* is shown very clearly in Figures 15.7 and 15.8, which present price and production figures for both non-OPEC and OPEC countries from 1973 to 2010. The prices shown for both the non-OPEC and OPEC groups are the same, as oil is fungible and there is only one international price. But look at the difference in the pattern of production. Between 1973 and 2010 the output of non-OPEC countries nearly doubled, rising steadily from 24 to 43 million barrels per day. This is what one would expect, as the world economy more than tripled in size over the same 37-year period.[41] In contrast, the OPEC production figures show no clear pattern; they jump up and down at random. This shows that the cartel

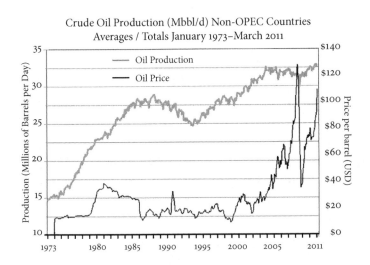

Crude Oil Production (Mbbl/d) Non-OPEC Countries
Averages / Totals January 1973–March 2011

FIGURE 15.7: *Non-OPEC oil production*
*and price, 1973–2010.*
(*Courtesy WTRG Economics*)

was engaged in tactical manipulation of the market. What is more striking, however, is the fact that *in 2010 OPEC production was no greater than it was in 1973.*

This is almost unbelievable, but just look at the data in Figure 15.8. In 1973, OPEC production was 30 million barrels per day. In 2010, OPEC production was 30 million barrels per day. That is, over a period during which the world economy grew threefold, OPEC production did not increase at all, despite the fact that the OPEC governments are sitting on top of 80 percent of the world's oil reserves, including all of the oil that is easiest to drill. In contrast, over the 30 years prior to 1973, while under the control of the Seven Sisters, the production of the countries that later became OPEC increased tenfold.[42]

The purpose of OPEC policy is to create a shortage of petroleum relative to the needs of the market, thereby driving prices up. The achievement of this contrived shortage has been greatly facilitated by the antihumanists in the United States and elsewhere, who have done everything in their power to prevent domestic drilling by Western

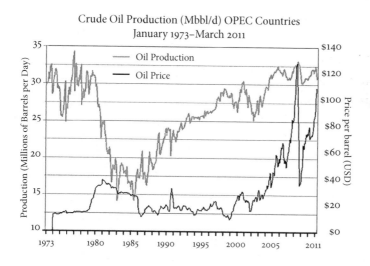

FIGURE 15.8: *OPEC oil production and price, 1973–2010.*

*(Courtesy WTRG Economics)*

nations. As a result, oil prices today are at least triple what they would be in a free-market economy.[43]

The effects of this huge tax on the world economy, levied by a conspiracy of some of the worst governments in the world, are appalling. American motorists are justly annoyed when they have to pay excessive prices for gasoline at the pump, but the effects of OPEC price rigging are much more serious than that, and severely impact the entire world. It is one thing to pay $75 per barrel when you live in a country like the United States, where the average worker makes over $20 per hour.[44] It is quite another if you live in a Third World nation where people make $3 per day. In 2008, oil spiked above $130 per barrel—ten times what it had cost in 1999.[45] America paid about $676 billion for the oil it used in 2008; when adjusted for inflation, that is six times what it paid just a decade earlier. In other words, even though the United States *only consumed 3 percent more oil* in 2008 than it did in 1998, the country *paid almost 500 percent more* for the oil it used.[46] Such a tax increase (mostly paid to Uncle Saud instead of Uncle Sam, but a tax all the same) is more than enough to cause a recession—and it did. Divided among 117 million American households, the $560 billion extra cost for oil in 2008 works out to about an extra $4,800 per household.[47] So each American household was paying about 12 percent of its after-tax income for that increased burden.[48] It is easy to see how the price spike in particular helped spark the deep economic recession that began in 2008. Indeed, some economists estimate that an increase of 10 percent in the price of crude oil drops the U.S. GDP by as much as 1 percent.[49]

The impact of OPEC's contrived shortages can be seen by looking at the effects of the oil-price hikes we have suffered for the past four decades, including those in 1973, 1979, 1991, 2001, and 2008. Each oil-price rise has been followed by a sharp rise in American unemployment. (See Figure 15.9.)

The distress to American workers caused by such events is manifest, but the economic damage goes far beyond the impact on the unemployed themselves. Since the United States imports 5 billion bar-

## Oil Price vs. U.S. Unemployment Rate

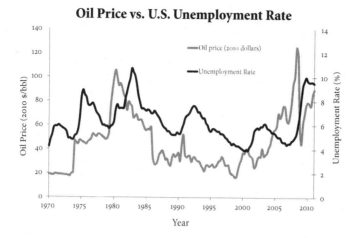

FIGURE 15.9: *Oil Price vs. U.S. Unemployment Rate.*

rels of oil per year, a sustained oil price of $100 per barrel contributes $500 billion to the U.S. balance-of-trade deficit. Furthermore, there is a direct and well-established relationship between unemployment rates and rates of mortgage defaults. The $130-per-barrel oil shock of 2008 threw 5 million Americans out of work, and in so doing it made many of them default on their home payments—and thus helped destroy the value of the mortgage-backed securities held by America's banks. This, in turn, threatened a general collapse of the financial system, with a bailout bill for $800 billion sent to the taxpayers as a result. But that is not all. The destruction of spending power of the unemployed and the draining of funds from everyone else to meet the direct and indirect costs of high oil prices reduced consumer demand for products of every type, thereby wrecking retail sales and the industries that depend upon them. And as the economy goes down, so do federal tax revenues, thereby exploding the national deficit.

Moreover, the oil tax didn't just hit us; it hit the entire globe. And a tax big enough to instigate recession in the United States can cause starvation in the Third World.

The events of 2008 may seem extreme—and they were—but even

under the conditions that have been considered "normal" since 1973, OPEC's oil tax has had its effect. While there have been periods of relative prosperity, and even rapid growth in certain places, the global postwar economic boom has not returned, and billions of people remain trapped in poverty as a result.

But there can be no doubt. If you want to reduce carbon emissions (and all other human activity), high oil prices are the way to go, and under this banner, the Islamist antihumanists of OPEC and the secular antihumanists of the global warming crusade stand united.

Because of its obviously detrimental effect on the U.S. economy, the need to break free from dependency on foreign oil has for some time been part of the canon recited by nearly every candidate running for high public office in the United States. There are, however, only two ways to accomplish this. The most obvious is to open up drilling development everywhere we can, but the political obstacles to doing so are enormous. The alternative is to make it possible for cars to run on fuels that are not dependent upon petroleum for their production. The best practical answer along these lines is methanol, which can be made from coal, natural gas, recycled trash, or any kind of biomass without exception, including crop and forestry residues.[50] It is cheap, too: the current price of methanol on the international market (without any subsidy) is about $1.25 per gallon.[51] The actual cost of manufacture is about $0.50 per gallon.[52] Methanol has about half the energy per gallon as gasoline, so you need to double these numbers to get the gasoline equivalent, but methanol is still highly competitive in price, and the resource base for its manufacture is essentially unlimited.[53]

But most importantly, there is a practical way to transition to a methanol fuel economy. Flex-fuel cars can be made that can run on gasoline, ethanol, and methanol, adding only about $100 to the cost of production.[54] If this feature were made the American standard, it would rapidly become the international standard, since foreign car makers would switch their lines over in order to be able to sell their vehicles here. In short order, every car being sold in significant numbers internationally would be a flex-fuel car, and within just a few years there would be tens of millions of such cars in the United States and hundreds of millions worldwide, granting their owners fuel choice.[55]

Under those conditions, there would be a global vehicle market for alcohol fuels, and market forces would impel many gas station owners in many countries to install alcohol pumps. Then gasoline would be forced to globally compete against both methanol and ethanol, and OPEC's power to set fuel prices would be broken.

This, however, is not the outcome desired by OPEC, nor by the global warming movement—which brings us to the subject of yet another means of denying fire to humanity.

## THE IRRATIONALITY OF "INDIRECT ANALYSIS"

The cap-and-trade scheme proposes to limit humanity's use of fire by controlling the issuance of permits. The oil cartel accomplishes the same goal by rigging up the price of fuel. There is a third method: preventive regulation of business in accord with a new principle called "indirect analysis."

A bit of background is in order here. For a number of years, environmentalists had supported the production of ethanol, on the principle that since it is a product of plant photosynthesis, using ethanol adds less $CO_2$ to the atmosphere than the gasoline it displaces. This was in keeping with traditional environmentalist practice of voicing support for many futuristic technologies that offer advantages against current industries, so long as the novelties remain impractical. By claiming to support ethanol, environmentalists could argue that new domestic drilling was unnecessary—a nice diversion so long as ethanol remained insignificant. But the corn ethanol industry eventually solved its technical problems, and starting around 2003, it took off, growing fourfold over the next six years.[56] By 2007, U.S. ethanol production had risen to the point where it replaced 5 percent of U.S. gasoline consumption,[57] and, together with ethanol programs in other nations, was actually beginning to have a worldwide impact. In fact, ethanol caused a 15 percent erosion of global oil prices, according to a Merrill Lynch analyst.[58]

While of significant benefit to consumers, this outcome was not pleasing to either the masters of OPEC or the environmentalists, both of whom would like to see oil prices as high as possible. Furthermore, the recruitment of large numbers of U.S. corn growers to ethanol production threatened to create a political constituency linked to the formidable U.S. farm lobby that would have the power to obtain legislation requiring that all new cars sold in the United States be flex-fueled. The passage of such a bill, which was actually introduced into both the Senate and House of Representatives in 2008 and again in years since,[59] would represent disaster for the oil cartel.[60] In early 2008, a worldwide anti-ethanol campaign was unleashed, managed in part by the gigantic public relations firm Glover Park—the very same organization responsible for running Al Gore's global warming hysteria campaign (and which, incidentally, is listed by the U.S. Department of Justice as an agent of the United Arab Emirates).[61]

The centerpiece of this campaign was a very well publicized 2008 paper authored by Timothy Searchinger, now affiliated with Princeton University's Woodrow Wilson School.[62] (The study, widely circulated by the German Marshall Fund, was originally published in *Science*— although it is worth noting that Searchinger is not a scientist; he is a lawyer who recently worked as a staff attorney for the Environmental Defense Fund, the organization best known for its role in the banning of DDT.) In the paper, Searchinger agreed that, because it replaced gasoline derived from petroleum with fuel derived from biomass, using corn ethanol directly decreased carbon emissions. However, according to Searchinger, since the program also reduced corn exports to Third World countries, it *indirectly* increased net global carbon emissions by encouraging the expansion of agriculture abroad.

The Searchinger paper caused nearly every environmentalist organization to reverse its previous support for ethanol, but its effects went far beyond that.[63] In consequence of the wide acclaim accorded its very original methodology, the regulatory agencies of the state of California and then the U.S. Environmental Protection Agency announced that they would henceforth assess the *indirect* global warming consequences of any project, and issue or reject permits based on those assessments.[64] The implications of this are enormous.

Searchinger's methodology has been criticized by scientists, and rightly so.[65] His "indirect analysis" approach is systematically flawed and has nothing in common with the scientific method. Using the same sort of analysis employed by Searchinger—that is, making broad claims of global effects stemming from undemonstrated causal relationships—it is possible to "prove" practically anything.[66] Claims of indirect effects of the U.S. corn ethanol program—or any other domestic program—on agriculture or deforestation elsewhere are not measurable or falsifiable, and so are not scientific assertions.

A more cogent critique of Searchinger's approach, however, would also be a moral one. Searchinger's argument, now embraced by the Obama administration's EPA, asserts that it should be the proper goal of American policy to constrict the economic growth of underdeveloped nations. This is not just a matter of concern for the Third World. In fact, if accepted as regulatory guidance, "indirect analysis" prevents the implementation of any positive activities in the United States itself—not just in biofuel production, but in any field of endeavor whatsoever.

Consider: If an American shops for groceries, regardless of their origin, he or she is acting to bid up the price of agricultural commodities internationally, encouraging the growth of agriculture everywhere, and thus plausibly deforestation. So anything that allows Americans to buy more groceries can be said to cause deforestation and thus global warming. Therefore, according to indirect analysis, any policy or technological development that contributes to income growth or an increased employment rate in the U.S. needs to be prevented. Instead of seeking to stimulate the economy, we should be seeking to depress it.

But that is not all. We should think twice about encouraging high-fuel-economy cars because, by reducing the amount that consumers spend on gas, such vehicles indirectly allow more to be spent on groceries and thereby contribute to deforestation. According to indirect analysis, public education should also be shut down because it leads to higher incomes. Health care should be gutted and the EPA's commendable activity in combating toxic air pollution should be reversed because they are extending the lives of millions of Americans, allowing them to buy things and heat up the planet.

The standard of indirect analysis turns ethics on its head. Everything good must be classed as evil, and all evil praised as good. What might be the next target—vitamins? Prior to the discovery of vitamins, millions of poor people with limited diets were weakened or killed by nutritional deficiencies. Now these people survive and they have a huge collective carbon footprint. Indirect analysis leads us to conclude that vitamins are bad, and that antibiotics and vaccines are much worse. But even these pale before the global warming threat posed by public sanitation and clean drinking water. To take this topsy-turvy approach to its logical conclusion, an environmental impact statement would have to be required every time a midwife assists in the birth of a child (if not earlier).

According to indirect analysis, all measures—including individual acts—that improve the economy, education, health, the environment, or technology are to be condemned. So long as humanity engages in any activities that cause carbon emissions, anything that helps humanity can also be said to cause global warming. The ethic motivating indirect analysis should be recognized for what it really is: Malthusian ideology in its most brutal form. Not only conservatives, but liberals, too, should be wary of making common cause with it, because all of the proudest accomplishments of both modern and historical liberalism—child labor laws, minimum wage laws, public schools, libraries, urban sanitation, childhood vaccinations, public health services, rural electrification, transportation infrastructure, social security, clean air and water laws, civil rights laws, and even emancipation, popular enfranchisement, representative government, and independence from colonial rule—all indirectly contribute to carbon emissions. The standard of indirect analysis would have us reject every one of these advances.

## CREATING A GLOBAL ANTIHUMAN CULT

The global warming crusade contains a threat that goes well beyond societal regulation and enforced economic stagnation. Unlike the campaigns against DDT, nuclear power, and genetically modified crops—but very much like the eugenics movement—the global warming cause is universal enough to serve as the basis of a pseudo-religion.[67] This potential is the subject of remarks by the movement's leaders themselves. In *An Inconvenient Truth*, leading global warming demagogue Al Gore says:

> The climate crisis also offers us the chance to *experience* what very few generations in history have had the *privilege of knowing*: a *generational mission*; the *exhilaration* of a *compelling moral purpose*; a *shared and unifying cause*; the *thrill* of being forced by circumstances to put aside the pettiness and conflict that so often stifle the restless *human need for transcendence*; the opportunity to *rise*. . . . When we rise, *we will experience an epiphany* as we discover that this crisis is not really about politics at all. It is a *moral and spiritual challenge*.[68]

In other words, it is clear that for Gore, global warming agitation is not really about climate change at all. Put simply, it's not about weather, it's about power. The movement is everything, the goal is nothing. It's not about curbing $CO_2$ emissions; it's about creating a mob—a mass cult whose legions empower its shamans, and whose systematic antihuman ideology serves as a basis for reorganizing society along totalitarian lines.

With practically unlimited funds and media support, the campaign to create the cult is now well underway. Leading from the front has been Gore himself, who became a worldwide superstar by producing his *Inconvenient Truth* in the form of a sensational documentary predicting an imminent global apocalypse of rising sea levels, droughts, plagues, heat waves, hurricanes, and conflagrations unless swift and forceful action is taken to rein in humanity. Cheered on by enraptured press that blacked out all scientific criticism—including even that of the establishment global warming crowd at the IPCC—Gore's film was boosted to become one of the most successful propaganda pieces of all time: it pulled in $49 million at the box office, with Gore netting an Oscar and a Nobel Prize.[69] Building on this success, Gore went on to collect a galaxy of Hollywood and rock music celebrities to hold colossal events designed to spread the "thrill" and "exhilaration" of joining the new "shared and unifying cause."

Like all cults, this new one adeptly represses heresy. While previous incarnations of the antihuman movement may have wished to block out contrary viewpoints, none of them, with the exception of openly totalitarian travesties like German Nazism and Chinese Maoism, has ever had the temerity to publicly demand the *silencing* of their opponents. Anti-nuclear activists certainly wanted to shut down the industry, but to the best of my knowledge, they never demanded that its publications be suppressed. Not so the global warming fanatics. In defiance of the Western scientific tradition, which maintains that skepticism of inferences drawn from observation is always in order, and that all accepted conclusions are always subject to review and potential overthrow by new data, the climate catastrophists insist that "the science is settled" (science is *never* "settled") and that therefore no debate, and no new data, can or should be entertained.[70] Those wishing to advance theories or data contrary to the accepted orthodoxy are not merely wrong, but criminal "deniers" who should be silenced, vilified, and if possible, prosecuted.

James Hansen, a leading global warming activist at NASA's Goddard Institute for Space Studies in New York, testified before Congress on June 23, 2008 that "fossil fuel companies choose to spread doubt about global warming. . . . CEOs of fossil energy companies know what they are doing and are aware of the long-term consequences of continued business as usual. In my opinion, these CEOs should be tried for high crimes against humanity and nature."[71] Going further, British barrister Polly Higgins has submitted a proposal to the U.N. that would define "ecocide" as an international crime comparable to genocide, thereby making "deniers" (a term chosen to vilify such skeptics by comparing them to Holocaust deniers) subject to prosecution for conspiracy to commit "crimes against peace."[72] Not to be outdone, *New York Times* columnist and Nobel Prize-winning economist Paul Krugman has denounced all those who speak or vote against cap-and-trade legislation as being guilty of "treason against the planet."[73] (In the United States, treason carries the death penalty.)

It would be a mistake to dismiss these strident voices as mere maniacal ravings. As such radical proposals are repeated, they lose their shock value, and eventually become respectable. Moreover, simply by being advanced, they serve the purpose of severely denigrating the skeptics so that their arguments need not be entertained. Over the past several years, many climate scientists have presented data that call into question much of the orthodoxy of the IPCC.[74] On the basis of the most recent information, it appears that global warming is slowing down. Correlations have also been identified between the current and previous warming periods and solar cycles, suggesting that the influence of $CO_2$ on current climate change may be less important than previously believed. Anomalies have surfaced, including measurements taken by 3,000 submersible robots that show no increase at all in ocean temperatures over the past five years.[75] If correct, these findings would disintegrate any semblance of a case for undertaking the destructive measures advocated by the climate fear-mongers.

It could be that the climate alarmists have answers to rebut these critics and their data, but if so, they are not showing it. Rather than engaging in scientific debate, they have evaded it, choosing instead to try to stop dissenting publications and cut off the funding of their opponents. That is not the way to do science. That is the way to do fraud.

## CHAPTER SIXTEEN

# The Mind Imprisoned or the Soul Unchained

*The mind is its own place, and in it self*
*Can make a Heav'n of Hell, a Hell of Heav'n.*
JOHN MILTON, *Paradise Lost*[1]

MEN ARE BORN free and equal; naturally endowed not only with life, but liberty, and the right to pursue happiness. To turn such beings into slaves, oppressors require means of constraint: chains and fetters, dungeons and jails. This is the service that antihumanism renders—it seeks to put humanity in a pen, one whose bars are invisible because they are made not of mere steel but of thought; a torture chamber of unlimited expanse, equipped with shackles for every soul; a locked compound within whose walls compassion cannot exist; a prison far more confining than any Bastille, because it binds its victims not by their flesh, but by their minds.

In a world of plenty, antihumanism declares that the hungry may not eat. Where there is space enough for everyone, antihumanism insists that myriads must be slain to make room for others. Where cures are available to avert disease, antihumanism demands that they not be employed. When new technology could make power cheaper and cleaner, antihumanism cries halt. When improved crops offer more food with fewer chemicals, antihumanism says no. Instead of welcoming the human spark of inventive genius, antihumanism decries it as a threat. When the human race improves nature, antihumanism condemns it for doing so, and calls for arrest and severe punishment. Where democracy allows for freedom of thought and conscience, antihumanism seeks to submerge reason and compassion and turn citizens into a herd. Where means exist on every side to make life on Earth a Heaven, antihumanism demands they be forgone to sentence ourselves to Hell.

Humanity today thus stands at a crossroads, facing a choice between two very different visions of the future. On one side stands antihumanism, which, disregarding its repeated prior refutations, continues to postulate a world of limited supplies, whose fixed constraints demand ever-tighter controls upon human aspirations. On the other side stand those who believe in the power of unfettered creativity to invent unbounded resources, and so, rather than regret human freedom, insist upon it. The contest between these two views will determine our fate.

If the idea is accepted that the world's resources are fixed with only so much to go around, then each new life is unwelcome, each unregulated act or thought is a menace, every person is fundamentally the enemy of every other person, and each race or nation is the enemy of every other race or nation. The ultimate outcome of such a worldview can only be enforced stagnation, tyranny, war, and genocide. The horrific crimes advocated or perpetrated by antihumanism's devotees over the past two centuries prove this conclusively. Only in a world of unlimited resources can all men be brothers.

That is why we must reject antihumanism and embrace instead an ethic based on faith in the human capacity for creativity and invention. For in doing so, we make a statement that we are living not at the end of history, but at the beginning of history; that we believe in freedom and not regimentation; in progress and not stasis; in love rather than hate; in life rather than death; in hope rather than despair.

# ACKNOWLEDGMENTS

I wish to acknowledge my debt to *New Atlantis* interns A. Barrett Bowdre, Elias Brockman, Nathaniel J. Cochran, Jonathan Coppage, Brendan Foht, and Edward A. Rubin, who put in many weeks at the Library of Congress verifying, and where necessary correcting, every fact, quote, and footnote in this book. Thanks, too, to *New Atlantis* intern Samuel Matlack for his fine work indexing the book, and to Pioneer Astronautics employees Heather Rose and Alyssa Piccinni for their help with graphics and proofreading.

I am grateful to the Ethics and Public Policy Center and the Witherspoon Institute for their support. I would also like to express my appreciation to *New Atlantis* editors Caitrin Nicol, Ari N. Schulman, and most especially Adam Keiper, who edited the manuscript of this work into its current form, greatly improving it in the process. Added thanks must go to Adam Keiper for nominating the manuscript to Encounter Books for publication, and to Encounter Books publisher Roger Kimball and director of production Heather Ohle, for seeing the merit in the project and shepherding it through to successful completion.

Most of all I would like to give my deepest thanks to my old friend Jamie Lutton, the proprietor of Seattle's great Twice Sold Tales used bookstore and bibliophile beyond compare, whose encyclopedic knowledge and intellectual companionship were of invaluable assistance in seeking, finding, and drawing together the strands that comprise this book. Thanks, Jamie. Without you, this tale could never have been told.

# NOTES

## PREFACE

1 William Shakespeare, *Hamlet*, Act II, scene ii, lines 308–313.

2 Mihajlo Mesarovic and Eduard Pestel, *Mankind at the Turning Point: The Second Report to the Club of Rome* (New York: Dutton, 1974), 1. The Club of Rome authors attribute this quotation to Dr. Alan Gregg, a longtime official at the Rockefeller Foundation. Gregg's full quotation was as follows: "To say that the world has cancer, and that the cancer cell is man, has neither experimental proof nor the validation of predictive accuracy; but I see no reason that instantly forbids such a speculation." Alan Gregg, "A Medical Aspect of the Population Problem," *Science* 121, no. 3172 (1955): 681.

## CHAPTER ONE · THOMAS MALTHUS, THE MOST DISMAL SCIENTIST

1 John P. Holdren and Paul R. Ehrlich, *Global Ecology: Readings Towards a Rational Strategy for Man* (New York: Harcourt Brace Jovanovich, 1971), 7.

2 Henry George, *Progress and Poverty* (London: William Reeves, 1884), 100.

3 Thomas Malthus, *Essay on Population*, 6th ed. (London: John Murray, 1826), bk. IV, chap. 5, 300–301.

4 *Ibid.*, bk. iii, chap. 7, especially 371–375; *ibid.*, bk. iv, chap. 1.

5 On Engels, see Allan Chase, *The Legacy of Malthus: The Social Costs of the New Scientific Racism* (New York: Alfred A. Knopf, 1977), 58–59; On Dickens, see *ibid.*, 628; On Nightingale, see note 28 below.

6 Henry George, *Progress and Poverty*, 74–75.

7 *Ibid.*, 99.

8 "Marcus" was the pseudonym adopted by an unknown British satirist who in 1838 published a Swiftian pamphlet entitled *On the Possibility of Limiting Populousness*. The pamphlet ridiculed Malthus by wholeheartedly embracing his theory, thereby recommending government enforcement of a two-and-a-half child per family policy, with those born in excess of quota disposed of "painlessly." Unfortunately, as we shall see in later chapters, this satire became a horrifying reality in the twentieth century, as Malthusians enforced precisely such policies upon the people of India, China, and other Third World nations.

9  Friedrich Engels, "Outlines of a Critique of Political Economy," *Deutsche-Französische Jahrbücher* (1844), quoted in Ronald Meek, *Marx and Engels on the Population Bomb* (Berkeley, CA: Ramparts Press, 1971), 56–73.

10  Holdren and Ehrlich, 7.

11  Nicholas C. Edsall, *The Anti-Poor Law Movement: 1834–44* (Totowa, New Jersey: Rowman & Littlefield, 1971), 2.

12  Letter from Thomas Malthus to David Ricardo, 1817, cited in John Cunningham Wood, ed., *Thomas Robert Malthus: Critical Assessments* (London: Routledge, 1994), 262.

13  See, for example, Paul Ehrlich, Anne Ehrlich, and John Holdren, *Ecoscience: Population, Resources, Environment* (San Francisco: W.H. Freeman, 1977), 232, where the Irish potato famine is referred to acting as a "safety valve" against unrestrained population growth.

14  Roderick Floud and Paul Johnson, ed., *The Cambridge Economic History of Modern Britain, Vol. 1: Industrialisation, 1700–1760* (Cambridge: Cambridge University Press, 2004), 65; United Kingdom, Government Statistical Service, Julie Jeffries, "The UK Population Past, Present, and Future," Focus on People and Migration (2005), available at http://www.statistics.gov.uk/downloads/theme_compendia/fom2005/01_fopm_population.pdf; United Kingdom, Census Office, *The Census of Great Britain in 1851* (London: Longman, Brown, Green, and Longmans, 1854), 90; Geographical comparison relies on data from the *CIA World Factbook*: https://www.cia.gov/library/publications/the-world-factbook/, accessed on August 14, 2011. The demographic data for 1846 is obtained by interpolating from the census data of 1841 and 1851.

15  Christine Kinealy, *The Great Irish Famine: Impact, Ideology and Rebellion* (New York: Palgrave, 2002), 105–111.

16  William Cobbett, *Political Register*, 1834, reprinted in *Cobbett on Ireland: A Warning to England*, Denis Knight, ed. (London: Lawrence and Wishart, 1984), 272.

17  John Prest, *Lord John Russell* (London: MacMillan, 1972), 271.

18  Jim Handy, "'Almost Idiotic Wretchedness': A Long History of Blaming Peasants," *Journal of Peasant Studies* 36, no. 2 (2009): 332.

19  Charles Trevelyan, *The Irish Crisis* (London: Longman, Brown, Green and Longmans, 1848), 201.

20  *Ibid.*, 1.

21  John Hughes, "A Lecture on the Antecedent Causes of the Irish Famine in 1847," (New York: 1847; University of Virginia, 2004).

22  Kinealy, *The Great Irish Famine*, 2.

23  Mike Davis, *Late Victorian Holocausts: El Niño Famines and the Making of the Third World* (New York: Verso, 2001), 7.

24  *Ibid.*, 27.

25  *Ibid.*, 32.

26  *Ibid.*, 38.

27 *Ibid.*, 40.

28 *Ibid.*, 46.

29 *Ibid.*, 48.

30 Florence Nightingale, "The People of India," *The Nineteenth Century*, August 1878, quoted in Davis, *Late Victorian Holocausts*, 25.

31 B.H. Baden Powell, *Land Systems of British India* (London: Henry Frowde, 1892), cited in Kingsley Davis, *The Population of India and Pakistan* (Princeton, NJ: Princeton University Press, 1951), 203.

32 Davis, *Late Victorian Holocausts*, 7.

33 In the 2008 movie *The Boy in the Striped Pajamas*, the commandant of a Nazi concentration camp, who is no crude thug but a solid family man with clear managerial ability, explains to his young son that "we're working very hard to make this world a better place." This was indeed the view of many of those who devoted themselves to the Nazi cause, as well as most of those involved in the population control movement down to this day. They are trying to make the world better—by getting rid of undesirable people. *The Boy in the Striped Pajamas*, DVD, directed by Mark Herman (2008; Miramax Lionsgate, 2011).

34 In the figures that follow, data for total world Gross Domestic Product are estimates published by J. Bradford DeLong of the Department of Economics, U.C. Berkeley, on his website. J. Bradford DeLong, "Estimating World GDP: 1 Million BC to Present" (1998), http://econ161.berkeley.edu/TCEH/1998_Draft/World_GDP/Estimating_World_GDP.html. Population estimates are those compiled by Wikipedia from various experts, see Wikipedia, "World Population," http://en.wikipedia.org/wiki/World_population, accessed on August 14, 2011; Wikipedia, "World Population Estimates," http://en.wikipedia.org/wiki/World_population_estimates, accessed on August 14, 2011. See also resources published by the United Nations Department of Economic and Social Affairs, Population Division, especially United Nations, Population Division, "The World at Six Billion" (UN, 1999), http://www.un.org/esa/population/publications/sixbillion/sixbilpart1.pdf; United Nations, Population Division, "Highlights," in *World Population Prospects: The 2002 Revision* (UN, 2003), http://www.un.org/esa/population/publications/wpp2002/WPP2002-HIGHLIGHTSrev1.PDF.

35 Paul R. Ehrlich, *The Population Bomb* (New York: Ballantine Books, 1968); Paul Ehrlich, Anne Ehrlich, and John Holdren, *Ecoscience: Population, Resources, Environment* (San Francisco: W. H. Freeman, 1977); Holdren and Ehrlich, *Global Ecology*; Donella Meadows *et al.*, *The Limits to Growth: A Report for the Club of Rome's Project on the Predicament of Mankind* (New York: New American Library, 1972).

36 For example, "Why did I pick on the next nine years instead of the next 900 for finding a solution to the population crisis? One answer is that the world, especially the undeveloped world, is rapidly running out of food. And famine, of course, could be one way to reach a death rate solution to the population problem. In fact, the battle to feed humanity is already lost, in the sense that we will not be

able to prevent large-scale famines in the next decade or so." P. Ehrlich, *The Population Bomb*, 36.

37 Julian L. Simon, *The Ultimate Resource* (Princeton: Princeton University Press, 1981); Julian L. Simon, *The Ultimate Resource 2* (Princeton: Princeton University Press, 1986). The second book is an update and substantial expansion of the original edition. The newer volume includes an excellent discussion of how the predictions in the first edition turned out (they were almost all correct), as well as refutations of arguments advanced against the first edition by Simon's critics. This book is the best systematic refutation of Malthusian theory ever written.

38 Simon, *The Ultimate Resource 2*.

## CHAPTER TWO · DARWIN'S MORAL INVERSION

1 Charles Darwin, *The Descent of Man and Selection in Relation to Sex* (London: John Murray, 1871). Reprinted in *The Origin of Species and The Descent of Man* (New York: The Modern Library, 1977), 521. Citation is to the 1977 edition.

2 Washington Irving, *Knickerbocker's History of New York: From the Beginning of the World to the Fall of the Dutch Dynasty* (New York: G.P. Putnam, 1809; Project Gutenberg, 2004), http://www.gutenberg.org/files/13042/13042-h/13042-h.htm.

3 Herbert Spencer did not coin the phrase "survival of the fittest" until 1864, after reading *The Origin of Species*. But Spencer's earlier works influenced Darwin's thinking, and Darwin embraced Spencer's phrase with enthusiasm and incorporated it in later editions of his book.

4 Charles Darwin, *On the Origin of Species by Means of Natural Selection, or the Preservation of Favored Races in the Struggle for Life* (London: John Murray, 1859; 6th ed. 1872). Reprinted in *The Origin of Species and The Descent of Man* (New York: The Modern Library, 1977), 51. Citation is to the 1977 edition.

5 In science, it is often the case that a theory that is useful for understanding some simple class of natural phenomenon becomes invalid when applied to more complex situations. For example, while the laws of gravity, inertia, and aerodynamics may provide an adequate foundation to predict the trajectory of a rock tossed by a human hand, they fail utterly if the projectile in question is a live sparrow. No one would be so obtuse as to try to predict bird flight based on inanimate ballistics. Yet essentially the same error has been made over and over again by Malthusians—for example by John Holdren and Paul Ehrlich, when they proposed to understand the human global economy based upon the model of fruit flies sealed in an agar jar. By ignoring the creative and communicative aspects of human nature, the Malthusians inevitably and repeatedly draw conclusions that are wildly incorrect. Following Malthus, Charles Darwin made the same fundamental mistake. His theory of natural selection represents a significant contribution to biology, and helps to explain much of the workings of evolution as it occurs in the animal and plant

world. But it falls apart completely when applied to the development of human society. Few errors in the history of science have been so disastrous.

6 Darwin, *The Descent of Man*, 496–97.

7 Christopher Hitchens, *God Is Not Great* (New York: Twelve, 2007), 66.

8 Karl Marx to Friedrich Engels, June 18, 1862, in *Marx/Engels Collected Works* 41:380, available at http://www.marxists.org/archive/marx/works/1862/letters/62_06_18.htm.

9 Friedrich Engels to Pyotr Lavrov, November 12–17, 1875, available at Marx/Engels Internet Archive (2000), http://www.marxists.org/archive/marx/works/1875/letters/75_11_17-ab.htm.

10 Clémence Royer, preface to *L'Origine de especes*, by Charles Darwin (Paris: Reinwald, 1882), 38, English translation quoted in André Pichot, *The Pure Society: From Darwin to Hitler* (London: Verso, 2009), 304.

11 Darwin, *The Descent of Man*, 501. Darwin sought to distance himself from the obvious conclusion of this line of thinking, writing that "if we were intentionally to neglect the weak and helpless, it could only be for a contingent benefit, with an overwhelming present evil. We must therefore bear the undoubtedly bad effects of the weak surviving and propagating their kind." (*Ibid.*, 502.) Clearly this half-hearted note of caution proved insufficient for Darwin's followers, who took his larger argument to its more obvious conclusion.

12 Darwin, *The Origin of Species*, 374.


CHAPTER THREE · THE BIRTH OF EUGENICS

1 Editorial on the death of Frederick Douglass, *New York Times*, February 27, 1895, 4.

2 Francis Galton, *Hereditary Genius: An Inquiry into its Laws and Consequences* (London: Macmillan, 1869); Francis Galton, "Eugenics: Its Definition, Scope, and Aims," *American Journal of Sociology* 10, no. 1 (1904), available at http://galton.org/essays/1900-1911/galton-1904-am-journ-soc-eugenics-scope-aims.htm. For the coining of the term "eugenics," see Francis Galton, *Inquiries into Human Faculty and its Development* (Macmillan: 1883); also, Francis Galton, *Inquiries into Human Faculty and its Development*, 2nd ed. (J.M. Dent, 1907), 7, available at http://galton.org/books/human-faculty/text/html/index.html.

3 Galton, *Hereditary Genius*.

4 *Ibid.*, 34.

5 *Ibid.*, 338–339.

6 Francis Galton, letter to the editor, *Times of London*, June 5, 1873.

7 Galton, *Hereditary Genius*, 339.

8 *Ibid.*, 36.

9 Francis Galton, "Hereditary Improvement," *Fraser's Magazine*, January 1873, 118.

10 Galton, *Hereditary Genius*, 361.

1 1  *Ibid.*, 1 4.

1 2  Galton, "Hereditary Improvement," 1 2 9.

1 3  *Daily News* (London), December 1 5, 1 8 6 9, no. 7 3 7 1.

1 4  Review of *Hereditary Genius*, *The Times*, January 7, 1 8 7 0, quoted in Martin Brookes, *Extreme Measures: The Dark Visions and Bright Ideas of Francis Galton* (New York: Bloomsbury Publishing, 2 0 0 4), 1 6 8–1 6 9, available at http://www.dnalc.org/view/1 1 9 2 2-Review-of-Hereditary-Genius-The-Times–1–7–1 8 7 0-.html.

1 5  Brookes, *Extreme Measures*, 2 7 0.

1 6  Sidney Webb, "Eugenics and the Poor Law: The Minority Report," *Eugenics Review* 2, no. 3 (1 9 1 0): 2 3 7. This was "An extended précis of a lecture delivered to the Eugenics Society at Denison House, Vauxhall Bridge Road, S.W., on December 1 5 th, 1 9 0 9."

CHAPTER FOUR · DEUTSCHLAND ÜBER ALLES

1  Francis Darwin, ed., *The Life and Letters of Charles Darwin* (New York: 1 9 1 9) 2:2 6 5, available at http://darwin-online.org.uk/content/frameset?viewtype=side&itemID=F1 4 6 1&pageseq=2 8 6.

2  Emile Boutroux, preface to *Le Darwinisme et la Guerre*, by Peter Chalmers-Mitchell, trans. Maurice Solovine (Paris: Alcan, 1 9 1 6), available in French at HathiTrust Digital Library, http://hdl.handle.net/2 0 2 7/mdp.3 9 0 1 5 0 6 4 4 5 4 8 8 0.

3  Robert C. Stauffer, "Haeckel, Darwin, and Ecology," *The Quarterly Review of Biology* 3 2, no. 2 (1 9 5 7): 1 3 8–1 4 4. The idea that "ontogeny recapitulates phylogeny" was discredited many decades ago, although the euphonious phrase lingers on in some quarters, and it remains true that "ontogeny does *appear* to recapitulate phylogeny." Marc C. Hammerman, "Recapitulation of Phylogeny by Ontogeny in Nephrology," *Kidney International* 5 7 (2 0 0 0): 7 4 2–7 5 5.

4  Carl C. Swisher III, Garniss H. Curtis, and Roger Lewin, *Java Man: How Two Geologists Changed Our Understanding of Human Evolution* (Chicago: University of Chicago, 2 0 0 0), 5 2.

5  See Peter C. Caldwell, review of *H.G. Bronn, Ernst Haeckel, and the Origins of German Darwinism: A Study in Translation and Transformation*, Sander Gliboff, and *The Tragic Sense of Life: Ernst Haeckel and the Struggle over Evolutionary Thought*, Robert J. Richards, *German History* 2 7, no. 3 (2 0 0 9): 4 4 3–4 4 5; Daniel Gasman, *The Scientific Origins of National Socialism: Social Darwinism in Ernst Haeckel and the German Monist League* (New York: American Elsevier, 1 9 7 1), 1 5 7–1 5 9; Richard Weikart, *From Darwin to Hitler: Evolutionary Ethics, Eugenics, and Racism in Germany* (New York: Palgrave MacMillan, 2 0 0 4), 1 6 5, 1 8 7.

6  See Weikart, *From Darwin to Hitler*, 1 2–1 3, 2 5, 7 6, 9 0, 1 0 7–0 9.

7  André Pichot, *The Pure Society: From Darwin to Hitler* (London: Verso, 2 0 0 9), 2 5 0–2 5 6.

8  Ernst Haeckel, *The Wonders of Life: A Popular Study of Biological Philosophy*, trans. Joseph McCabe (New York: Harper, 1904), 390.

9  Weikart, *From Darwin to Hitler*, 65–67.

10  *Ibid.*, 145–148.

11  Daniel Gasman, *The Scientific Origins of National Socialism*, 91, 103.

12  *Ibid.*, 95, 103.

13  G. Vacher de Lapouge, preface to his translation of E. Haeckel, *Le Monisme, lien entre la religion et la science* (Paris: Schleicher, n.d.), 1–2, quoted in an English translation in André Pichot, *The Pure Society: From Darwin to Hitler* (London: Verso, 2009), 317–318.

14  Gasman, *The Scientific Origins of National Socialism*, 20, 147–150.

15  Pichot, *The Pure Society*, 183.

16  Friedrich Hellwald, *Culturgeschichte in ihrer natürlichen Entwicklung bis zur Gegenwart* (Augsburg: Lampart & comp., 1875), 44–45, 58, quoted in Weikart, *From Darwin to Hitler*, 169. *Culturgeschichte* is available in the German original at HathiTrust Digital Library, http://hdl.handle.net/2027/mdp.39015059445802.

17  Heinrich Ernst Ziegler, *Die Naturwissenschaft und die Socialdemokratische Theorie, ihr Verhältnis dargelegt auf Grund der Werke von Darwin und Bebel* (Stuttgart: Verlag von Ferdinand Enke, 1893), 167–168, quoted in Weikart, *From Darwin to Hitler*, 171. *Die Naturwissenschaft* is available in the German original at HathiTrust Digital Library, http://hdl.handle.net/2027/uc1.b21748.

18  Otto Ammon, *Die Gesellschaftsordnung*, 3rd ed. (Jena, Germany: G. Fischer, 1900), 164, quoted in Weikart, *From Darwin to Hitler*, 197. Emphasis in the original. *Die Gesellschaftsordnung* is available in the German original at HathiTrust Digital Library, http://hdl.handle.net/2027/nyp.33433081930871.

19  Gasman, *The Scientific Origins of National Socialism*, 148; Weikart, *From Darwin to Hitler*, 93, 119–22.

20  Helene Stöcker, "Rassenhygiene und Mutterschutz," *Die neue Generation* 13 (1917): 138–42, quoted in Weikart, *From Darwin to Hitler*, 202.

21  Weikart, *From Darwin to Hitler*, 176.

22  *Ibid.*, 206.

23  *Ibid.*, 205.

24  *Ibid.*, 174.

25  Barbara Tuchman, *The Guns of August* (1962; repr., New York: Ballantine Books, 1994), 12–13.

26  *Ibid.*, 130.

## CHAPTER FIVE · EUGENICS COMES TO AMERICA

1  Charles Davenport, letter to Madison Grant, April 7, 1925. Quoted in Allan Chase, *The Legacy of Malthus: The Social Costs of the New Scientific Racism* (New York: Alfred A. Knopf, 1977), 301.

2 Geoffrey Hellman, *Bankers, Bones, and Beetles: The First Century of The American Museum of Natural History* (Garden City, NY: The Natural History Press, 1969), 17–19, 27.

3 Chase, *The Legacy of Malthus*, 113.

4 Francis Amasa Walker, "Restriction of Immigration," *Atlantic Monthly*, June 1896, 822–29, quoted at length in Chase, *The Legacy of Malthus*, 108–110. The sentences in the quotation have been rearranged in this excerpt for brevity and clarity. Italics added.

5 Chase, *The Legacy of Malthus*, 114–118.

6 Decades later, Mary Harriman would go on to be friends and roommates with Frances Perkins, the Secretary of Labor in Franklin D. Roosevelt's administration.

7 Jonathan Peter Spiro, *Defending the Master Race: Conservation, Eugenics, and the Legacy of Madison Grant* (Burlington, VT: University of Vermont Press, 2009), 127; Chase, *The Legacy of Malthus*, 118–120; Daniel J. Kevles, *In the Name of Eugenics: Genetics and the Uses of Human Heredity* (Cambridge, MA: Harvard University Press, 1998), 54–55; "Scientific Notes and News," *Science* 46 (1917): 635.

8 Chase, *The Legacy of Malthus*, 16, 133–135.

9 *Ibid.*, 16–17; See also *Relf v. Weinberger*, 372 F. Supp. 1196 (Dist. D.C. 1974).

10 *Ibid.*, 212.

11 *Ibid.*, 207–208; See also Joseph Goldberger and G.A. Wheeler, "The Experimental Production of Pellagra in Human Subjects by Means of Diet," *Hygienic Laboratory Bulletin* (Washington: Government Printing Office, 1920), repr. in Milton Terris, ed., *Goldberger on Pellagra* (Baton Rouge: Louisiana State Press, 1964), 55–94.

12 Chase, *The Legacy of Malthus*, 213–215; see also Charles Benedict Davenport, *Heredity in Relation to Eugenics* (New York: Henry Holt & Co., 1913), 213.

13 Chase, *The Legacy of Malthus*, 213–220; and see also the *Third Report of the Robert M. Thompson Pellagra Commission of the New York Post-Graduate Medical School and Hospital*, excerpted in *Archives of Internal Medicine*, vol. xviii (1916), online here: http://books.google.com/books?id=CyYBAAAAYAAJ.

14 *Ibid.*, 24, 201–225, 639.

15 *Ibid.*, 226–273, 283.

16 Henry Fairfield Osborn, "The Approach to the Immigration Problem through Science," *Proceedings of the National Immigration Conference, Special Report No. 26* (New York: 1923), 44–53, quoted in Stephen Jay Gould, *The Mismeasure of Man* (New York: W.W. Norton, 1996), 261.

17 Grant's book had respectable sales in the United States (more than 16,000 copies during his lifetime; see "Madison Grant, 71, Zoologist, is Dead," *New York Times*, May 31, 1937, 15), but sold vastly more copies overseas. It sold wildly in Germany in translation under the title *Der Untergang der grossen Rasse*.

18 Madison Grant, *The Passing of the Great Race; Or the Racial Basis of European His-*

*tory*, 4th ed. (New York: Charles Scribner's Sons, 1936), 193, 5, 16, 48, 49, 263, available online at http://www.archive.org/details/passingofgreatraoogranuoft.

19 Jonathan Peter Spiro, *Defending the Master Race: Conservation, Eugenics, and the Legacy of Madison Grant* (Burlington, VT: University of Vermont Press, 2009), 6–7.

20 *Ibid.*, 357.

21 Spiro, *Defending the Master Race*, 3–142, 266–296.

22 Theodore Roosevelt, "Foundations of the Nineteenth Century," *The Outlook*, July 1911, 729, quoted in Theodore Roosevelt, *The Works of Theodore Roosevelt*, vol. 26, *History as Literature and Other Essays* (New York: Scribner, 1913), 231–243.

23 Konrad Heiden and Ralph Manheim, *The Führer* (Castle Books, 2002), 198; and Peter Viereck, *Metapolitics: From Wagner and the Romantics to Hitler*, expanded edition (New Brunswick, NJ: Transaction, 2004), 148–149. See also Berthold Hoeckner, "Wagner and the Origin of Evil," *Opera Quarterly* 23, no. 2–3 (Spring-Summer 2007): 160–162, 180–181 n. 61.

24 William L. Shirer, *The Rise and Fall of the Third Reich* (New York: Simon and Schuster, 1960), 103.

25 Chase, *The Legacy of Malthus*, 289–291.

26 C.C. Little, "The Second International Congress of Eugenics," *Eugenics Review* 13, no. 4 (January 1922), 511–524; "The Second International Congress of Eugenics," *Natural History.* xxi, no. 3 (May-June 1921), 246–249; "Personnel of the Second International Congress of Eugenics," *Natural History.* xxi, no. 5 (September-October 1921), 542–544; Chase, *The Legacy of Malthus*, 277–279.

27 Chase, *The Legacy of Malthus*, 279.

28 Madison Grant *et al.*, "Report of the Committee on Selective Immigration of the Eugenics Committee of the United States of America," *Eugenical News*, February 1924, 21.

29 H. F. Perkins, ed., *A Decade of Progress in Eugenics: Scientific Papers of the Third International Congress of Eugenics* (Baltimore: Williams and Wilkins Company, 1934), 511–526.

30 Chase, *The Legacy of Malthus*, 54–55, 482.

31 Michael Burleigh, *The Third Reich: A New History* (New York: Hill and Wang, 2000), 233.

32 André Pichot, *The Pure Society: From Darwin to Hitler* (London: Verso, 2009), 168–173. For more on Muller's life, see his Nobel biography: www.nobelprize.org/nobel_prizes/medicine/laureates/1946/muller-bio.html. For Muller's sperm bank project, see David Plotz, *The Genius Factory: The Curious History of the Nobel Prize Sperm Bank* (New York: Random House, 2005).

33 Charles B. Davenport, "Presidential Address: The Development of Eugenics" in H. F. Perkins, ed., *A Decade of Progress in Eugenics: Scientific Papers of the Third International Congress of Eugenics*, 21–22.

34 *Ibid.*, 22.

35 Henry Fairfield Osborn, "Birth Selection versus Birth Control," H. F. Perkins, ed., *A Decade of Progress in Eugenics: Scientific Papers of the Third International Congress of Eugenics*, 29–41.

36 Harry H. Laughlin, "Historical Background to the Third International Congress of Eugenics," in H. F. Perkins, ed., *A Decade of Progress in Eugenics: Scientific Papers of the Third International Congress of Eugenics*, 10; and Pichot, *The Pure Society: From Darwin to Hitler*, 183.

37 Bernard Schreiber, *The Men Behind Hitler: A German Warning to the World* (Les Mureaux: La Haye-Mureaux, 1975), 160, available at http://www.toolan.com/hitler/index.html.

38 Pichot, *The Pure Society: From Darwin to Hitler*, 183.

39 Stefan Kühl, *The Nazi Connection* (New York: Oxford University Press, 1994), 32–33. Although Laughlin missed the 1935 Berlin conference, he was certainly no stranger to Nazi Germany, its scientists, and its activists. See Paul A. Lombardo, "'The American Breed': Nazi Eugenics and the Origins of the Pioneer Fund," *Albany Law Review* 65, no. 3 (2002), 743–830.

40 "Population Parley is Set," *New York Times*, August 22, 1935, 11.

41 "Population Parley Hears Nazi Praise," *New York Times*, August 28, 1935, 4.

42 *Ibid.*

43 *Ibid.*

44 "Germany: Praise for Nazis," *Time*, September 9, 1935.

CHAPTER SIX · THE NAZI HOLOCAUST

1 Francis Galton, "Hereditary Improvement," *Fraser's Magazine*, January 1873, 119.

2 Stefan Kühl, *The Nazi Connection* (New York: Oxford University Press, 1994), 36.

3 Martin Gilbert, *The Second World War: A Complete History* (New York: Henry Holt, 1989), 243.

4 Michael Burleigh, *The Third Reich: A New History* (New York: Hill and Wang, 2000), 284; Bryan Mark Rigg, *Hitler's Jewish Soldiers: The Untold Story of Nazi Racial Laws and Men of Jewish Descent in the German Military* (n.p.: University Press of Kansas, 2002), 72.

5 John M. Efron, *Medicine and the German Jews: A History* (New Haven: Yale University Press, 2001), 234.

6 Daniel Charles, *Master Mind: The Rise and Fall of Fritz Haber, the Nobel Laureate Who Launched the Age of Chemical Warfare* (New York: Ecco, 2005).

7 United States Holocaust Memorial Museum, "Nazi Camps," *Holocaust Encyclopedia*, http://www.ushmm.org/wlc/en/article.php?ModuleId=10005144; Agence France-Presse, "20,000 Nazi camps, ghettos in WWII Europe," June 9, 2009; Michael Burleigh, *The Third Reich: A New History*, 394.

8 Daniel Goldhagen, *Hitler's Willing Executioners* (New York: Knopf, 1996), 8, 164–178.

9 *Ibid.*, 244–248.

10 Richard J. Evans, *The Coming of the Third Reich* (New York: Penguin, 2003), 174–175, 340.

11 *Ibid.*, 344.

12 Goldhagen, *Hitler's Willing Executioners*, 100–102.

13 *Ibid.*

14 Richard Weikart, *From Darwin to Hitler: Evolutionary Ethics, Eugenics, and Racism in Germany* (New York: Palgrave MacMillan, 2004), 233.

15 Burleigh, *The Third Reich: A New History*.

16 Richard J. Evans, *The Third Reich in Power* (New York: Penguin, 2005).

17 Michael Burleigh and Wolfgang Wipperman, *The Racial State: Germany 1933–1945* (Cambridge, UK: Cambridge University Press, 1991), 103, 152–153, 251.

18 Janet Biehl and Peter Staudenmaier, *Ecofascism: Lessons from the German Experience* (San Francisco: AK Press, 1995), 10–12, available at http://www.scribd.com/doc/8750846/Eco-Fascism-Fascist-Ideology-the-Green-Wing-of-the-Nazi-Party-and-Its-Historical-Antecedents-by-Peter-Staudenmaier; Ludwig Klages, *Man and Earth*, trans. Joe Pryce, available at http://www.revilo-oliver.com/Writers/Klages/Man_and_Earth.html. Klages considered himself neither a Nazi nor a Darwinian, but as Biehl and Staudenmaier note, his extreme Romantic rejection of rationality combined with "a political subtext of cultural despair" formed an ideal basis for authoritarianism and made him "the intellectual pacemaker of the Third Reich."

19 Jonah Goldberg, *Liberal Fascism: The Secret History of the American Left, from Mussolini to the Politics of Change* (New York: Broadway Books, 2007), 384.

20 Peter Staudenmaier, "Fascist Ecology: The 'Green Wing' of the Nazi Party and its Historical Antecedents," in Biehl and Staudenmaier, *Ecofascism*.

21 *Ibid.*, 17.

22 Inge Scholl and Dorothee Sölle, *The White Rose: Munich 1942–1943* (Hannover, NH: Wesleyan University Press, 1970), 73–74.

23 *Ibid.*, 78–79.

24 *Ibid.*, 85–86.

25 Allan Chase, *The Legacy of Malthus: The Social Costs of the New Scientific Racism* (New York: Knopf, 1977), 349–350.

26 Michael Burleigh, *The Third Reich: A New History*, 384–394, 404; Robert J. Lifton, *The Nazi Doctors: Medical Killing and the Psychology of Genocide* (United States: Basic Books, 2000), 142.

27 Michael Burleigh, *Death and Deliverance: Euthanasia in Germany, 1900–1945* (Cambridge, UK: Cambridge University Press, 1994); Karl Binding and Alfred Hoche, *Allowing the Destruction of Life Unworthy of Life, Die Freigabe der Vernichtung lebensunwerten Lebens* (Leipzig: Verlag von Felix Meiner, 1920); Wesley J. Smith, "Killing Babies Compassionately," *Weekly Standard Online*, May 27,

2006. Available at http://www.weeklystandard.com/Content/Public/Articles/ 000/000/012/003dncoj.asp.

28  William L. Shirer, *Berlin Diary: The Journal of a Foreign Correspondent 1934–1941* (Baltimore: Johns Hopkins University Press, 2002), 574.

29  Suzanne E. Evans, *Forgotten Crimes: The Holocaust and People with Disabilities* (Chicago: Ivan R. Dee, 2004), 87–88.

30  Burleigh, *The Third Reich: A New History*, 403–404.

31  Burleigh, *The Third Reich: A New History*, 294–298.

32  *Ibid.*, 318.

33  Arthur D. Morse, *While Six Million Died: A Chronicle of American Apathy* (Norwich: Fletcher & Son, 1968), 199–220.

34  Jonathan Peter Spiro, *Defending the Master Race: Conservation, Eugenics, and the Legacy of Madison Grant* (Burlington, VT: University of Vermont Press, 2009), 365–370; Allan Chase, *The Legacy of Malthus*, 353; Morse, *While Six Million Died*, 252–269.

35  Morse, *While Six Million Died*, 270–288; William H. Tucker, *The Science and Politics of Racial Research* (Chicago: University of Illinois Press, 1996), 127.

36  Sarah A. Ogilvie and Scott Miller, *Refuge Denied: The St. Louis Passengers and the Holocaust* (Madison, WI: University of Wisconsin Press, 2006), 174–175.


CHAPTER SEVEN · EUGENICS REBORN

1  William Vogt, *The Road to Survival* (New York: William Sloane Associates, 1948), 279.

2  Donald T. Critchlow, *Intended Consequences: Birth Control, Abortion, and the Federal Government in Modern America* (New York: Oxford University Press, 1999), 32.

3  Allan Chase, *The Legacy of Malthus: The Social Costs of the New Scientific Racism* (New York: Knopf, 1977), 352–353, 367.

4  Guy Irving Burch and Elmer Pendell, *Population Roads to Peace and War* (Washington, D.C.: Population Reference Bureau, 1945). Burch was a director of the Population Reference Bureau and the American Eugenics Society, and a charter member of the Population Association of America. A leading light in Margaret Sanger's American Birth Control League and the pro-Nazi Coalition of Patriotic Societies, Burch succinctly explained his motivations in a 1934 letter: "I have long worked with the American Coalition of Patriotic Societies to prevent the American people from being replaced by alien or Negro stock, whether it be by immigration or by overly high birth rates among others in this country." Pendell, a professor at Baldwin-Wallace College in Ohio, was a member of the board of the radical eugenicist Birthright, Inc. organization. See Chase, *The Legacy of Malthus*, 366–371; David M. Kennedy, *Birth Control in America: The Career of Margaret Sanger* (New Haven: Yale, 1970), 119–120.

5  Burch and Pendell, *Population Roads to Peace and War*, 47.

6  Lothrop Stoddard, *The Rising Tide of Color Against White World Supremacy* (New York: Charles Scribner's Sons, 1920). None other than Madison Grant provided an introduction to the first edition of Stoddard's book. Here are some samples from Stoddard's text (taken from pages 300–308): "All these marvelous achievements [of civilization] were due solely to superior heredity, and the mere maintenance of what had been won depended absolutely upon the prior maintenance of race-values. Civilization of itself means nothing. It is merely an effect, whose cause is the creative urge of superior germ-plasm. Civilization is the body; the race is the soul. Let the soul vanish, and the body moulders into the inanimate dust from which it came.... There is no immediate danger of the world being swamped by black blood. But there is a very imminent danger that the white stocks may be swamped by Asiatic blood.... Unless we set our house in order, the doom will sooner or later overtake us all. And that would mean that the race obviously endowed with the greatest creative ability, the race which had achieved most in the past and which gave the richer promise for the future, had passed away, carrying with it to the grave those potencies upon which the realization of man's highest hopes depends. A million years of human evolution might go uncrowned.... One element should be fundamental to all the compounding of the social pharmacopoeia. That element is *blood*.... Asia should be given clearly to understand that we cannot permit either migration to white lands or penetration of the non-Asiatic tropics ... even within the white world, migrations of lower human types like those which have worked such havoc in the United States must be rigorously curtailed." Stoddard's second book was even worse. Lothrop Stoddard, *Revolt Against Civilization: The Menace of the Under Man* (New York: Charles Scribner's Sons, 1922).

   Stoddard traveled to Nazi Germany in 1940, where he was given a personal audience with Adolf Hitler and allowed to sit in as a guest judge as part of the three-person panel comprising a Nazi Eugenics Court, passing sentences of forced sterilization on various individuals considered undesirable by the Nazis. From this inside position, Stoddard wrote back dispatches to Americans to clear up any unfortunate misunderstandings that Jewish propaganda may have given them about the Third Reich. As Stoddard explained in one of his writings: "Inside Germany, the Jewish problem is regarded as a passing phenomenon, already settled in principle and soon to be settled in fact by the physical elimination of the Jews themselves from the Third Reich. It is the regeneration of the Germanic stock with which public opinion is most concerned.... Their attitude is voiced by Professor [eugenicist Hans F.K.] Günther when he writes: ' ... The question is not so much whether we men now living are more or less Nordic; the question put to us is whether we have the courage to make ready for future generations a world cleansing itself racially and eugenically.'" (Chase, *The Legacy of Malthus*, 347–348.)

7 Fairfield Osborn, *Our Plundered Planet* (Boston: Little Brown and Company, 1948).

8 Vogt, *The Road to Survival*, see note 1. The 1948 hardcover edition of the book includes a preface by Bernard Baruch, an advisor to Presidents Woodrow Wilson and Franklin Roosevelt, as well as endorsements by writers Christopher Morley, Dorothy Canfield Fisher, and Clifton Fadiman, and Wilderness Society founder Aldo Leopold. Chase, *The Legacy of Malthus*, 377–378; Matthew Connelly, *Fatal Misconception: The Struggle to Control World Population* (Cambridge, MA: Belknap Press, 2008), 129.

9 Osborn, *Our Plundered Planet*, 41, 201.

10 Vogt, *The Road to Survival*, 186, 224–225, 281–282, 227–228.

11 *Ibid.*, 218, 238.

12 James Stewart Martin, *All Honorable Men* (New York: Little Brown, 1950). Draper had been Secretary-Treasurer of Dillon, Read & Company in the 1930s when the firm underwrote the bonds that financed the Nazi industrial and rearmament programs. During the post-war occupation, Draper's top consultant was Dr. Alexander Kreuter, a financier who, during the war, had helped to create a banking syndicate for German-occupied Europe. Kreuter had also been manager of the collaborationist bank, and was a financial contributor to the Nazi SS.

Martin was chief of the U.S. military's decartelization branch during the first two years of the postwar occupation of Germany. His book presents extensive material accusing Draper of acting to protect the Nazi industrial cartel power structure from war crimes prosecution, denazification, and decartelization, which had been ordered by President Truman.

Martin was not the only one to make such accusations. In October 1946, American military governor General Lucius D. Clay reprimanded Draper for speaking out against denazification and decartelization. In November 1948, President Truman ordered Secretary of the Army Kenneth Royal to send an investigating commission to Germany to check into allegations that denazification policies were being sabotaged by members of the military government. In testimony before the commission, occupation administration attorney Alexander Sacks said: "The policies of the Roosevelt and Truman Administrations have been flagrantly disregarded by the very individuals who were charged with the highest responsibility for carrying them out. . . . It is no secret that the operations of the decartelization program have been hampered by Major General Draper and his associates in military government. . . . They have done whatever they could, by innuendo and misstatement, to discredit a program which they either did not understand, or did not like." In April 1949, the commission reported its findings—to wit, that the men "with direct responsibility for carrying out the work of the Decartelization Branch have not had the record of accomplishment in connection with decartelization, and particularly with deconcentration, that one would like to see in persons in such positions. . . . Some, including those who are responsible for the review of actions, have not always been in complete sympathy with the program." The commissioners also found no evidence to substantiate Draper's claim that elimination of "excessive concentration of economic power" would interfere with German economic recovery. In response to the report, Draper, by then Under Secretary of the Army, resigned and returned to his job as vice president of Dillon, Read & Company.

13 Connelly, *Fatal Misconception,* 135–141.

14 *Ibid.,* 139.

15 *Ibid.,* 141.

16 Pierre Desrochers and Christine Hoffbauer, "The Post War Intellectual Roots of the Population Bomb—Fairfield Osborn's 'Our Plundered Planet' and William Vogt's 'Road to Survival' in Retrospect," *Electronic Journal of Sustainable Development* 1, no. 3, http://www.ejsd.org/public/journal_article/12. Osborn, it is worth noting, had by 1940 succeeded Madison Grant as head of the bluestocking New York Zoological Society.

17 Michael Barker, "The Philanthropic Roots of Corporate Environmentalism," *Swans Commentary,* November 3, 2008, http://www.swans.com/library/art14/barker07.html.

18 Eric B. Ross, *The Malthus Factor: Poverty, Politics and Population in Capitalist Development* (London: Zed Books, 1998), 155–156; "Class Notes," Stanford Magazine, July-August 1997, available at http://www.stanfordalumni.org/news/magazine/1997/julaug/classnotes/obituaries.html.

19 "American Conservation Association," Sourcewatch, http://www.sourcewatch.org/index.php?title=American_Conservation_Association, accessed on August 17, 2011.

20 Connelly, *Fatal Misconception,* 159; Ross, *The Malthus Factor,* 91; H. F. Perkins, ed., *A Decade of Progress in Eugenics: Scientific Papers of the Third International Congress of Eugenics* (Baltimore: Williams and Wilkins Company, 1934), 511.

21 Ross, *The Malthus Factor,* 90–91; Ansley J. Coale, "Frank W. Notestein, 1902–1983," Population Index 49, no. 1 (1983): 3–12. For a fuller history of the Population Council, see also Population Council, *The Population Council: A Chronicle of the First Twenty-Five Years, 1952–1977* (New York: The Council, 1978).

22 A leading Nazi race scientist, Verschuer was the head of the Kaiser Wilhelm Institute for Anthropology, Human Genetics, and Eugenics, whose work was funded by the Rockefeller Foundation from 1927 through 1939. Verschuer's institute listed its 1935 activities as follows: "the training of SS doctors; racial hygiene training; expert testimony for the Reich Ministry of the Interior on cases of dubious heritage; collecting and classifying skulls from Africa; studies in race crossing; and experimental genetic pathology." Josef Mengele, Verschuer's student and subordinate, took a post at Auschwitz in order to be able to perform experiments on captives, including many children. Most of Mengele's experiments were fatal to their subjects. Many of those who survived were killed by Mengele afterwards,

so that he could forward their remains along with the rest to Verschuer for autopsies and further scientific study. After the war, Mengele disappeared. Verschuer was appointed professor of genetics at the University of Münster in West Germany, where he continued his eugenics studies until his death in 1969. See André Pichot, *The Pure Society: From Darwin to Hitler*, 79–80, 184–185; Rebecca R. Messall, "Eugenics, Rockefeller, and *Roe v. Wade*," Catholic League for Religious and Civil Rights, July 2005, http://www.catholicleague.org/printer.php?p=rer&id=118; Stefan Kühl, *The Nazi Connection* (New York: Oxford University Press, 1994), 20–21.

23 Connelly, *Fatal Misconception*, 159.

24 "Intelligent or Unintelligent Birth Control?" Editorial from *American Medicine*, *The Birth Control Review*, May 1919, 12, available at http://library.lifedynamics.com/Birth%20Control%20Review/1919-05%20May.pdf.

25 Margaret Sanger, *The Pivot of Civilization* (New York: Brentano's, 1922), 282, available at http://www.gutenberg.org/files/1689/1689-h/1689-h.htm. The book features an introduction by H. G. Wells.

26 "About Margaret Sanger: American Birth Control League," The Margaret Sanger Papers Project, New York University, 2010, http://www.nyu.edu/projects/sanger/secure/aboutms/organization_abcl.html.

27 Connelly, *Fatal Misconception*, 63–64.

28 "About Margaret Sanger: Birth Control Federation of America," The Margaret Sanger Papers Project, New York University, 2010, http://www.nyu.edu/projects/sanger/secure/aboutms/organization_bcfa.html; Perkins, *A Decade of Progress in Eugenics*, 511; Adele E. Clark, *Disciplining Reproduction: Modernity, American Life Sciences, and "The Problems of Sex"* (Berkeley: University of California Press, 1998), 185.

29 "About Margaret Sanger: Birth Control Federation of America."

30 Betsy Hartmann, *Reproductive Rights and Wrongs: The Global Politics of Population Control*, rev. ed. (Boston: South End Press, 1995), 102.

31 Chase, *The Legacy of Malthus*, 382–383.

32 Steven Mosher, *Population Control: Real Costs, Illusory Benefits* (New Brunswick: Transaction Publishers, 2009), 37–39; T. O. Greissimer, *The Population Bomb* (New York: The Hugh Moore Fund, 1954).

33 Connelly, *Fatal Misconception*, 186–187; Critchlow, *Intended Consequences*, 42–43; Mosher, *Population Control*, 38–39; Hartmann, *Reproductive Rights and Wrongs*, 105.

34 Donald T. Critchlow, *Intended Consequences*, 43; Hartmann, *Reproductive Rights and Wrongs*, 105.

35 Dwight D. Eisenhower, "The President's News Conference of December 2, 1959," *Public Papers of the President of the United States Dwight D. Eisenhower: 1959: Containing the Public Messages, Speeches, and Statements of the President, January 1 to December 31, 1959*, Washington, D.C., 288, 785–794. Also available at *The*

*American Presidency Project,* http://www.presidency.ucsb.edu/ws/index.php? pid=11587#axzz1JtQdi7l2.

36 Critchlow, *Intended Consequences,* 44; "Presidential Politics: Margaret Sanger in the Voting Booth," *The Margaret Sanger Papers Project Newsletter,* Fall 1992, available at http://www.nyu.edu/projects/sanger/secure/newsletter/articles/presidential_politics.html.

37 "Margaret Sanger is Dead at 82; Led Campaign for Birth Control," *New York Times,* September 7, 1966.

38 Connelly, *Fatal Misconception,* 189.

39 Allan Chase, *The Legacy of Malthus,* 382–387.

40 Connelly, *Fatal Misconception,* 231. The Draper Fund was founded within the Population Crisis Committee in 1975; it was named after General Draper, who had died in 1974. See, for instance, "A Decade of Family Planning Progress," *Draper Fund Report,* no. 13 (June 1984), http://pdf.usaid.gov/pdf_docs/PNAAU716.pdf.

41 Lyndon B. Johnson, "Address in San Francisco at the 20th Anniversary Commemorative Session of the United Nations: June 25, 1965," *Public Papers of the President of the United States Lyndon B. Johnson: 1965 (in two books): Containing the Public Messages, Speeches, and Statements of the President,* Washington, D.C., bk. 2, 331, 703–706. Also available at *The American Presidency Project,* http://www.presidency.ucsb.edu/ws/index.php?pid=27054#axzz1JWJ8iGM1.

42 Fred Pearce, *The Coming Population Crash and Our Planet's Surprising Future* (Boston, MA: Beacon Press, 2010), 60.

43 See, e.g., Julian L. Simon, *Population Matters: People, Resources, Environment, and Immigration* (New Brunswick, NJ: Transaction Publishers, 1996), 557–558.

CHAPTER EIGHT · IN DEFENSE OF MALARIA

1 Winston Churchill, radio broadcast, September 28, 1944, quoted in T. F. West and G. A. Campbell, *DDT: The Synthetic Insecticide* (London: Chapman and Hall, 1946), 11.

2 Juurd Eijsvoogel, "Alexander King, the Activist: The Human Lemmings," in Janny Groen, Eefke Smit, Juurd Eijsvoogel, ed., *The Discipline of Curiosity: Science in the World* (New York: Elsevier, 1990), 43.

3 Rick Atkinson, *The Day of Battle: The War in Sicily and Italy, 1943–1944* (New York: Henry Holt, 2007), 448.

4 DDT stands for dichlorodiphenyltrichloroethane.

5 Darwin Stapleton, "The Short-Lived Miracle of DDT," *American Heritage Invention and Technology Magazine* 15, no. 3 (2000): 34–41.

6 Stapleton, "The Short-Lived Miracle of DDT"; Atkinson, *The Day of Battle,* 448.

7 Atkinson, *The Day of Battle,* 146.

8 *Ibid.,* 572.

9   Stapleton, "The Short Lived Miracle of DDT."

1 0   G. Fischer, "The Nobel Prize in Physiology or Medicine 1948 Presentation Speech," in *Nobel Lectures: Physiology or Medicine 1942–1962* (Amsterdam: Elsevier, 1964), available at www.nobelprize.org/nobel_prizes/medicine/laureates/1948/press.html.

1 1   Roger Bate, "The Rise, Fall, Rise, and Imminent Fall of DDT," AEI Health Policy Outlook Series, no. 14 (November 2007), http://www.aei.org/outlook/27063.

1 2   Bate, "The Rise, Fall, Rise, and Imminent Fall of DDT; Amir Attaran *et al.*, "Balancing Risks on the Backs of the Poor," *Nature Medicine* 6, no. 7 (2000): 729.

1 3   Nicholas Murray, *Aldous Huxley: A Biography* (New York: Thomas Dunne Books, 2002), 276, 416, 454; Aldous Huxley, *Brave New World Revisited* (New York: Harper & Row, 1958; New York: Harper & Row Perennial Edition, 1965), 8. Citations are to the Perennial edition. The general dissemination of pleasure-producing recreational drugs is prevalent in *Brave New World*, and Huxley would later openly advocate recreational psychopharmacology, including psychedelic drugs like LSD, which he used.

1 4   Aldous Huxley, "Racial History," review of *The Conquest of a Continent*, by Madison Grant, Hearst, February 7, 1934, reprinted in Aldous Huxley, *Complete Essays* (Chicago: Ivan R. Dee, 2000), 3:377–378. Huxley's review quibbled with certain aspects of Grant's racial vision that revealed much about his own: "The trouble begins when Mr. Grant interprets the facts he has collected and passes judgments of value upon them. For the interpretation is throughout in terms of race and the judgments are based on the assumption of Nordic superiority. With some of Mr. Grant's conclusions almost everyone will agree. Miscegenation should be prevented, because there is good evidence to show that cross-breeding between individuals of widely different race is biologically unsound.... Now, it seems unquestionable that much of the new immigration [to America] was of rather poor quality. But was this a *racial* defect?... No branch of the white race has a monopoly of intelligence.... The thing that immigration officers should discriminate against is not race (except in those cases where miscegenation leads to biologically undesirable results) but stupidity. A country's first need is good brains, not blue eyes."

1 5   Aldous Huxley, review of *The Melting Pot*, by Israel Zangwill, *Westminster Gazette*, December 9, 1920, 6.

1 6   Huxley, *Brave New World Revisited*, 17.

1 7   In 1958, Rachel Carson contacted E. B. White, a contributor to *The New Yorker*, suggesting someone should write about DDT; he declined, but the magazine's editor, William Shawn, suggested that Carson herself write it. The ensuing articles, supplemented by additional material, became *Silent Spring*, for which Carson signed a contract with Houghton Mifflin in August 1958. Linda Lear, *Rachel Carson: Witness for Nature* (New York: Henry Holt, 1997), 316–326.

1 8   Rachel Carson, *Silent Spring* (New York: Houghton Mifflin, 1962; New York:

Mariner Books 40th Anniversary Edition, 2002), 1–3. Citations are to Mariner edition.

19 See the focus section later in this chapter for an analysis of Carson's claims.

20 Carson, *Silent Spring*, 16, 22, 225.

21 J. Gordon Edwards, "DDT: A Case Study in Scientific Fraud," *Journal of American Physicians and Surgeons* 9, no. 3 (2004): 86.

22 Attaran *et al.*, "Balancing Risks on the Backs of the Poor," 729.

23 National Academy of Sciences, Committee on Research in the Life Sciences of the Committee on Science and Public Policy, *The Life Sciences: Recent Progress and Application to Human Affairs, The World of Biological Research, Requirements for the Future* (Washington, DC: GPO, 1970), 432.

24 Edmund M. Sweeney, "Consolidated DDT Hearing: Hearing Examiner's Recommended Findings, Conclusions, and Orders," Environmental Protection Agency, 40 CFR 164.32 (April 25, 1972), 12, 93–94.

25 "A Decade of Family Planning Progress," *Draper Fund Report*, no. 13, 1984, 29.

26 Bate, "The Rise, Fall, Rise, and Imminent Fall of DDT," 4.

27 Edwards, "DDT: A Case Study in Scientific Fraud," 86; Environmental Protection Agency, William Ruckelshaus, "Environmental Protection Agency: Consolidated DDT Hearings, Opinion and Order of the Administrator," *Federal Register* 37, no. 131, July 7, 1972: 13369–13376. As it happened, in August 1970, while Ruckelshaus was still assistant attorney general, he had stated in a brief filed with the U.S. Court of Appeals for the District of Columbia Circuit that "DDT is not endangering the Public Health. To the contrary, DDT is an indispensable weapon in the arsenal of substances used to protect human health and has an amazing and exemplary record of safe use. . . . DDT, when properly used at recommended concentrations, does not cause a toxic response in man or other mammals and is not harmful." Brief for the Respondents, William D. Ruckelshaus and Environmental Protection Agency, *Environmental Defense Fund, Inc. v. Ruckelshaus*, No 23813 (DC App filed August 31, 1970).

28 USAID's environmental procedures are laid out in USAID, "Agency Environmental Procedures," 22 CFR 216, October 9, 1980, available online at http://www.usaid.gov/our_work/environment/compliance/22cfr216.htm. In a statement on the USAID website, undated but apparently from the last decade, the agency takes great pains to explain that it has no regulation formally forbidding funding of DDT projects in other countries—but not once does it explicitly mention any DDT projects that it has funded since the 1970s. See USAID, "USAID Support for Malaria Control in Countries Using DDT," http://pdf.usaid.gov/pdf_docs/PDACH948.pdf. An apparently more recent USAID statement, also undated, does acknowledge a new interest in funding projects that use DDT on a small scale and indoors only. See USAID, "USAID and Malaria," http://www.usaid.gov/our_work/global_health/id/malaria/news/afrmal_ddt.html.

29 See, for example, the 1986 statement by Secretary of State George Schultz: "The

U.S. cannot, repeat cannot . . . participate in programs using any of the following: (1) lindane, (2) BHC, (3) DDT, or (4) dieldrin." Edwards, "DDT: A Case Study in Scientific Fraud," 87. As recently as 2004, one USAID official admitted that the reason her agency "doesn't finance DDT is that doing so would require a battle for public opinion. 'You'd have to explain to everybody why this is really O.K. and safe every time you do it,' she said." In short, public perception has been allowed to trump scientific fact in the debate over this life-saving chemical. Tina Rosenberg, "What the World Needs Now Is DDT," *New York Times Magazine*, April 11, 2004, 41.

30 Agency for Toxic Substances and Disease Registry (ATSDR, "Toxicological Profile for DDT, DDE, and DDD," 2002, 222, available at http://www.atsdr.cdc.gov/toxprofiles/tp35.pdf.

31 In Africa alone, numerous studies suggest a figure of one million malaria deaths per year since the 1960s. See Robert W. Snow and Judy A. Omumbo, *Disease and Mortality in Sub-Saharan Africa* (Washington, DC: World Bank, 2006), available at http://www.ncbi.nlm.nih.gov/books/NBK2286/. Other estimates are higher; one World Health Organization researcher estimated in the 1990s that there were "1.5 to 2.7 million deaths" from malaria per year in Africa. Thomas C. Nchinda, "Malaria: A Reemerging Disease," *Emerging Infectious Diseases* 4, no. 3 (1998), available at http://www.cdc.gov/ncidod/eid/vol4no3/nchinda.htm. Although malaria deaths have begun to decline in recent years—see the World Health Organization's annual *World Malaria Report* for estimates—the total global death toll from malaria since the publication of *Silent Spring* is probably between 60 and 150 million.

32 E.J.L. Soulsby and William R. Harvey, "Disease Transmission by Arthropods," *Science* 176, no. 4039 (1972): 1153–1155.

33 Charles T. Rubin, *The Green Crusade* (Lanham, MD: Rowman & Littlefield, 1994), 38–44. Rubin, unlike other critics of *Silent Spring*, closely compares some of Carson's claims to the original studies she cites as sources for her information. He finds a pattern in which she misrepresents the studies or takes claims out of context so as to make "the harm of pesticides seem greater, more certain, or more unprecedented than the original source indicates." *Ibid.*, 39–40.

34 R.E. Duggan and P.E. Corneliussen, "Dietary Intake of Pesticide Chemicals in the United States (III), June 1969-April 1970," *Pesticides Monitoring Journal* 5, no. 4 (1972): 331–341, available online at http://www.archive.org/details/pesticidesmonitoo5unit. This comprehensive multi-year study, conducted by scientists working for the Food and Drug Administration, was cited by EPA reports well into the 1970s. My figure of 30 micrograms per day is an extrapolation from their data, assuming an average weight of around 68 kg (150 pounds) and working from the fact that the study assumed a diet "almost twice the 'average' intake of the 'average' individual."

35 World Health Organization, *DDT in Indoor Residual Spraying: Human Health Aspects* (Geneva: WHO, 2011), 71, available at http://www.who.int/ipcs/publications/ehc/ehc241.pdf.

36 D. Ditraglia *et al.*, "Mortality Study of Workers Employed at Organochlorine Pesticide Manufacturing Plants," *Scandinavian Journal of Work, Environment & Health* 7, no. 4 (1981): 140–146; Wong *et al.*, "Mortality of Workers Potentially Exposed to Organic and Inorganic Brominated Chemicals, DBCP, TRIS, PBB, and DDT," *British Journal of Industrial Medicine* 41, no. 1 (1984): 15–24; H. Austin *et al.*, "A Prospective Follow-Up Study of Cancer Mortality in Relation to Serum DDT," *American Journal of Public Health* 79, no. 1 (1989): 43–46; Cocco *et al.*, "Proportional Mortality of Dichloro-Diphenyl-Trichloroethane (DDT) Workers: A Preliminary Report," *Archives of Environmental Health* 52, no. 4 (1997): 299–303; P. Cocco *et al.*, "Cancer Mortality and Environmental Exposure to DDE in the United States," *Environmental Health Perspectives* 108, no. 1 (2000): 1–4; Cocco *et al.*, "Cancer Mortality Among Men Occupationally Exposed to Dichlorodiphenyltrichloroethane," *Cancer Research* 65, no. 20 (2005): 9588–9594; Purdue *et al.*, "Occupational Exposure to Organochlorine Insecticide and Cancer Incidence in the Agricultural Health Study," *International Journal of Cancer* 120, no. 3 (2007): 642–649.

37 World Health Organization, *DDT in Indoor Residual Spraying*, 71–83. There is, however, some evidence that exposure to DDT before puberty may be linked to breast cancer later in life; see *ibid.*, 71–75.

38 *Ibid.*, 52–61.

39 *Ibid.*, 61–64.

40 Alice Ottoboni, "Effect of DDT on the Reproductive Life-Span in the Female Rat," *Toxicology and Applied Pharmacology* 22, no. 3 (1972): 497–502.

41 Alice Ottoboni, Glenn D. Bissell, and Alfred C. Hexter, "Effects of DDT on Reproduction in Multiple Generations of Beagle Dogs," *Archives of Environmental Contamination and Toxicology* 6, no. 1 (1977): 83–101.

42 ATSDR, "Toxicological Profile for DDT, DDE, and DDD," 2002, 25.

43 Sweeney, "Hearing Examiner's Recommended Findings, Conclusions, and Orders," 93.

44 Carson, *Silent Spring*, 103–127.

45 *Ibid.*, 104–109. When I was a little boy growing up in Brooklyn in the late 1950s, my mother frequently took me for neighborhood walks during which we looked for birds. We saw plenty of robins (and pigeons, crows, sparrows, and gulls, as well as ducks and geese during their migration time). This was in Brooklyn, no less, where the birds had to face not only pesticides but the polluting emissions from millions of cars and homes and businesses, not to mention the predatory activities of innumerable small boys armed with slingshots and BB guns. The idea that the United States was in danger of running out of birds—particularly

robins!—in 1959 is so far from reality as to defy satire. I haven't been back to my old neighborhood in decades, but I am quite certain that the robins are still there, just as they are everywhere else.

46 National Audubon Society, 1942, The 42nd Christmas Bird Count, *Audubon Magazine*; National Audubon Society, 1961, The 61st Christmas Bird Count, *Audubon Field Notes* 15, no. 2. The Audubon Society keeps its data freely available online at http://birds.audubon.org/historical-results.

47 Carson, *Silent Spring*, 104.

48 J.W. Taylor, "Summaries of Hawk Mountain Migrations of Raptors: 1934–1970," *Hawk Mountain Sanctuary Newsletters*, quoted in Edwards, "DDT: A Case Study in Scientific Fraud," 84.

49 F. Graham, *Audubon Magazine*, January 1985, 17; Edwards, "DDT: A Case Study in Scientific Fraud," 84.

50 J. R. Sauer *et al.*, *The North American Breeding Bird Survey, Results and Analysis 1966–2009*, version 3.23.2011, USGS Patuxent Wildlife Research Center, Laurel, MD. http://www.mbr-pwrc.usgs.gov/bbs/.

51 ATSDR, "Toxicological Profile for DDT, DDE, and DDD," 134, D24–D26.

52 J. Gordon Edwards, "The Lies of Rachel Carson," *21st Century Science and Technology*, Summer 1992, available online at http://www.21stcenturysciencetech.com/articles/summo2/Carson.html.

53 Charles F. Wurster, Jr., "DDT Reduces Photosynthesis by Marine Phytoplankton," *Science* 159, no. 3822 (1968): 1474–75.

54 DDT can be dissolved in seawater at concentrations higher than 1.2 ppb if the water contains other components, and of course DDT that is not dissolved can still be carried in suspension. But even so, Wurster was unable to find any examples in nature of water with DDT levels at 500 ppb, even though he took samples from locations that had very recently been treated with DDT, and the highest concentrations he found were short-lived and very localized—hardly sufficient to pose a serious threat to the world's oceans. Wurster, "DDT Reduces Photosynthesis by Marine Phytoplankton," 1475.

55 Thomas H. Jukes, "*Silent Spring* and the Betrayal of Environmentalism," *21st Century Science and Technology* 7, no. 3 (Fall 1994).

56 Paul Ehrlich, "Eco-Catastrophe!" *Ramparts*, September 1969, 24–28.

CHAPTER NINE · SCRIPTURES FOR THE DOOM CULT

1 From a 1967 speech at a University of Texas symposium, quoted in Allan Chase, *The Legacy of Malthus: The Social Costs of the New Scientific Racism* (New York: Knopf, 1977), 398, 421.

2 Paul R. Ehrlich and Anne H. Ehrlich, "The Population Bomb Revisited," *Electronic Journal of Sustainable Development* 1, no. 3 (2009): 73–97, http://www.ejsd.org/docs/The_Population_Bomb_Revisited.pdf.

3 Paul R. Ehrlich, *The Population Bomb* (New York: Ballantine Books, 1968; New York: Ballantine Books, 1975), xi-xii. Citations are to the 1975 edition. Italics added.

4 *Ibid.*, 1.

5 *Ibid.*, 152.

6 *Ibid.*, 151–152.

7 *Ibid.*, 152.

8 *Ibid.*, 132–133.

9 *Ibid.*, 130–131.

10 *Ibid.*, 131.

11 *Ibid.*, 131–132.

12 *Ibid.*, 155–156.

13 *Ibid.*, 133–134.

14 Larry D. Barnett, "Zero Population Growth, Inc.," *BioScience* 21, no. 14 (1971): 759; Ehrlich, *The Population Bomb*, 131; Editorial, "Population Policy Needed," *Sarasota Herald Tribune*, Jan 1, 1980, available at http://news.google.com/news papers?nid=1755&dat=19800101&id=wCMhAAAAIBAJ&sjid=wWcEAAA AIBAJ&pg=2699,38509. According to the editorial, "Congress is now consid- ering legislation to declare a national policy goal of population stabilization and to establish an Office of Population Policy in the White House. . . . In introducing the bill, Rep. Richard Ottinger (D-NY) reminded his colleagues in the House of Representatives that the measure asks for nothing the United States does not already advocate to the less developed nations of the world." Ottinger's legisla- tion, H.R. 5062 ("A bill to declare a national policy goal of national population stabilization, and to establish an Office of Population Policy"), can be found online at http://hdl.loc.gov/loc.uscongress/legislation.96hr5062.

15 Club of Rome, "Founding the Club of Rome," http://www.clubofrome.at/ peccei/clubofrome.html.

16 Pentti Malaska and Matti Vapaavuori, ed., "Club of Rome Dossiers: 1965–1984," (Finnish Association for the Club of Rome, 2005), http://www.clubofrome.at/ archive/pdf/dossiers.pdf; Donella Meadows *et al.*, *The Limits to Growth: A Report for the Club of Rome's Project on the Predicament of Mankind* (New York: New American Library, 1972), ix-x.

17 Meadows *et al.*, *The Limits to Growth*, xi.

18 Peter J. Henriot, "The Politics of Ecology," America, June 17, 1972, 636, quoted in Charles T. Rubin, *The Green Crusade: Rethinking the Roots of Environ- mentalism* (Lanham, MD: Rowman and Littlefield, 1998), 133.

19 Meadows *et al.*, *The Limits to Growth*, 56–58.

20 Julian Simon and Herman Kahn, *The Resourceful Earth: A Response to Global 2000* (New York: Blackwell, 1984), 1–51; Julian Simon, *The Ultimate Resource 2* (Princeton, NJ: Princeton University Press, 1996), 509; The Council on Envi- ronmental Quality and U.S. Department of State, *The Global 2000 Report to*

*the President*, Gerald Barney, study director (Washington, DC: GPO, 1980).

21 Paul and Anne Ehrlich, *The End of Affluence: A Blueprint for Your Future* (New York: Ballantine Books, 1974), 7.

22 Meadows *et al.*, *The Limits to Growth*, 56–58.

23 Julian Simon, *The Ultimate Resource* (Princeton, NJ: Princeton University Press, 1980), 27.

24 Simon, *The Ultimate Resource* 2, 35.

25 Meadows *et al.*, *The Limits to Growth*, 56–58.

26 James F. Carlin, Jr., "Tin," in *Metal Prices in the United States Through 1998*, U.S. Geological Survey, 1998, available at http://minerals.usgs.gov/minerals/pubs/metal_prices/metal_prices1998.pdf. Prices are in 1992 dollars.

27 The wager has been analyzed many times since 1990, usually by those who wish to show that Simon's victory was a fluke. See, for example, Alex Tabarrok, "Revisiting Simon-Ehrlich," *Marginal Revolution*, 2010, http://marginalrevolution.com/marginalrevolution/2010/02/revisiting-simonehrlich.html.

28 Simon, *The Ultimate Resource* 2, 35–36.

29 I would prefer to continue to call the trio geniuses but, given the facts of the case, fear loss of credibility should I persist in doing so. So in deference to the sensibilities of my more skeptical readers, I will relent and simply call them suckers, as I feel I can do without worry of contradiction.

30 Simon, *The Ultimate Resource* 2, 45.

## CHAPTER TEN · THE BETRAYAL OF THE LEFT

1 H. Tudor and J. M. Tudor, eds., *Marxism and Social Democracy: The Revisionist Debate* 1896–1898 (Melbourne: Cambridge University Press, 1988), 169.

2 For example, Ronald Meek, ed., *Marx and Engels on the Population Bomb* (Berkeley, CA: Ramparts Press, 1971).

3 Richard Neuhaus, *In Defense of People: Ecology and the Seduction of Radicalism* (New York: Macmillan, 1971), 33.

4 *Ibid.*, 59–60, 214–216. Neuhaus would go on to leave the left altogether, chiefly over the issue of abortion, and in 1990 founded the magazine *First Things*.

5 Paul Ehrlich, "Eco-Catastrophe!" *Ramparts*, September 1969, 24–28.

6 Allan Chase, *The Legacy of Malthus: The Social Costs of the New Scientific Racism* (Chicago: University of Illinois Press, 1980), 382–86; Jacqueline Kasun, *The War Against Population: The Economics and Ideology of Population Control* (San Francisco: Ignatius, 1988), 218.

7 Lawrence Lader, *Breeding Ourselves to Death* (New York: Ballantine Books, 1971), 81.

8 Chase, *The Legacy of Malthus*, 386–87.

9 *Kraft durch Freude* ("Strength through Joy") was a German organization in the

1930s and 40s that sought to promote Nazi ideals through sport and leisure activities.

10 Chase, *The Legacy of Malthus*, 386–387.


CHAPTER ELEVEN · THE ANTI-NUCLEAR CRUSADE

1 Paul R. Ehrlich and Richard L. Harriman, *How to Be a Survivor* (New York: Ballantine, 1971), 72.

2 Petr Beckmann, *The Health Hazards of Not Going Nuclear* (Boulder, CO: Golem Press, 1976), 86–87, 124.

3 "Coal Workers' Pneumoconiosis-Related Years of Potential Life Lost Before Age 65 Years—United States, 1968–2006," *Morbidity and Mortality Weekly Report* 58, no. 50 (2009). The exact figure is 28,912 deceased persons aged at least 25 due to black lung disease between 1968 and 2006; assuming the average of 300 deaths per year from 2002–2006 carried forward, the number of deaths due to black lung from 1968–2011 would be well over 30,000. Moreover, the report notes that this is likely an *underestimate* due to many black lung deaths being misattributed on death certificates to other causes. Note also that, while incidence of black lung disease had been falling dramatically since federal regulations began in 1969, the total number of years of potential life lost before age 65 (YPLL) has been increasing since 2002, and the YPLL per deceased person has been increasing since the early 1990s—apparently due to slackening enforcement of safety standards and increased working hours per miner.

4 Michael Kruzer *et al.*, "Radon and Risk of Extrapulmonary Cancers: Results of the German Uranium Miners' Cohort Study, 1960–2003," *British Journal of Cancer* 99, no. 11 (2008): 1946–1953; Gunter Wolf *et al.*, "Chromosomal Aberrations in Uranium and Coal Miners," *International Journal of Radiation Biology* 80, no. 2 (2005): 147–153.

5 Beckmann, *The Health Hazards of Not Going Nuclear*, 82.

6 J. P. McBride *et al.*, "Radiological Impact of Airborne Effluents of Coal and Nuclear Power Plants," *Science* 202, no. 4372 (1978): 1045–1050.

7 John Lamarsh, *Introduction to Nuclear Engineering*, 2nd ed. (Reading, MA: Addison-Wesley, 1983), 351.

8 Robert C. Duncan, "Nuclear Power vs. Clean Coal's Dirty Mess," *Fort Worth Star-Telegram*, Feb. 8, 2009.

9 Beckmann, *The Health Hazards of Not Going Nuclear*, 121.

10 *Ibid.*, 88.

11 *Ibid.*

12 *Ibid.*

13 Duncan, "Nuclear Power vs. Clean Coal's Dirty Mess"; American Lung Association, "Toxic Air: Time to Clean Up Coal-Fired Power Plants," March 8, 2011,

http://www.lungusa.org/about-us/our-impact/top-stories/toxic-air-coal-fired-power-plants.html. The American Lung Association reports that more than 400 coal-fired power plants in the U.S. are estimated to kill approximately 13,000 people a year; replacing each plant would then prevent over 30 deaths annually, adding up to hundreds over the lifetime of the plant.

14  Beckmann, *The Health Hazards of Not Going Nuclear*, 11, 73.

15  Eric N. Skousen, *The War Against Nuclear Power* (Salt Lake City: The Freemen Institute, 1981), 46.

16  U.S. Energy Information Administration, *Annual Energy Review 2009* (Washington, DC: Energy Information Administration, 2010), 275, http://www.eia.gov/emeu/aer/pdf/pages/sec9.pdf. However, as of this writing, one nuclear plant is under construction in the United States, at the Watts Bar Nuclear Generating Station in Tennessee; construction there resumed in 2007 after a pause of nearly two decades. Meanwhile, the Nuclear Regulatory Commission is currently reviewing more than two dozen applications for new reactors, and some might receive construction permits over the next few years.

17  Using the figure of 98.079 quadrillion BTU of total energy consumption in the U.S. in 2010 from the Energy Information Administration, and the 2010 U.S. population of 308.7 million in the 2010 Census. This comes to 317.7 million BTU, or 10,629 watt-years, per capita. See U.S. Energy Information Administration, *August 2011 Monthly Energy Review*, August 19, 2011, 3, http://www.eia.gov/totalenergy/data/monthly/.

18  "A Survey of the Future of Energy: The Power and the Glory," *The Economist*, June 19, 2008.

19  See as one example of this philosophy, UNESCO, *Declaration on the Responsibilities of the Present Generations Towards Future Generations*, adopted November 12, 1997, article 4.

20  Robert Zubrin, *Energy Victory: Winning the War on Terror by Breaking Free of Oil* (Amherst, NY: Prometheus Books, 2007), 210. Also see: Ronald Knief, *Nuclear Energy Technology: Theory and Practice of Commercial Nuclear Power* (New York: McGraw Hill, 1981), 549; George A. Olah, Alain Goeppert, and G. K. Surya Prakash, *Beyond Oil and Gas: The Methanol Economy* (Weinheim, Germany: Wiley-VCH, 2006), 27–50; BP, "BP Statistical Review of World Energy, June 2011," 2011, www.bp.com/statisticalreview; and U.S. Bureau of the Census, "International Data Base: Total Midyear Population for the World: 1950–2050," June 2011, http://www.census.gov/population/international/data/idb/worldpoptotal.php.

21  U.S. Bureau of the Census, Population Clock, census.gov.

22  Christine Perham, "EPA's Role At Three Mile Island" *EPA Journal* 6, no. 9 (1980), available at http://www.epa.gov/aboutepa/history/topics/tmi/02.html.

23  Government of Japan, "Occurrence and Development of the Accident at the Fukushima Nuclear Power Stations" in *Report of Japanese Government to IAEA*

*Ministerial Conference on Nuclear Safety: Accident at TEPCO's Fukushima Nuclear Power Stations* (Nuclear Emergency Response Headquarters, June 2011), http://www.iaea.org/newscenter/focus/fukushima/japan-report/chapter–4.pdf.

24 Jonathan Tirone, Stuart Biggs, and Simon Lomax, "NRC Chief Warns of Risks as Japanese Flee Tsunami Region," *Bloomberg News*, March 16, 2011; Thomas H. Maugh II, "U.S. Officials Express Strong Concerns About Japan Nuclear Crisis," *Los Angeles Times*, March 16, 2011.

25 U.S. Navy 7th Fleet, "Seventh Fleet Repositions Ships after Contamination Detected," press release, March 14, 2011, http://www.navy.mil/search/display. asp?story_id=59065.

26 Robert Zubrin, "Fire NRC Chairman Gregory Jaczko," *National Review Online*, June 13, 2011, http://www.nationalreview.com/articles/269475/fire-nrc-chairman-gregory-jaczko-robert-zubrin.

27 The Chernobyl Forum, *Chernobyl's Legacy: Health, Environmental, and Socioeconomic Impacts* (Vienna, Austria: IAEA, 2005), 16.

28 Robert Pool, *Beyond Engineering: How Society Shapes Technology* (New York: Oxford University Press, 1997), 50–52.

29 J. Samuel Walker, *Three Mile Island: A Nuclear Crisis in Historical Perspective* (Berkeley, CA: University of California Press, 2004), 25. Walker cites a 1975 Harris poll revealing that only 24 percent of those polled believed that a power plant could not explode like an atomic bomb.

30 Senate Committee on Environment and Public Works, *Yucca Mountain: The Most Studied Real Estate on the Planet, Report to the Chairman*, prepared by majority staff, http://epw.senate.gov/repwhitepapers/YuccaMountainEPWReport.pdf.

31 U.S. Department of Energy, *Rev. 1 to DOE/RW–0539, Yucca Mountain Science and Engineering Report* (North Las Vegas, NV: U.S. DOE 2002), 4–463, http://pbadupws.nrc.gov/docs/ML0305/ML030580066.pdf.

32 Charles D. Hollister, D. Richard Anderson, and G. Ross Heath, "Subseabed Disposal of Nuclear Wastes," *Science* 213, no. 4514 (1981): 1321–1326. See also Scientia Press, "Sea-Based Nuclear Waste Solutions," http://www.scientiapress. com/findings/sea-based.htm.

33 Senate Committee on Environment and Public Works, "Yucca Mountain."

34 Hannah Northey, "GAO: Death of Yucca Mountain Caused by Political Maneuvering," *Greenwire* for NYtimes.com, May 10, 2011, http://www.nytimes.com/gwire/2011/05/10/10greenwire-gao-death-of-yucca-mountain-caused-by-politica–36298.html.

35 Senate Committee on Environment and Public Works, "Democrats' Mission to Kill Yucca Mountain Rejects Sound Science, American Energy Security, and American Jobs," press release, May 7, 2009, http://epw.senate.gov/public/index.cfm?FuseAction=Minority.PressReleases&ContentRecord_id=1c2f9d87-802a-23ad-4596-63977c942f69&Region_id=&Issue_id=.

36 U.S. Nuclear Regulatory Commission, "Fact Sheet on Biological Effects of

Radiation," January 2011, last reviewed/updated February 4, 2011, http://www.nrc.gov/reading-rm/doc-collections/fact-sheets/bio-effects-radiation.html. See also, National Council on Radiation Protection and Measurements, "Uncertainties in Fatal Cancer Risk Estimates Used in Radiation Protection," *NCRP Report*, no. 126 (1997).

37 Beckmann, *The Health Hazards of Not Going Nuclear*, 113–114; Health Physics Society, "What Are Some Sources of Radiation Exposure?" updated August 27, 2011, http://hps.org/publicinformation/ate/faqs/radsources.html; Stanley S. Johnson, "Natural Radiation," *Virginia Minerals* 37, no. 2 (1991), available at http://www.dmme.virginia.gov/DMR3/dmrpdfs/vamin/VAMIN_VOL37_NO02.PDF; U.S. Department of Energy Oak Ridge Office, "About Radiation," 2009, http://www.oakridge.doe.gov/external/PublicActivities/EmergencyPublicInformation/AboutRadiation/tabid/319/Default.aspx. The Environmental Protection Agency website offers a calculator that lets you estimate your annual radiation dosage: http://www.epa.gov/radiation/understand/calculate.html.

38 Richard Rhodes, "Radioactive Coal Ash," *New York Times*, September 8, 2010.

39 This is because commercial reactors keep their fuel in place for a long time, during which some of the $^{239}$Pu created in the reactor absorbs a further neutron to become $^{240}$Pu. The $^{240}$Pu seriously degrades the value of the plutonium for weapons purposes. However, in standalone atomic piles, such as those developed at the Hanford Site during the Manhattan Project, the fuel is not left in the system for long, so the plutonium produced is not spoiled. In the case of thorium reactors, which breed $^{232}$Th to $^{233}$U, the use of reactor fuel for bomb-making becomes even more difficult, making such systems ideal for use in situations where proliferation is of concern.

40 Hans Fantel, "Science Taps Star Power for Unlimited Energy," *Popular Mechanics* 145, no. 4 (1976): 71.

41 Robert W. Conn et al., "Lower Activation Materials and Magnetic Fusion Reactors," *Nuclear Technology/Fusion* 5, no. 3 (1984): 291–310.

42 George Liu et al., "The Rate of Methanol Production on a Copper-Zinc Oxide Catalyst: The Dependence on the Feed Composition," *Journal of Catalysis* 90, no. 1 (1984): 139–146.

43 Kevin Bonsor, "How Fusion Propulsion Will Work," Space Propulsion Systems, Inc., http://www.sps.aero/Key_ComSpace_Articles/TSA-005_Fusion_Propulsion_White_Paper.pdf.

44 European Fusion Development Agreement, "The Current Status of Fusion Research," 2010, http://www.efda.org/fusion_energy/fusion_research_today.htm.

45 Robert W. Conn, "Magnetic Fusion Reactors," in Edward Teller, ed., *Fusion: Magnetic Confinement*, vol. 1, pt. B (New York: Academic Press, 1981), 194–398.

46 Robert Zubrin, "A Deuterium-Tritium Ignition Ramp for an Advanced Fuel Field-reversed Configuration Reactor," *Fusion Technology* 9, no. 1 (1986): 97–100.

47 In view of the extraordinary potential benefits of controlled fusion, it is amazing that the U.S. Department of Energy's annual budget for fusion research is limited to about $400 million per year. When compared to the cost of a single space shuttle flight, this number is truly remarkable. Though NASA for years claimed that each flight costs only $450 million, over the lifetime of the program the average cost for a single space shuttle launch was closer to $1.5 *billion* dollars. By contrast, very little funding has been made available to build the next machine to advance on the fusion accomplishments achieved by the Princeton Plasma Physics Lab TFTR, built circa 1980. The same pattern can be observed in the European, Russian, and Japanese programs, none of which has been funded to build any new fusion experimental machines of consequence since the late 1980s. This is why, in contrast to the earlier period, there has been no advance in experimental achievement in the fusion field since 1995. This period of stagnation can be laid at the doorstep of the bureaucrats of the U.S. Department of Energy and their counterparts in the European, Japanese, and Russian programs, who decided in the mid–1980s to replace their (supposedly wasteful, but actually quite productive) competing national programs with a single international cooperative program, called ITER (for International Tokamak Experimental Reactor, to which the United States funds 9 percent of the program's budget). Lacking competitive spur, the ITER consortium has not achieved anything—not even a single experiment since it was launched almost a quarter century ago.

This must certainly please the Malthusians, who made their true feelings about fusion clear in 1989, when an (unfortunately false) report appeared in the media that two chemists had made a breakthrough enabling cheap, practical, "cold fusion" energy without any radioactive wastes. In response to this apparent windfall for mankind, leading environmentalists could only express horror. On April 19, 1989, author Jeremy Rifkin told the *Los Angeles Times* that cold fusion was "the worst thing that could happen to our planet." In the same article, John Holdren, currently president Obama's science advisor, also expressed his dismay over the invention, saying "clean-burning, non-polluting, hydrogen-using bulldozers still could knock down trees or build housing developments on farmland." Holdren's mentor, *Population Bomb* author Paul Ehrlich, went further (as always), stating that "industrialized societies, so far, have not used power wisely"—and thus cold fusion, even if clean and cheap, would be "like giving a machine gun to an idiot child."

U.S. Department of Energy, *FY 2012 Congressional Budget: Science: Fusion Energy Sciences*, 207, http://science.energy.gov/~/media/budget/pdf/sc-budget-request-to-congress/fy-2012/Cong_Budget_2012_FES.pdf; Roger Pielke, Jr. and Radford Byerly, "Shuttle Programme Lifetime Cost," *Nature* 472, no. 7341 (2011): 38; Bjørn Lomborg, *The Skeptical Environmentalist* (Cambridge, UK: Cambridge University Press, 2001), 321.

CHAPTER TWELVE · POPULATION CONTROL: PREPARING
THE HOLOCAUST

1  Exodus, 1:9–22 (New American Bible).
2  Lyndon B. Johnson, "Address in San Francisco at the 20th Anniversary Commemorative Session of the United Nations: June 25, 1965," *Public Papers of the President of the United States Lyndon B. Johnson: 1965 (in two books): Containing the Public Messages, Speeches, and Statements of the President*, Washington, DC, bk. 2, 331, 703–706. Also available at *The American Presidency Project*, http://www.presidency.ucsb.edu/ws/index.php?pid=27054#axzz1JWJ8iGM1.
3  Matthew Connelly, *Fatal Misconception* (Cambridge, MA: Belknap, 2008).
4  U.S. National Security Council, Henry A. Kissinger, "National Security Study Memorandum 200: Implications of Worldwide Population Growth for U.S. Security and Overseas Interests," December 10, 1974, (also known as the Kissinger Report, and hereafter cited as NSSM 200), available at http://pdf.usaid.gov/pdf_docs/PCAAB500.pdf.
5  Angela Franks, *Margaret Sanger's Eugenic Legacy: The Control of Female Fertility* (Jefferson, NC: McFarland, 2005), 167–168.
6  Alexandra Minna Stern, "Sterilized in the Name of Public Health: Race, Immigration, and Reproductive Control in Modern California," *American Journal of Public Health* 95, no. 7 (2005): 1133.
7  Bonnie Mass, *Population Target: The Political Economy of Population Control in Latin America* (Toronto: Latin American Working Group, 1976), 101. The program in Puerto Rico, which began well before the federal commitment to population control, was run by Ernest Gruening, the first director of the U.S. Division of Territories and Island Possessions. Gruening and his wife had been delegates at Margaret Sanger's first American Birth Control League meeting, and they advocated population control throughout their lives. By the 1960s, Gruening was the first U.S. Senator from Alaska (he had previously been governor of the Alaska Territory) and a trustee of the Draper Fund/Population Crisis Committee. In 1966–67, he played a central role in orchestrating the Senate vote on population control funding, advocating access to family planning as a human right. With Puerto Rico, Gruening, a doctor turned journalist turned politician, had used money from the Department of Health, Education, and Welfare to develop a model that the Johnson administration looked to later when advocating worldwide population control. In 1968, in recognition for his efforts toward population control, Planned Parenthood awarded Senator Gruening the Margaret Sanger Award in World Leadership; see Planned Parenthood, "PPFA Margaret Sanger Award Winners," http://www.plannedparenthood.org/about-us/newsroom/politics-policy-issues/ppfa-margaret-sanger-award-winners-4840.htm.
8  Matthew Connelly, *Fatal Misconception: The Struggle to Control World Population* (Cambridge, MA: Belknap Press, 2008) 210–213. The study was "Lower

Birth Rates—Some Economic Aspects," by RAND economist Stephen Enke, February 12, 1965. Enke was an economist who shortly afterwards became Deputy Assistant Secretary of Defense under McNamara. A discount rate is the comparative value of money in the future vs. money today. Thus, at a discount rate of 15 percent, it takes $1.15 (in inflation-adjusted dollars) next year to equal $1 spent this year. For payback several years in the future, the yearly discount rate factor is compounded, so for example at a discount rate of 15 percent, it takes $1.15 raised to the 20th power, or $16.37, of inflation-adjusted dollars, paid back twenty years from now to equal $1 spent today, or $267.86 of inflation-adjusted dollars paid back forty years from now. Such a rate of return has never been obtained over time in any economy. For example, the U.S. Standard and Poor's 500 Index (S&P), a measure of the average value of five hundred of the leading stocks in America, was 92 in 1970, and stands at about 1,100 today, so that it has gone up twelvefold—unadjusted for inflation—over the past forty years. Adjusted for inflation, it has only gone up by about a factor of two. (The Consumer Price Index went from 38 in January 1970 to 216 in January 2010, a nearly sixfold increase.) Therefore, in real dollars, a person who put his money in the 500 leading American stocks over the past forty years would have seen his money merely double, not increase by a factor of 268, which is what a discount rate of 15 percent would require. The RAND study was thus complete nonsense, and had no intention other than to make an economic case—a cost-benefit analysis—for population control. Of course, while the equation is ludicrous even on its own terms, the notion of determining the value of children in this way in the first place is morally reprehensible, and is more worthy of Swiftian satirical refutation than of rebuttal via counter-calculations.

9 Attached covering memorandum to "Memorandum from Robert Komer of the National Security Council Staff to President Johnson," *Foreign Relations of the United States, 1964–1968*, vol. 34, Washington, April 27, 1965, 272, n. 1, available at http://history.state.gov/historicaldocuments/frus1964-68v34/d272.

10 See Neil Sheehan, *A Bright and Shining Lie: John Paul Vann and America in Vietnam* (New York: Vintage Books, 1988) and Karen Kampwirth, *Gender and Populism in Latin America: Passionate Politics* (University Park, PA: Penn State Press, 2010), 166–167. The "pacification program" meant the burning of Vietnamese villages (resulting in the deaths of 150,000 over three years in the Quang Nai province alone), destruction of livestock and crops, and the relocation of Vietnamese to "strategic hamlets" run by USAID. "Blowback" was inevitable, as many of the young men who escaped through the barbed wire were motivated to join the Viet Cong. Hatred of the American military soared, and not just in Vietnam. Many revolutionaries took advantage of the unpopular sterilization programs—the Sandinistas in Nicaragua abolished sterilization in 1979, stressing how vital it was for Nicaragua to be repopulated so the nation could work towards becoming more self-sufficient.

11 R. T. Ravenholt, "The AID Population and Family Planning Program—Goals, Scope, and Progress," *Demography* 5, no. 2 (1968): 561–573.

12 Steven W. Mosher, *Population Control: Real Costs, Illusory Benefits* (New Brunswick, NJ: Transaction Publishers, 2008), 40–41.

13 *Ibid.*

14 R. T. Ravenholt, "Africa's Population-Driven Catastrophe Worsens," unpublished paper dated June 2000, www.ravenholt.com, quoted in Mosher, *Population Control*, 65. Ravenholt has since edited this piece, altering the passage in question.

15 Matthew Connelly, *Fatal Misconception*, 232–234. As reported by Connelly: "[Population Council President Frank] Notestein became accustomed to a lifestyle he could hardly have imagined only a few years before. As he traveled the world promoting the IUD, with introductions from John D. Rockefeller III and World Bank President Eugene Black, this once obscure academic found doors opening to him before he even touched the handle. Heads of state and cabinet ministers sought his counsel, and everywhere family planning workers awaited his approval. With obvious relish, Notestein recorded the hospitality he received in diaries with datelines from such places as Cairo, Taipei, Karachi, and Seoul. They were true banquets, from which he 'staggered away from the table my soul content within me,' only to face 'another day of tremendous eating'. . . . Among his peers Notestein was not particularly conspicuous in his consumption. Alan Guttmacher [president of the Planned Parenthood Federation of America and vice resident of the American Eugenics Society] was in the habit of beginning letters to the Planned Parenthood membership with comments like 'This is written 31,000 feet aloft as I fly from Rio to New York.' He insisted on traveling with his wife, first class, with the IPPF picking up the tab. Ford [Foundation] officials flew first class with their spouses as a matter of policy. One wonders why [Ford Foundation India program director] Douglas Ensminger ever left his residence in Delhi—he was served by a household staff of nine, including maids, cooks, gardeners, and chauffeurs. He titled this part of his oral history 'The "Little People" of India.' Ensminger insisted on the need to pay top dollar and provide a plush lifestyle to attract the best talent, even if the consultants he recruited seemed preoccupied with their perks. One of these strivers ran his two-year-old American sedan without oil just so that the Ford Foundation would have to replace it with the latest model. The fund-raising consultants the IPPF hired advised that it had to spend money to make money. . . . Thus, while the new headquarters in London had 'an air of quality,' it still needed a director-general with . . . a salary and staff support costing twenty thousand pounds (equivalent to more than $450,000 today). The lifestyle of the leaders of the population control establishment reflected the power of an idea whose time had come as well as the influence of the institutions that were now backing it."

16 Mosher, *Population Control*, 43.

17 *Ibid.*

18 Barbara Ehrenreich, Stephen Minkin, and Mark Dowie, "The Charge: Gynocide," *Mother Jones*, Nov./Dec. 1979.

19 *Ibid.*

20 Julian Simon, *The Ultimate Resource* (Princeton, NJ: Princeton University Press, 1981), 292–293.

21 *Ibid.*, 292. Simon presents a table collecting figures for primary sources of "international population assistance funds" from 1965–1976. It is interesting to note that after the United States government, with a total of $867 million over the period in question, the next largest donor for this period was the tiny nation of Sweden, whose outsized contribution of $134 million exceeded that of the United Kingdom ($25 million), West Germany ($23 million), Japan ($22 million), Canada ($34 million), Denmark ($19 million), Belgium ($2.4 million), Australia ($1.6 million), and the OPEC countries ($2.6 million) *combined*. This remarkable effort on the part of Sweden to reduce the world's nonwhite population can be credited to the persistence in the Nordic paradise of a powerful domestic eugenics movement since the 1920s, strongly reinforced by the large number of Nazi refugees who found a safe haven in the neutral nation during the war's immediate aftermath. Championed by welfare-state theoreticians Alva and Gunnar Myrdal (see, for example, their 1934 book *The Crisis in the Population Question*) and the Swedish Society for Eugenics, forced sterilization laws resembling those of Nazi Germany were instituted in Sweden in 1934 and remained on the books until 1976.

22 Jacqueline Kasun, *The War Against Population: the Economics and Ideology of Population Control* (San Francisco: Ignatius, 1988), 163–164; Donald Critchlow, *Intended Consequences: Birth Control, Abortion, and the Federal Government in Modern America* (New York: Oxford University Press, 1999), 161–173; Commission on Population Growth and the American Future, John D. Rockefeller III, chairman, *Population Growth and the American Future* (Washington, DC: GPO, 1972), online at http://www.population-security.org/rockefeller/001_population_growth_and_the_american_future.htm.

23 NSSM 200, 8. Italics added to this and the subsequent quotes from NSSM 200, for readability.

24 *Ibid.*

25 *Ibid.*, 10.

26 *Ibid.*, 14.

27 *Ibid.*, 40.

28 *Ibid.*, 52.

29 *Ibid.*, 63–64.

30 *Ibid.*, 77.

31 *Ibid.*

32 *Ibid.*, 13.

33 *Ibid.*, 81.

34 U.S. National Security Council, Brent Scowcroft, "National Security Decision Memorandum 314: Implications of Worldwide Population Growth for U.S. Security and Overseas Interests," November 26, 1975, Box 1, National Security Decision Memoranda and Study Memoranda, Gerald R. Ford Library, available online at http://www.ford.utexas.edu/library/document/nsdmnssm/nsdm314 a.htm.

35 "Under Secretaries Committee Population Task Force, First Progress Report," National Security Council (1976), 26, quoted in Mosher, *Population Control*, 219.

CHAPTER THIRTEEN · POPULATION CONTROL:
IMPLEMENTING THE HOLOCAUST

1 Bernard Berelson and Jonathan Lieberson, "Government Efforts to Influence Fertility: The Ethical Issues," *Population and Development Review*, December 1979, 609. Population and Development Review is the official journal of the Population Council.

2 Steven W. Mosher, *Population Control: Real Costs, Illusory Benefits* (New Brunswick, NJ: Transaction Publishers, 2008), 133–136. On October 22, 1998, President Clinton signed legislation—called the Tiahrt Amendment, after the Kansas congressman who authored it—that bans U.S. government funding for foreign population control programs that employ quotas or numerical targets, incentives or rewards for program personnel or acceptors, disincentives for non-acceptors, false or obscure representations, or unsafe drugs or medical devices. All of these are standard practice in USAID's population control campaigns. USAID has essentially ignored the law and continued business as usual.

3 Betsy Hartmann, *Reproductive Rights and Wrongs: The Global Politics of Population Control* (Boston: South End Press, 1995).

4 Mosher, *Population Control*, 170–198.

5 *Ibid.*, 128–130.

6 *Ibid.*, 140.

7 *Ibid.*, 141.

8 Michael Benge, "Terrifying Abuses in Vietnam," Commentary Forum, *Washington Times*, January 13, 2002.

9 Mosher, *Population Control*, 140–141.

10 *Ibid.*, 163–198. Also see, for example, the arguments that sterilization is being used to continue, now before birth, the genocide against Hutus in Rwanda: African SurViVors International, "Eugenic sterilization is one of the many indispensable measures that RPF programs use to numerously REDUCE the number of the hated Hutu Rwandans," July 3, 2009, http://survivorsnetworks.blogspot.com/2009/07/eugenic-sterilization-is-one-of-many.html.

11 "International Planned Parenthood Celebrates 40th Anniversary," *Margaret*

*Sanger Papers Project Newsletter*, no. 3 (Fall 1992), available at http://www.nyu.edu/projects/sanger/secure/newsletter/articles/ippf_fortieth.html.

12 Matthew Connelly, *Fatal Misconception: The Struggle to Control World Population* (Cambridge, MA: Belknap Press, 2008), 221–222; Joseph A. Califano, *The Triumph and Tragedy of Lyndon Johnson: The White House Years* (College Station, TX: Texas A&M Press, 2000), 154–155; Joseph A. Califano, *Inside: A Public and Private Life* (New York: Public Affairs, 2004), 172–173.

13 Connelly, *Fatal Misconception*, 222.

14 *Ibid.*, 217.

15 *Ibid.*, 227.

16 *Ibid.*, 222–223.

17 *Ibid.*, 222–225.

18 Mosher, *Population Control*, 87.

19 Alaka M. Basu, "Family Planning and the Emergency," *Economic and Political Weekly* 20, no. 10 (1985): 423.

20 Paul R. Ehrlich, *The Population Bomb* (New York: Ballantine Books, 1968; New York: Ballantine Books, 1975), 40–41. Citations are to the 1975 edition.

21 From a 1967 speech at a University of Texas symposium, quoted in Allan Chase, *The Legacy of Malthus: The Social Costs of the New Scientific Racism* (New York: Knopf, 1977), 398.

22 Basu, "Family Planning and the Emergency," 423.

23 *Ibid.*, 318.

24 *Ibid.*, 318–321; Mosher, *Population Control*, 142; Angela Franks, *Margaret Sanger's Eugenic Legacy: The Control of Female Fertility* (Jefferson, NC: McFarland and Co, 2005), 171–172.

25 Connelly, *Fatal Misconception*, 321.

26 Molly Moore, "Teeming India Engulfed by Soaring Birthrate," *Washington Post*, August 21, 1994.

27 Connelly, *Fatal Misconception*, 321.

28 *Ibid.*, 322–323.

29 *Ibid.*, 322–323.

30 *Ibid.*, 325–326. The surprise electoral landslide that ended nearly three decades of Congress Party rule was a crushing rebuke by India's people to the population control campaign. Both Indira Gandhi and her son Sanjay were defeated in their home districts. The Congress Party lost 141 out of 142 seats in the states that had registered the largest number of sterilizations. In the previous election, Congress had won 80 percent of the vote in these states. In Delhi, crowds stayed up through the night to cheer the results. Unfortunately, however, international pressure remained on India to implement population control measures, so rather than terminating completely, the campaign was merely reduced dramatically in scale and intensity, with sterilizations falling from 8 million in 1976 to about 1.5 million per year in 1977 and 1978.

31 Warren C. Robinson and John A. Ross, eds., *The Global Family Planning Revolution: Three Decades of Population Policies and Programs* (Washington, DC: World Bank, 2007), 310–322, available at http://siteresources.worldbank.org/INTPRH/Resources/GlobalFamilyPlanningRevolution.pdf.

32 John A. Ross, Douglas H. Huber, and Sawon Hong, "Worldwide Trends in Voluntary Sterilization," *International Family Planning Perspectives* 12, no. 2 (1986): 34–39.

33 Paul Murphy, "Killing Baby Girls Routine in India," *San Francisco Examiner*, May 21, 1995; Satinder Bindra, "Grim Motives Behind Infant Killings," CNN, July 7, 2003, http://articles.cnn.com/2003-07-07/world/india.infanticide.pt1_1_baby-girls-killings-fewer-girls.

34 Christophe Z. Guilmoto, "The Sex Ratio Transition in Asia," *Population and Development Review* 35, no. 3 (2009): 519–549.

35 Office of the Registrar General and Census Commissioner of India, "Provisional Population Totals: Census 2011," http://censusindia.gov.in/2011-prov-results/indiaatglance.html. Because of the timing of the rise in India's sex selection practices, and also because Indian women (like women in most countries) tend to live longer than men, the effect is more pronounced if you do not include population cohorts that are older. So, for example, if you only count the Indian population under the age of 65, there are almost 43 million more men than women.

36 Robinson and Ross, eds., *The Global Family Planning Revolution*, 235–238. The coup and genocidal jihad that followed from 1965 to 1969 were allegedly coordinated by Marshall Green, the U.S. ambassador to Indonesia. In 1975, Green became the first coordinator of the State Department's Office of Population Affairs. Upon retiring from government in 1979, he joined the board of the Draper Fund/Population Crisis Committee.

37 Hartmann, *Reproductive Rights and Wrongs*, 74.

38 *Ibid.*, 76–79.

39 *Ibid.*, 76–79.

40 *Ibid.*, 76–79.

41 *Ibid.*, 76–79.

42 Infant mortality in Indonesia now stands at 27.95 deaths per 1,000 live births. In Thailand it is 16.39 and in Malaysia it is 15.02. *CIA World Factbook*, Indonesia, "People: Infant Mortality," updated August 23, 2011, https://www.cia.gov/library/publications/the-world-factbook/geos/id.html; *CIA World Factbook*, Thailand, "People: Infant Mortality," updated August 23, 2011, https://www.cia.gov/library/publications/the-world-factbook/geos/th.html; *CIA World Factbook*, Malaysia, "People: Infant Mortality," updated August 23, 2011, https://www.cia.gov/library/publications/the-world-factbook/geos/my.html.

43 Mosher, *Population Control*, 122–126.

44 *Ibid.*

45 *Ibid.*

46 *Ibid.*, 136–139. Peru, Congress of the Republic of Peru, Subcommittee Investigating the Persons and Institutions Involved in Voluntary Surgical Contraception, *Final Report Concerning Voluntary Surgical Contraception During the Years 1990–2000*, June 2002. It should be noted that relative to the small size of Peru's population (about 27 million people in 2000) the 314,000 women sterilized under Fujimori would be proportional to a program sterilizing 3.3 million women in the United States.

47 Mosher, *Population Control*, 143–145. IPPF was involved through its Peruvian subsidiary, the Instituto Peruano de Paternidad Responsible; see International Planned Parenthood Federation, "Country Profiles; Peru," archived at http://web.archive.org/web/20041114212838/http://ippfnet.ippf.org/pub/IPPF_Regions/IPPF_CountryProfile.asp?ISOCode=PE.

48 Susan Greenhalgh, *Just One Child: Science and Policy in Deng's China* (Berkeley, CA: University of California Press, 2008), 125–168. Song has denied that he plagiarized the Club of Rome, but Greenhalgh's textual analysis of his writings, which include not only the Club's standard phrases and metaphors, but whole paragraphs lifted in their entirety from *Blueprint for Survival*, leaves little room for doubt as to the source of Song's genius.

49 Greenhalgh, *Just One Child*, 158.

50 Jacqueline Kasun, *The War Against Population: the Economics and Ideology of Population Control* (San Francisco: Ignatius Press, 1988), 73.

51 Greenhalgh, *Just One Child*, 161–162.

52 *Ibid.*, 180–184.

53 Ehrlich, *The Population Bomb*, 130.

54 Connelly, *Fatal Misconception*, 341–342. The permits read as follows: "Based on the nationally issued population plan targets, combined with the need for late marriage, late birth, and fewer births, it is agreed that you may give birth to a child during the year 198-; the quota is valid for this year and cannot be transferred."

55 Connelly, *Fatal Misconception*, 347; Mosher, *Population Control*, 74.

56 Mosher, *Population Control*, 71–95.

57 Connelly, *Fatal Misconception*, 343.

58 Michele Vink, "Abortion and Birth Control in Canton, China," *Wall Street Journal*, November 30, 1981, quoted in Mosher, *Population Control*, 79–80 and Connelly, *Fatal Misconception*, 346.

59 Christopher Wren, "China's Birth Goals Meet Regional Resistance," *New York Times*, May 15, 1982.

60 Mosher, *Population Control*, 80.

61 Connelly, *Fatal Misconception*, 347–348; Mosher, *Population Control*, 75.

62 Connelly, *Fatal Misconception*, 350. Qian's reference to "raising population quality" is worth noting. The Chinese population control program had a significant eugenic component, and in fact, sample copies of earlier American eugenics laws were supplied to the program by none other than the IPPF's Penny Kane

(*Fatal Misconception*, 345). The system's provision of dealing with unauthorized second children through 20,000 yuan ($2,000) fines has clear eugenic intent, as this sum is impossible for rural peasants but readily manageable by ranking Communist Party insiders and other urban elites. Mosher also reports a special emphasis of the campaign targeting reductions in China's Uyghur minority population (*Population Control*, 140–141). Other sources report Chinese use of population control to eliminate the native Tibetan population; see Tibet Support Group, "The Quality Baby: Birth Control Policies in Tibet," *Tibet Facts* 9, http://tibet.dharmakara.net/TibetFacts9.html.

63 Mosher, *Population Control*, 79. See also Bryan T. Johnson, "The World Bank and Economic Growth: 50 Years of Failure," *The Backgrounder*, no. 1082, Heritage Foundation, May 16, 1996, available at http://www.heritage.org/research/reports/1996/05/bg1082nbsp-the-world-bank-and-economic-growth.

64 Mosher, *Population Control*, 86.

65 Wei Xing Zhu, Li Lu, and Therese Hesketh, "China's Excess Males, Sex Selective Abortion, and One Child Policy: Analysis of Data from 2005 National Intercensus Survey," *BMJ* 338:b1211 (2009), http://www.bmj.com/content/338/bmj.b1211.full.pdf.

66 Mosher, *Population Control*, 82–89, 130.

67 Stephen Karanja, "Health System Collapsed," *PRI Review* 7, no. 2 (1997): 10.

68 Stephen W. Mosher, "The Sword of Damocles," *PRI Review* 10, no. 5 (2000).

69 Mosher, *Population Control*, 166–169.

70 *Ibid.*, 170–198.

71 See the website of the United Nations Statistics Division, http://data.un.org/.

72 Joint United Nations Program on HIV/AIDS (UNAIDS), *Global Report: UNAIDS Report on the Global AIDS Epidemic: 2010* (UNAIDS, 2010), 20, 23, 25–31, http://www.unaids.org/globalreport/documents/20101123_Global-Report_full_en.pdf.

73 *Ibid.*, 18.

74 *Ibid.*, 26, 181.

75 *Ibid.*, 27.

76 *Ibid.*, 180. Figures calculated in combination with 2009 population data from the World Bank. The data show 33.3 million people around the world living with HIV, 22.5 million of them in sub-Saharan Africa. The world population in 2009 was about 6,775 million people, with 840 million living in sub-Saharan Africa. So inside sub-Saharan Africa, 22.5 million people out of 840 million have HIV (coming to 26.8 per thousand), while outside sub-Saharan Africa, 10.8 million people out of 5,935 million have HIV (coming to 1.8 per thousand).

77 *Ibid.*, 50.

78 *Ibid.*, 25, 130, 182. Of the 22.5 million people in sub-Saharan Africa infected with HIV, 12.1 million (53.8 percent) are women. Of the 10.8 million people outside sub-Saharan Africa infected with HIV, 3.8 million (35.2 percent) are women.

79 In 1997, Dr. Mary Meaney, an American tourist visiting Kenya, encountered a very ill woman lying by the side of the road. Taking action, Meaney picked the woman up and drove her to the nearest government hospital, some five hours away. There she found "no gloves, no syringes, no vitamins, no basic medical supplies . . . but 75,000 condoms from USAID." Mosher, *Population Control*, 167. The stereotypes regarding African promiscuity underlying this gambit are crude and racist, though the population controllers are too politic to state them outright.

80 Mosher, *Population Control*, 179.

81 David Gisselquist, Devon Brewer, Richard Rothenberg, *et al.*, "Mounting Anomalies in the Epidemiology of HIV in Africa: Cry the Beloved Paradigm," *International Journal of STD and AIDS*, 2003, 14:145.

82 *Ibid.*, 188; Steven W. Mosher, "We will never turn you away . . . AIDS, Abortion and Effective U.S. Policy," *Research*, Population Research Institute, http://www.pop.org/content/we-will-never-turn-you-away-aids-abortion-and-effective-us-policy-900.

83 Mosher, *Population Control*, 186–189; World Health Organization (WHO), "Wastes from Health-Care Activities," Fact Sheet 253, reviewed November 2007, http://www.who.int/mediacentre/factsheets/fs253/en/index.html; WHO, "Injection Safety," Fact Sheet 231, revised October 2006, http://www.who.int/mediacentre/factsheets/fs231/en/index.html.

84 WHO, "Injection Safety."

85 WHO, "Wastes from Health-Care Activities."

86 Mosher, *Population Control*, 187.

87 UNAIDS, *Report on the Global AIDS Epidemic: 2010*, 16. Fortunately, the President's Emergency Plan for AIDS Relief, which President George W. Bush first announced in 2003, has provided antiretroviral treatments to more than two million people—but even this act of American generosity is insufficient to help the vast majority of those infected with HIV.

CHAPTER FOURTEEN · BETTER DEAD THAN FED:
GREEN POLICE FOR WORLD HUNGER

1 Hassan Adamu, "We'll Feed Our People As We See Fit," *Washington Post*, September 11, 2000.

2 Dave Emory, "It's Not Easy Being Green: Nazi Infiltration and Cooptation of the Green Party," For the Record, SpitfireList, no. 628, March 8, 2008, http://spitfire list.com/for-the-record/ftr-628-its-not-easy-being-green-nazi-infiltration-and-co-option-of-the-green-party/.

3 Martin A. Lee, *The Beast Reawakens* (New York: Little Brown, 1997), 216–217.

4 *Ibid.*, 217.

5 Jonah Goldberg, *Liberal Fascism: The Secret History of the American Left, from Mussolini to the Politics of Change* (New York: Broadway Books, 2007), 384.

6 Mark Hertsgsard, "Who Killed Petra Kelly," *Mother Jones*, January/February 1993, available at http://motherjones.com/politics/1993/01/motherjones-jf93-who-killed-petra-kelly.

7 George L. Mosse, *The Crisis of German Ideology: Intellectual Origins of the Third Reich* (New York: Grosset and Dunlap, 1964).

8 Peter Staudenmaier, "Anthroposophy and Ecofascism," Institute for Social Ecology, January 10, 2009, http://www.social-ecology.org/2009/01/anthroposophy-and-ecofascism-2/.

9 Janet Biehl and Peter Staudenmaier, *Ecofascism: Lessons from the German Experience* (San Francisco: AK Press, 1995), 17–20.

10 *Ibid.*, 16, 20–24.

11 Staudenmaier, "Anthroposophy and Ecofascism"; Anna Bramwell, *Ecology in the 20th Century: A History* (New Haven: Yale University Press, 1999), 199–208.

12 "Otto Schily," Wikipedia, http://en.wikipedia.org/w/index.php?title=Otto_Schily.

13 C. S. Prakash and Gregory Conko, "Agricultural Biotechnology Caught in a War of Giants," in Jon Entine, ed., *Let Them Eat Precaution: How Politics Is Undermining the Genetic Revolution in Agriculture* (Washington DC: American Enterprise Institute, 2006), 35–55.

14 *Ibid.*, 38–39, 47.

15 *Ibid.*, 42–43.

16 National Agricultural Statistics Service, "USDA Crop Production Historical Track Records: April 2011," 2011, http://usda.mannlib.cornell.edu/usda/current/htrcp/htrcp-04-26-2011.pdf.

17 Roger Elmore and Lori Abendroth, "Are We Capable of Producing 300 Bu/Acre Corn Yields?," Iowa State University Agronomy Extension, http://www.agronext.iastate.edu/corn/production/management/harvest/producing.html; Michael D. Edgerton, "Increasing Crop Productivity to Meet Global Needs for Feed, Food, and Fuel," *Plant Physiology* 149, no. 1 (2009): 7–13.

18 Prakash and Conko, "Agricultural Biotechnology Caught in a War of Giants," 41, 46; Robert Paarlberg, *Starved for Science: How Biotechnology is Being Kept Out of Africa* (Cambridge, MA: Harvard University Press, 2008), 159–170.

19 Xudong Ye et al., "Engineering the Provitamin A (β-Carotene) Biosynthetic Pathway into (Carotenoid-Free) Rice Endosperm," *Science* 287, no. 5451 (2000): 303–305.

20 J. H. Humphrey, K. P. West, Jr., and A. Sommer, "Vitamin A Deficiency and Attributable Mortality Among Under-5-Year-Olds," *Bulletin of the World Health Organization* 70, no. 2 (1992): 225–232; World Health Organization (WHO), "Micronutrient Deficiencies: Vitamin A Deficiency," http://www.who.int/nutrition/topics/vad/en/; WHO, *Guidelines on Food Fortification With Micronutrients* (France: WHO, 2006), 51.

21 P. Lucca, R. Hurrell, and I. Potrykus, "Genetic Engineering Approaches to

Improve the Bioavailability and the Level of Iron in Rice Grains," *Theoretical and Applied Genetics* 102, no. 2 (2001): 392; World Health Organization, *Worldwide Prevalence of Anaemia 1993–2005* (Geneva: WHO, 2008): 7.

22 Jon Entine, "Beyond Precaution," in *Let Them Eat Precaution*, 6–7; Indur Goklany, *The Precautionary Principle: A Critical Appraisal of Environmental Risk Assessment* (Washington, DC: Cato Institute, 2001); "Beware the Precautionary Principle," Social Issues Research Center, http://www.sirc.org/articles/beware.html. Robert Paarlberg, "Let Them Eat Precaution: Why GM Crops Are Being Over-Regulated in the Developing World," in *Let Them Eat Precaution: How Politics Is Undermining the Genetic Revolution in Agriculture*, Jon Entine, ed. (Washington, DC: American Enterprise Institute, 2006), 92–112.

23 *Ibid.*

24 California Department of Food and Agriculture, "A Food Foresight Analysis of Agricultural Biotechnology," January 2003, 3.

25 Paarlberg, "Let Them Eat Precaution," 102–105.

26 Paul Driessen, *Eco-Imperialism: Green Power, Black Death* (Bellevue, WA: Free Enterprise Press, 2004), 45–64.

27 J.L. Araus *et al.*, "The Historical Perspective of Dryland Agriculture: Lessons Learned from 10,000 Years of Wheat Cultivation," *Journal of Experimental Botany* 58, no. 2 (2007): 131–145.

28 Ramakrishna Nemani *et al.*, "Recent Trends in Hydrologic Balance Have Enhanced the Terrestrial Carbon Sink in the United States," *Geophysical Research Letters* 29, no. 10 (2002): 106.1–106.4.

29 A.O. Richardson and J.D. Palmer, "Horizontal Gene Transfer in Plants," *Journal of Experimental Botany* 58 (2006): 1–9; O. Piskurek and N. Okada, "Poxviruses as Possible Vectors for Horizontal Transfer of Retroposons from Reptiles to Mammals," *PNAS* 29 (2007): 12046–12051. The transfer of genetic material between distantly related organisms is not unique to biotechnology, or even agriculture. It sometimes occurs in nature as well. The flowering plant Amborella, for example, has been shown to have DNA transferred from both mosses and algae—two entirely different phyla of plants. Gerbils have been found with snake DNA, apparently transferred by viruses. The fact that DNA developed in one species line can sometimes make its way into other unrelated life forms is an aid to evolution, as it enhances the number of variations that nature can experiment with.

30 Prakash and Conko, "Agricultural Biotechnology Caught in a War of Giants," 39.

31 Alan L. Olmstead and Paul W. Rhode, "Adapting North American Wheat Production to Climatic Challenges, 1839–2009," *PNAS* 108, no. 2 (2011): 480–485.

32 "Norman Borlaug, Feeder of the World, Died on September 12th, Aged 95," *The Economist*, September 19, 2009.

33 Olmstead and Rhode, "Adapting North American Wheat Production to Climatic Challenges, 1839–2009."

34 "Norman Borlaug, Feeder of the World," *The Economist*. *The Economist* has writ-

ten a great deal about the Green Revolution, as well as worthwhile criticism of how corporations have yielded too quickly to the unreasonable demands of eco-fascists; see, for example, "Irresponsible: The Dangers of Corporate Social Responsibility," *The Economist*, November 21, 2002.

35 Matt Ridley, *The Rational Optimist: How Prosperity Evolves* (New York: Harper Collins, 2010), 141–143.

36 Norman Borlaug, "Nobel Prize Acceptance Speech," December 10, 1970, available at http://nobelprize.org/nobel_prizes/peace/laureates/1970/borlaug-acceptance.html.

37 Norman Borlaug, "Ending World Hunger. The Promise of Biotechnology and the Threat of Antiscience Zealotry," *Plant Physiology* 124, no. 2 (2007): 487–490.

38 Ridley, *The Rational Optimist*, 151–152. Green activist claims that Bt corn endangers the monarch butterfly, while oft repeated, have been shown to be entirely false. These claims are based on a study done by a Cornell researcher who killed some monarch butterfly caterpillars by force-feeding them milkweed leaves heavily dusted with Bt pollen. However, in the wild, monarch butterfly caterpillars avoid eating corn pollen on milkweed leaves. Thus a USDA study concluded, "This 2-year study suggests that the impact of Bt corn pollen from current commercial hybrids on monarch butterfly populations is negligible." M.K. Sears *et al.*, "Impact of Bt Corn Pollen on Monarch Butterfly Populations: A Risk Assessment," *Proceedings of the National Academy of Sciences of the United States of America* 98, no. 21 (2001): 11937–11942. See also Ronald Bailey, *Liberation Biology* (Amherst, NY: Prometheus Books, 2005), 207–208.

39 Bailey, *Liberation Biology*, 188.

40 Peggy G. Lemaux, "Genetically Engineered Plants and Foods: A Scientist Reviews the Issues (Part I)," *Annual Review of Plant Biology* 59 (2008): 777. Lemaux's article is an excellent and thorough analysis and defense of biotechnology.

41 Donald Danforth Plant Science Center, "About Our Plants," http://www.danforthcenter.org/get_involved/what_we_do/about_our_plants.asp.

42 Driessen, *Eco-Imperialism*, 51.

43 Bailey, *Liberation Biology*, 193–194.

44 Xudong Ye *et al.*, "Engineering the Provitamin A (β-Carotene) Biosynthetic Pathway into (Carotenoid-Free) Rice Endosperm," 303–305.

45 Humphrey, West, and Sommer, "Vitamin A Deficiency and Attributable Mortality Among Under-5-Year-Olds," 225–232; WHO, "Micronutrient Deficiencies: Vitamin A Deficiency"; WHO, *Guidelines on Food Fortification With Micronutrients*, 51.

46 Bailey, *Liberation Biology*, 194–195.

47 Steven H. Strauss, Stephen P. DiFazio, and Richard Meilan, "Genetically Modified Poplars in Context," *Forestry Chronicle* 77, no. 2 (2001).

48 Bailey, *Liberation Biology*, 200–201.

49 Bailey, *Liberation Biology*, 197–198.

5 0 Saltwater fish are largely unchanged since the beginning of human history. Many freshwater fish have been altered by breeding done by pond-fish farmers since ancient times.

5 1 Bailey, *Liberation Biology*, 1 9 6 – 1 9 7. The FDA approval process for AquaBounty's salmon, currently underway, is facing stiff opposition from lawmakers in the American Northwest. See http://www.nytimes.com/gwire/2 0 1 1 /0 6 /1 6 /1 6 greenwire-houese-moves-to-ban-modified-salmon–8 4 1 6 5 .html.

CHAPTER FIFTEEN · QUENCHING HUMANITY'S FIRE:
GLOBAL WARMING AND THE MADNESS OF CROWDS

1 Terence Corcoran, "Global Warming: The Real Agenda," *Calgary Herald*, December 2 6 , 1 9 9 8 .

2 Marc Morano, "Gore Uses Religion to Attract 'Global Warming' Converts," CNSNews, May 2 6 , 2 0 0 6 , available at http://web.archive.org/web/2 0 0 8 0 4 0 6 0 4 4 9 2 2 /http://www.cnsnews.com/ViewCulture.asp?Page=/Culture/archive/2 0 0 6 0 5 /CUL2 0 0 6 0 5 2 6b.html.

3 Richard Wrangham, "Cooking as a Biological Trait," *Comparative Biochemistry and Physiology - Part A: Molecular & Integrative Physiology* 1 3 6 , no. 1 (2 0 0 3 ): 3 5 –4 6 ; Rachael Moeller Gorman, "Cooking Up Bigger Brains," *Scientific American*, January 2 0 0 8 , 1 0 2 – 1 0 5 .

4 Strictly based on the one-fourth power law, Venus's absolute temperature should be 1 .1 9 times as great as Earth's. Multiplying this factor by a typical Earth temperature of 2 8 3 K (1 0 °C or 5 0 °F), we get an absolute temperature of 3 3 7 K for Venus, which is equal to 6 4 °C or 1 4 7 °F.

5 National Aeronautics and Space Administration (NASA), "A Meeting with the Universe—Planetary Exploration," http://history.nasa.gov/EP–1 7 7 /toc.html. Today we know that Venus's mean temperature is 4 6 4 °C (8 6 7 °F).

6 NASA, "Venus Fact Sheet," http://nssdc.gsfc.nasa.gov/planetary/factsheet/venus fact.html.

7 The first person to propose the existence of a planetary greenhouse effect caused specifically by atmospheric carbon dioxide was the Swedish scientist Svante Arrhenius, writing in the 1 8 9 0 s. As the *Oxford English Dictionary* notes, the term itself was in circulation by the early twentieth century. The discovery of the atmospheric conditions of Venus, however, did much to bring the subject to the mainstream scientific and public attention.

8 Charles D. Keeling, "The Concentration and Isotopic Abundances of $CO_2$ in the Atmosphere," *Tellus* 1 2 , no. 2 (1 9 6 0 ): 2 0 0 – 2 0 3 .

9 Kenneth R. Lang, *The Cambridge Guide to the Solar System*, 2 nd ed. (Cambridge, UK: Cambridge University Press, 2 0 1 1 ), 2 2 2 .

1 0 The Impact Team, *The Weather Conspiracy: The Coming of the New Ice Age* (New York: Ballantine Books, 1 9 7 7 ).

11 Paul R. Ehrlich and John P. Holdren, "Overpopulation and the Potential for Ecocide," in *Global Ecology: Readings Toward a Rational Strategy for Man*, eds. John P. Holdren and Paul R. Ehrlich (New York: Harcourt Brace Jovanovich, 1971), 76–77. Noteworthy in view of current claims about the danger posed by the global-warming-induced melting of the Antarctic ice sheet is this, from page 77: "This number [0.2 °C of industry-caused cooling already achieved] seems small until it is realized that a decrease of only 4 °C would probably be sufficient to start another ice age. . . . The effects of a new ice age on agriculture and the supportability of large human populations scarcely need elaboration here. Even more dramatic results are possible, however; for instance a sudden outward slumping in the Antarctic ice cap, induced by added weight, could generate a tidal wave of proportions unprecedented in recorded history."

12 See, for example, Stephen Schneider and Randi Londer, *The Coevolution of Climate and Life* (San Francisco: Sierra Club Books, 1984).

13 See, for example, Patrick J. Michaels, *Meltdown: The Predictable Distortion of Global Warming by Scientists, Politicians, and the Media* (Washington, DC: Cato Institute, 2004).

14 Andrew Shepherd and Duncan Wingham, "Recent Sea-Level Contributions of the Antarctic and Greenland Ice Sheets," *Science* 315, no. 5818 (2007): 1529–1532.

15 Ralph F. Keeling *et al.*, "Atmospheric $CO_2$ Values (ppmv) Derived from In Situ Air Samples Collected at Mauna Loa, Hawaii, U.S.A," Carbon Dioxide Research Group, February 2009, http://cdiac.ornl.gov/ftp/trends/co2/maunaloa.co2.

16 Carroll L. Wilson and William H. Matthews, eds., *Inadvertent Climate Modification, Report of Conference: Study of Man's Impact on Climate* (SMIC) (MIT Press, 1971), 234, quoted in *The Discovery of Global Warming*, December, 2009, http://www.aip.org/history/climate/xKeeling7 1–2.htm.

17 James Kasting, "The Carbon Cycle, Climate, and the Long-Term Effects of Fossil Fuel Burning," *Consequences* 4, no. 1 (1998), http://www.gcrio.org/CONSEQUENCES/vol4no1/carbcycle.html.

18 Assume each doubling, or increase by a factor of 2, of $CO_2$ concentration increases the temperature by 1.5–5 °C. An increase of 20 percent is a factor of 1.2, which is roughly the fourth root of 2 ($\log_2 1.2 \approx 0.26$), should cause a temperature increase of roughly one-fourth of a full doubling of $CO_2$ —or, more precisely, an increase of 0.39–1.32 °C.

19 Intergovernmental Panel on Climate Change, "2.2 Drivers of Climate Change," http://www.ipcc.ch/publications_and_data/ar4/syr/en/mains2–2.html.

20 A gigatonne is a billion tonnes. A tonne is a metric ton, weighing 2,200 pounds (or 1.1 tons).

21 Humanity's current global carbon fuel usage is about 9 Gt per year. However in 1958, it was only about 2 Gt, with the average over the intervening period being about 5 Gt. Thus, in the past half century, we have cumulatively released about 250 Gt of carbon into the atmosphere.

22 A. B. Robinson *et al.*, "Environmental Effects of Increased Atmospheric Carbon Dioxide," *Climate Research* 13, (1999): 149–164. Oxygen comes naturally in two isotopes, the common "light" isotope $^{16}O$, and the rarer "heavy" isotope $^{18}O$. During periods of cold climate, such as an ice age, increased amounts of $^{16}O$ tend to be trapped in ice sheets near the poles. This leaves the ocean waters comparatively enriched in $^{18}O$, and the record of such past enrichment will be preserved in marine fossils laid down at that time. Thus, by measuring the ratio of $^{18}O/^{16}O$ in marine fossils, scientists can assess global temperatures in ages past; the higher the $^{18}O/^{16}O$ ratio, the colder the global climate. For more on this technique, see NASA Earth Observatory, "Paleoclimatology: The Oxygen Balance," http://earth observatory.nasa.gov/Study/Paleoclimatology_OxygenBalance/oxygen_ balance.html.

23 Schneider and Londer, *The Coevolution of Climate and Life*, 111.

24 J. R. Petit *et al.*, Vostok Ice Core Data for 420,000 Years, IGBP PAGES/World Data Center for Paleoclimatology Data Contribution Series #2001-076 (2001), NOAA/NGDC Paleoclimatology Program, Boulder CO. Available at ftp://ftp.ncdc. noaa.gov/pub/data/paleo/icecore/antarctica/vostok/deutnat.txt.

25 James Zachos *et al.*, "Trends, Rhythms, and Aberrations in Global Climate 65 Ma to Present," *Science* 292, no. 5517 (2001): 686–693; J. R. Petit *et al.*, "Climate and Atmospheric History of the Past 420,000 years from the Vostok Ice Core, Antarctica," *Nature* 399 (1999): 429–436; L. E. Lisiecki and M. E. Raymo, "A Pliocene-Pleistocene stack of 57 globally distributed benthic $\delta^{18}O$ records," *Paleoceanography* 20 (2005): PA1003.

26 Tim K. Lowenstein and Robert V. Demicco, "Elevated Eocene Atmospheric $CO_2$ and Its Subsequent Decline," *Science* 313, no. 5795 (2006): 1928.

27 Bonnie F. Jacobs, John D. Kingston, and Louis L. Jacobs, "The Origin of Grass-Dominated Ecosystems," *Annals of the Missouri Botanical Garden* 86, no. 2 (1999): 590–643.

28 Ramakrishna Nemani *et al.*, "Recent Trends in Hydrologic Balance Have Enhanced the Terrestrial Carbon Sink in the United States," *Geophysical Research Letters* 29, no. 10 (2002): 1468.

29 Oak Ridge National Laboratory (ORNL), "Carbon Dioxide Fertilization Is Neither Boon Nor Bust," press release, Feb 15, 2004, http://www.eurekalert.org/ pub_releases/2004-02/jaaj-cdfo20504.php. "Productivity" here is a measure of how much $CO_2$ is absorbed. Another, more recent article from *Nature* is more explicit about the increased crop yields, though it also worries about the nutritional value of those crops. One possible solution to the low-protein problem is said to be more fertilizers. Ned Stafford, "Future Crops: The Other Greenhouse Effect," *Nature* 448, no. 7153 (2007): 526–528.

30 This figure of one in seven is extrapolated from the measured 14 percent increase in the rate of plant growth over the continental United States, in conjunction with the laboratory experiments that show the effects of $CO_2$ on plant

growth. Nemani *et al.*, "Recent Trends in Hydrologic Balance"; ORNL, "Carbon Dioxide Fertilization is Neither Boon nor Bust."

31 United Nations Statistics Division, "Millennium Development Goals Indicators: Carbon Dioxide Emissions," http://mdgs.un.org/unsd/mdg/SeriesDetail.aspx?srid=749.

32 Congressional Budget Office (CBO), "The Costs of Reducing Greenhouse-Gas Emissions," November 23, 2009, available at http://www.cbo.gov/ftpdocs/104xx/doc10458/11-23-GreenhouseGasEmissions_Brief.pdf.

33 David Kreutzer, Karen Campbell, and Nicolas Loris, "CBO Grossly Underestimates Cost of Cap and Trade" (Heritage Foundation Webmemo #2503), July 24, 2009, http://www.heritage.org/research/reports/2009/07/cbo-grossly-underestimates-cost-of-cap-and-trade.

34 Environmental Protection Agency, "Unit Conversions, Emissions Factors, and Other Reference Data," November, 2004, http://www.epa.gov/appdstar/pdf/brochure.pdf. U.S. Energy Information Administration (EIA), "Coal Explained: Coal Prices and Outlook," last updated July 14, 2011, http://www.eia.gov/energyexplained/index.cfm?page=coal_prices.

35 CBO, "Climate-Change Policy and $CO_2$ Emissions from Passenger Vehicles," October 6, 2008, available at http://www.cbo.gov/ftpdocs/98xx/doc9830/10-06-ClimateChange_Brief.pdf. The CBO does not appear to have considered the effects on gasoline prices specifically of the Waxman-Markey bill. This analysis considers the effects of the America's Climate Security Act of 2007. The effects would be similar.

36 David F. Burg, *A World History of Tax Rebellions: An Encyclopedia of Tax Rebels, Revolts, and Riots from Antiquity to the Present* (New York: Routledge, 2004), 6–7.

37 Today's governments still use similar techniques. New York City's taxi medallion system provides a modern-day example: the local government regulates and restricts the number of taxi drivers by requiring them to purchase a "medallion" to operate. These medallions can be bought and sold on the market, and the price has increased eightfold (in real terms) over the last forty years, with individual medallions now being sold by speculators for over $600,000 and corporate medallions going for as much as $850,000. Current possessors of licenses strongly oppose changing the system lest they lose their value. The medallion system is not precisely an instance of tax farming, since the government did not pick any single entity to act on its behalf, but the effect is much the same. Medallion Financial Corp., *2010 Annual Report*, 2–3; Michael M. Grynbaum, "Taxi-Industry Battle Continues, with Echoes of 1971," *New York Times*, City Room blog, August 1, 2011, http://cityroom.blogs.nytimes.com/2011/08/01/a-taxi-industry-battle-continues-with-echoes-of-1971.

38 *American Clean Energy and Security Act of 2009*, H.R. 2454, 111th Congr., 1st sess., Title 3, Subtitle A, § 311, http://www.gpo.gov/fdsys/pkg/BILLS-111hr2454eh/pdf/BILLS-111hr2454eh.pdf, page 682.

39 Depending on what energy source is used—coal, natural gas, or other hydrocarbons—making a tonne of fertilizer can produce anywhere from one to four tonnes of carbon dioxide.

40 Raymond J. Learsy, *Over a Barrel: Breaking the Middle East Oil Cartel* (Nashville, TN: Nelson Current, 2005), see quoted with discussion in Robert Zubrin, "Achieving Energy Victory," *The New Atlantis*, no. 18 (2007), http://www.the newatlantis.com/publications/achieving-energy-victory.

41 Earth Policy Institute, "Gross World Product, 1950–2009," January 12, 2011, http://www.earth-policy.org/data_center/C26. Between 1973 and 2009, Gross World Product increased from $21.7 trillion to $73.2 trillion (or $5,319 to $10,728 per capita).

42 American Petroleum Institute, *API Basic Petroleum Data Book*, vol. 19, no. 1, Table VII, January 1, 1999.

43 Zubrin, "Achieving Energy Victory," 5–6.

44 U.S. Bureau of Labor Statistics, "Economy at a Glance," http://www.bls.gov/eag/ eag.us.htm, data extracted on September 2, 2011.

45 WTRG Economics, "Oil Price History and Analysis," regularly updated at http://www.wtrg.com/prices.htm.

46 These figures were derived using data from the U.S. government. The United States consumed an average of 19.5 million barrels of petroleum per day in 2008 and 18.92 million per day in 1998, paying an average of $94.74 per barrel in 2008 and $12.52 per barrel in 1998. That comes to a cost of $676 billion in 2008 and $86 billion in 1998. When the 1998 figure is put in terms of 2008 dollars (adjusting for the 32 percent inflation rate between 1998 to 2008), it comes to $114 billion spent for petroleum in 1998. So the United States paid almost six times as much for oil in 2008 in real terms as it paid in 1998, even though the amount of oil the country consumed only increased by 3 percent. See EIA, Table 1, "Crude Oil Prices," http://www.eia.gov/pub/oil_gas/petroleum/data_publica tions/petroleum_marketing_annual/current/txt/tableso1.txt; Bureau of Transportation Statistics, "Table 4-1: Overview of U.S. Petroleum Production, Imports, Exports, and Consumption," http://www.bts.gov/publications/ national_transportation_statistics/html/table_04_01.html; Bureau of Labor Statistics, "CPI Inflation Calculator," http://www.bls.gov/data/inflation_calcu lator.htm.

47 U.S. Bureau of the Census, "Table 689. Money Income of Households—Percent Distribution by Income Level, Race, and Hispanic Origin, in Constant (2008) Dollars: 1980–2008," in *Statistical Abstract of the United States: 2011*, 452, available at http://www.census.gov/compendia/statab/2011/tables/11s0689.pdf.

48 The average U.S. household income before taxes in 2008 was about $50,000, *ibid.* Since the average household tax rate is around 20 percent, the average after-tax income is about $40,000. Catherine Rampell, "How Much Americans Actually Pay in Taxes," *New York Times*, Economix blog, April 8, 2009, http://economix.

blogs.nytimes.com/2009/04/08/how-much-americans-actually-pay-in-taxes/.

49 International Monetary Fund, *World Economic Outlook: April 2011* (IMF, 2011), 122, http://www.imf.org/external/pubs/ft/weo/2011/01/pdf/c3.pdf.

50 Victor Phillips and Patrick Takahashi, "Methanol from Biomass," *Environmental Science & Technology* 24, no. 8 (1990): 1136–1137.

51 ICIS, "Methanol (US Gulf)," Lane Kelley, ed., February 25, 2011, http://www.icispricing.com/il_shared/Samples/SubPage135.asp.

52 Air Products Liquid Phase Conversion Company, "Commercial-Scale Demonstration of the Liquid Phase Methanol (LPMEOH) Process: Project Performance Summary: Clean Coal Technology Demonstration Program," prepared for the Department of Energy, June 2004, 6, http://www.netl.doe.gov/technologies/coalpower/cctc/resources/pdfs/lpmeoh/LPMEOH_PPS.pdf.

53 T. B. Reed and R. M. Lerner, "Methanol: A Versatile Fuel for Immediate Use," *Science* 182, no. 4119 (1973), 1299–1304.

54 Josh Voorhees, "Detroit Automakers Spurn Ethanol Mandate," *Scientific American*, Greenwire blog, May 21, 2009, http://www.scientificamerican.com/article.cfm?id=detroit-automakers-ethanol-mandate.

55 See my book *Energy Victory: Winning the War on Terror by Breaking Free of Oil* (Amherst, NY: Prometheus Books, 2007) for an in-depth treatment of the problem posed by OPEC and the method for defeating it through the creation of fuel choice.

56 Renewable Fuels Association, "Statistics," http://www.ethanolrfa.org/pages/statistics#C.

57 Robert Zubrin, "In Defense of Biofuels," *The New Atlantis*, no. 20 (2008): 5; John M. Urbanchuk, "Contribution of the Ethanol Industry to the Economy of the United States," Renewable Fuels Association, 3, http://www.ethanolrfa.org/page/-/objects/documents/1537/2007_ethanol_economic_contribution.pdf?nocdn=1.

58 Patrick Barta, "As Biofuels Catch On, Next Task Is to Deal With Environmental, Economic Impact," *Wall Street Journal*, March 24, 2008.

59 The bill, known as the Open Fuel Standards Act, has been introduced into both the House and Senate repeatedly since 2008. Its 2010 bill numbers were S. 835 and H.R. 1476. A bipartisan group of lawmakers, led by Senators Maria Cantwell (D.-Wash.), Sam Brownback (R.-Kansas), Joe Lieberman (I.-Conn.), Susan Collins (R.-Maine), John Thune (R.-S.D.), Amy Klobuchar (D.-Minn.), and Reps. Eliot Engel (D.-N.Y.), Steve Israel (D.-N.Y.), Bob Inglis (R.-S.C.), and Roscoe Bartlett (R.-Md.), are among the sponsors.

60 Muriel Boselli, "Saudi Oil Minister Slams Biofuels, Supports Solar Energy," *Reuters*, April 10, 2008; *MarketWatch*, "OPEC President Blames Ethanol for Crude-Price Rise," July 6, 2008; Associated Press, "Chavez Calls Ethanol Production 'Crime,'" April 26, 2008.

61 U.S. Department of Justice, "Report of the Attorney General to the Congress of the United States on the Administration of the Foreign Agents Registration Act

of 1938, as amended, for the six months ending June 30, 2007," (Washington, DC), 230, http://www.fara.gov/reports/June30-2007.pdf. For the exposé of Glover Park's role in orchestrating the 2008 anti-ethanol campaign see Anna Palmer, "Beating Up on Ethanol," *Roll Call*, May 14, 2008. Palmer's article included documents showing that the Grocery Manufacturers Association, represented by Scott Faber—a former staff member with the Environmental Defense Fund—had paid Glover Park $300,000 to launch an "aggressive public relations campaign" to "obliterate whatever intellectual justification might still exist for corn-based ethanol among policy elites."

62  Timothy Searchinger *et al.*, "Use of U.S. Croplands for Biofuels Increases Greenhouse Gases through Emissions from Land-Use Change," *Science* 319, no. 5867 (2008): 1238–1240; Timothy Searchinger, "The Impacts of Biofuels on Greenhouse Gases: How Land Use Change Alters the Equation," German Marshall Fund, February 7, 2008, http://www.gmfus.org/cs/publications/publication_view?publication.id=602.

63  Anna Palmer, "Enviros Take on Ethanol," *Roll Call*, May 12, 2008.

64  For California regulations, see Wyatt Buchanan, "Air Resources Board Moves to Cut Carbon Use," *San Francisco Chronicle*, April 24, 2009. For the EPA adoption see Stephen Power, "If a Tree Falls in the Forest, Are Biofuels To Blame? It's Not Easy Being Green," *Wall Street Journal*, November 11, 2008.

65  Seungdo Kim and Bruce E. Dale, "Indirect Land Use Change for Biofuels: Testing Predictions and Improving Analytical Methodologies," *Biomass and Bioenergy* 35, no. 7 (2011): 3235–3240; Michael Wang and Zia Haq, "Letter to *Science*," revised version, March 14, 2008, http://www.transportation.anl.gov/pdfs/letter_to_science_anldoe_03_14_08.pdf.

66  For example, using Searchinger's "indirect analysis" approach you can "prove" that increasing the mileage standards for vehicles contributes to global warming. Consider: Every gallon of gasoline not used by a motorist saves him $3.50 at today's prices. He can use that money to buy other things. For example, at current prices (about $80 per ton), $3.50 could buy him about 90 pounds of coal. Burning that coal would obviously produce far more carbon dioxide emissions than burning the 6 pounds of carbon in one gallon of gas. So higher mileage standards for cars cause global warming. Q.E.D.

67  Joel Garreau, "Environmentalism as Religion," *The New Atlantis*, no. 28, (2010): 61–74.

68  Al Gore, *An Inconvenient Truth* (New York: Rodale, 2006), 11. Italics added.

69  Box Office Mojo, "An Inconvenient Truth," http://boxofficemojo.com/movies/?id=inconvenienttruth.htm.

70  This is especially true in the public sphere and the media. As just one example of how this pressure intrudes on the scientific process, Mike Hulme, a prominent British climate scientist and an avowed believer in anthropogenic climate change, noted, "I have found myself increasingly chastised by climate change campaigners

when my public statements and lectures on climate change have not satisfied their thirst for environmental drama and exaggerated rhetoric." Mike Hulme, "Chaotic World of Climate Truth," *BBC News*, November 4, 2006, http://news.bbc.co.uk/2/hi/science/nature/6115644.stm.

71 James E. Hansen, "Global Warming Twenty Years Later," *World Watch Institute*, http://www.worldwatch.org/node/5798.

72 Polly Higgins, *Eradicating Ecocide*, (London: Shepheard-Walwyn, 2010). Higgins is a member of the board of a group called DESERTEC, which describes itself as "a charitable initiative of the Club of Rome."

73 Paul Krugman, "Betraying the Planet," *New York Times*, June 28, 2009, http://www.nytimes.com/2009/06/29/opinion/29krugman.html.

74 Christopher Booker, *The Real Global Warming Disaster* (London: Continuum, 2009); S. Fred Singer and Dennis T. Avery, *Unstoppable Global Warming: Every 1,500 Years* (Lanham, MD: Rowman and Littlefield, 2007); Roy W. Spencer, *Climate Confusion* (New York: Encounter Books, 2008); Patrick J. Michaels, *Meltdown: The Predictable Distortions of Global Warming by Scientists, Politicians, and the Media* (Washington, DC: Cato Institute, 2004); Ian Plimer, *Heaven and Earth: Global Warming, the Missing Science* (Lanham, MD: Rowman and Littlefield, 2009).

75 John M. Lyman, Josh K. Willis, and Gregory C. Johnson, "Recent Cooling of the Upper Ocean," *Geophysical Research Letters* 33, (2006): L18604. It is worth noting that the authors of this article have since conceded that their data seem significantly flawed. J. K. Willis, J. M. Lyman, G. C. Johnson, and J. Gilson, "Correction to 'Recent Cooling of the Upper Ocean,'" *Geophysical Research Letters* 34, (2006): L16601.

76 Richard Lindzen, "Climate of Fear," *Wall Street Journal*, April 12, 2006.

CHAPTER SIXTEEN · MINDS IMPRISONED OR THE SOUL UNCHAINED

1 John Milton, *Paradise Lost*, bk. 1, lines 254–255.

# ILLUSTRATION CREDITS

Right: Courtesy The Select Committee on Energy Independence and Global Warming, U.S. House of Representatives. Public domain.

115 Courtesy J. Rennie Whitehead.

119 Courtesy Indur M. Goklany, from www.masterresource.org/2010/04/popula tion-consumption-carbon-emissions-and-human-well-being-in-the-age-of-industrialization-part-i-revisiting-the-julian-simon-paul-ehrlich-bet/.

123 Courtesy Indur M. Goklany, *ibid.*

126 Public domain.

129 Hugh Moore Fund Collection.

131 Top: Courtesy National Archives, ARC Identifier 542002/Local Identifier 306-SSM-4A-35-6. Bottom: Courtesy Boston University Photography.

135 Copyright N. T. Stobbs. Creative Commons license.

137 Clamshell Alliance Papers, Milne Special Collections, University of New Hampshire.

151 Courtesy Princeton Plasma Physics Laboratory, U.S. Department of Energy. Public domain.

155 Hugh Moore Fund Collection.

160 Courtesy Reimert T. Ravenholt.

175 Copyright Nick Rain, flickr.com/photos/nickrainimages/.

181 Courtesy Francisco Pérez García, Agencia de Noticias Spacio Libre.

186 Courtesy Care of China's Orphaned and Abandoned, www.cocoa.org.uk.

187 Left: Associated Press/Michel Lipchitz. Right: Reprinted by permission of All Girls Allowed, allgirlsallowed.org, 2010. Data from World Health Organization, World Bank, Centers for Disease Control and Prevention, *British Medical Journal*, and Women's Rights Without Frontiers.

192 Author's Graph. Data from 2010 UNAIDS report.

194 Courtesy USAID. Public domain.

197 Copyright DPA Picture-Alliance.

199 Both public domain.

202 Left: Courtesy Dr. William Charles Caccamise, Sr., M.D., EyeRounds.org. Right: Courtesy International Rice Research Institute. Creative Commons license.

205 Author's photograph.

211 Courtesy International Rice Research Institute. Creative Commons license.

218 Courtesy AquaBounty.

224 Courtesy Robert Rohde, GlobalWarmingArt.com.

225 Courtesy Robert Rohde, GlobalWarmingArt.com.

227 Courtesy *Journal of American Physicians and Surgeons*.

229 Courtesy Robert Rohde, GlobalWarmingArt.com.

232 Screenshot from *An Inconvenient Truth* (2006). Fair Use.

238 Courtesy James L. Williams, WTRG Economics.

239 Courtesy James L. Williams, WTRG Economics.

# INDEX

## A NOTE ON THE TYPE

MERCHANTS OF DESPAIR *has been set in Minion, a type designed by Robert Slimbach in 1990. An offshoot of the designer's researches during the development of Adobe Garamond, Minion hybridized the characteristics of numerous Renaissance sources into a single calligraphic hand. Unlike many early faces developed exclusively for digital typesetting, drawings for Minion were transferred to the computer early in the design phase, preserving much of the freshness of the original concept. Conceived with an eye toward overall harmony, Minion's capitals, lowercase letters, and numerals were carefully balanced to maintain a well-groomed "family" appearance—both between roman and italic and across the full range of weights. A decidedly contemporary face, Minion makes free use of the qualities Slimbach found most appealing in the types of the fifteenth and sixteenth centuries. Crisp drawing and a narrow set width make Minion an economical and easygoing book type, and even its name evokes its adaptable, affable, and almost self-effacing nature, referring as it does to a small size of type, a faithful or favored servant, and a kind of peach.*

SERIES DESIGN BY CARL W. SCARBROUGH

Made in the USA
San Bernardino, CA
19 March 2016